WOODY ALLEN
FILM BY FILM

For Tessa, Cy and Seve – Love is too weak a word for what I feel

THIS IS A CARLTON BOOK
Published in Great Britain in 2015 by
Carlton Books Limited
20 Mortimer Street
London W1T 3JW

Text copyright © 2015 Jason Solomons
Design and layout © 2015 Carlton Books

A CIP catalogue for this book is available from the British Library.

Project Editor: Matt Lowing
Editorial: Caroline Curtis and Chris Parker
Design: Lucy Coley, Katie Baxendale and Barbara Zuniga
Picture Research: Steve Behan
Production: Maria Petalidou
Index: Colin Hynson

ISBN: 978 1 78097 673 0

Printed in Slovenia

10 9 8 7 6 5 4 3 2 1

WOODY ALLEN
FILM BY FILM

JASON SOLOMONS

CARLTON
BOOKS

Contents

Woody Allen Film by Film

The 1960s

The 1970s

> "The two biggest myths about me are that I'm an intellectual, because I wear these glasses, and that I'm an artist because my films lose money."
>
> Woody Allen

The 1980s

The 1990s

The 2000s

Foreword by Alfonso Cuarón

Cinema is illusion but what I love most about Woody Allen is how he makes that illusion appear so effortless.

Everybody, particularly every other film maker, knows that making movies is not easy and yet for Woody Allen it comes across as pure pleasure. In a way, it's a very old-fashioned style but he is such an important and unique link in cinematic history, connecting the traditions of Old Hollywood with those of French cinema and linking them to the most contemporary film-making styles.

The stories he tells and the images he creates add up to the purest release of the form of cinema, a blend of escapism that is romantic and comic but also combined with the bleakest confrontations of human existence.

Yet what you always feel watching a Woody Allen film is his amazing love of the cinema of the 1940s, that same sense of wonder he had when he was a kid and falling in love with movies. He has a gift of transmitting that love, that pleasure to his audience. I find it thrilling.

Perhaps contemporary audiences have become disconnected from those kinds of movies, removed from the experience and emotion of watching those kinds of movies, but Woody reminds us what it means to be truly in love with cinema.

To current, younger audiences, it may be as if he's speaking a dead language, like Latin or Sanskrit, but that doesn't mean the poetry of those languages isn't still beautiful and powerful. Anyone can see that beauty immediately in Woody Allen's movies. They are a magical link to an amazing world.

Watching *Magic in the Moonlight* recently, a film set in the 1920s and made well into the 21st century, I felt I was being transported back to the 1940s, when the movies were, above all things, about wonder. That film was full of questions and wonder and done with such an effortless charm. But what is amazing is that he can also,

just a few months earlier, make a film like *Blue Jasmine* with Cate Blanchett, that is modern and satirical and funny with the most wonderful part for any actress, no matter what period. Jasmine is an absolute classic screen role, as relevant now as it would have been 100 years ago.

Looking back over the history of cinema – and Woody Allen films practically oblige you to do so – there are many directors who have prolific filmographies, masters such as John Ford. But John Ford didn't write his own scripts. In German cinema, there has been Fassbinder who managed a prolific and original output as writer, director and performer, but Woody Allen has matched all that, without the cocaine.

The fact that Woody is still so active at 80 years old is remarkable but longevity is not the real surprise or the reason to celebrate. The greatest danger is to take him for granted. Because what is truly inspiring is that the quality of his stories remains so high and so varied in range that even now, after all these years and all these stories which we can immediately identify as his, we still cannot pigeonhole him. We don't know what he will do next. That is an extraordinary achievement for an artist.

I have always loved the misconception of him as this rather insecure character. That's probably the biggest joke of his career. I never stop laughing at that one – no way is this an insecure man. His screenplays and his dramatic structures are always flawless and you just have to sit back and wonder at the confidence of such storytelling.

Alfonso Cuarón, Oscar-winning director of *Gravity*, *Y Tu Mama Tambien* and *Children of Men*.

The Woody Allen Interview

Cannes could be an ordeal for anybody. It's hot and noisy and busy and your film screens late at night. Yet for a man in his 80th year, he looks well and fresh and apart from the occasional cough – he's particular about air-conditioning – he is happy to reflect and share his wit and wisdom.

JS: I'm so pleased to see you're in such good health.

WA: Not nearly as pleased as I am, I can bet you that…

JS: How is the circus of Cannes treating you?

WA: It's always a little embarrassing promoting your own movie. I made it, so of course I'm going to say it's wonderful and we all did such a good job, but I'm lying essentially. Things like that are not realistically for me to say. It's for others to decide if I did a good job or not.

JS: The movie business has changed a lot in recent years, so you really have to fight to get attention, especially for old-fashioned films like yours with no super heroes or explosions. Things aren't like the old days. You have to boast about your own movie.

WA: That's right. These days I gotta go out and sell my movie, which is hard for me because it's not like I make can openers or something. I'm supposed to be selling a work of art here, but you can't imagine Picasso knocking on doors and saying, "Hello, I made this painting, you can buy it, but if you don't like it, or it's too blue, I can put maybe a little bit more red in it …" So, you know, I understand you gotta let people know your movie's out there, but for me, it's an awkward situation.

JS: *Irrational Man* was well received in Cannes, as was *Midnight in Paris* and *Vicky Cristina Barcelona*. But that's not always the case. *Hollywood Ending* did not go down well in 2002. Cannes can be a brutal place to open a movie the critics don't like.

WA: Ah, well, that doesn't apply to me, or it doesn't affect me, because I never ever read about myself and that's because people always get everything wrong. Even when they want to be very nice, they're still wrong, so I never read about myself. I have found that the less you can think about yourself, the better off you are. The more you read: *He's wonderful, He's terrible, His movie is a masterpiece* or *It's a miserable failure*, then the more it stays in your mind and it can be a bother. So I don't read the critics, or the interviews in case I read back what I said and I know I'll hate it and wish I could take it back or say it better.

JS: You say you try not to think about yourself, but your films are full of thoughts and worries and musings about your place in the universe. It seems to me that you actually never stop thinking about yourself.

WA: Yes, well, I do a lot of worrying about my mortality. In that respect you're right. I think we all ponder on that, don't we? I don't suppose I do more than anyone else, but maybe it looks that way because it's the subject of my work. And those questions have always bothered me. I'm political as a citizen but not as an artist – I vote, I donate to campaigns, but in art I'm interested in those questions about our existence. And those are the things I want to talk about in movies and usually make jokes about, actually.

JS: When did you start worrying about such things?

WA: I became aware of it at about five years old. It's not so unusual, you know, you do become aware of it. Psychologists have studied and generally agree that children can be very aware of it …

JS: OK, so you knew your parents were going to die, and that you were going to die and everyone around you, but you at five years old took that philosophically rather than just going to your room to read comic books?

WA: Right. There are some people who are better adjusted than me who can say, "Oh well, that's the human condition, I accept that, and now I'm going to get on and enjoy myself," but I couldn't do that. I felt very clearly that *Gee this ruins everything*, and I was spoiled, you know. I said, *If that's it, I'm taking my ball and I'm going home, I don't want to play. If that's the rule, I don't like the game.* I had a bad reaction.

JS: For someone who felt so bad about life, you've had what we might call a very good innings.

WA: I was very lucky that way – jokes saved my life. I was not scholarly at school. I was interested in playing baseball and listening to jazz and I was thrown out of college and they threw me out of New York University for being a terrible student. But for some reason, and I really don't know why, I could write jokes. Nobody in my family ever wrote jokes or was in show business, nobody, and I was able to do good jokes. When I was 15, I could write them and sell them and make people laugh, and it really saved my life. I made money, I wrote, I worked in clubs and cabarets, telling jokes, on television and in theatre. And you make an exaggerated amount of money – you know, very quickly I made more selling jokes than my mother, who was a florist, and my father who did a lot of jobs – jeweller, taxi driver, bartender – more than they made put together … It's like an ear for music. I had an ear for jokes and if I hadn't had it, who knows what I'd have done? Many people have ears for jokes and they're amusing and they come to the wedding and the funeral or round for dinner and they can be funny, but I was a step ahead, I could do it professionally.

JS: How did your parents feel about that? Did they think you were funny?

WA: My parents were thrilled I was making money – they didn't know if I was funny. Only in later years when they saw my movies were being accepted by the public they felt comfortable. They weren't discouraging, they never said *Don't go into show business*, but they had no real opinion if it was funny or not funny. They were out of it.

JS: There's an old joke about the vaudevillian on his death bed, when his family are around him and saying it must be so hard to be slipping away and he says: "Dying is easy. Comedy is hard." You seem, however, not to rate comedy that highly.

WA: I wanted to write tragedies, but nobody would give me the chance to be Bergman, or Eugene O'Neill or Tennessee Williams. I always got hired to write jokes. They would say *But comedy is so much more valuable, so few people can do it, so we need you*. And they wouldn't put their money into me doing a serious picture – only after *Annie Hall*, United Artists let me, finally relenting to my whining. You know, for me, I felt the same way about comic things. I enjoyed a Bergman film more than a comedy at the movies. I'd enjoy the comedies and they entertained me, but I wasn't moved long after. If I went to a serious picture, even *Gone with the Wind*, I was more enthralled, more in awe. Comedy is like a dessert, but a serious film is a full meal.

JS: But you have made comedy into a life philosophy, a way of coping. The way you have used it, it's a legitimate response to the human condition. So why isn't being funny enough?

WA: I think there are a few reasons. That which comes naturally you tend to take for granted. You know, when I see someone who can draw, it's amazing to me. There was a girl next to me in class at school who would suddenly draw a horse, and it was perfect, like with the hair and the legs, it would be just like that, looking like a horse and because I'm someone who can't draw – I don't know how she does it. But to her it's nothing. So I said to her, "Wow! Drawing a horse like that is so hard," and she'd say, "No, it's easy, that's just how it comes out." So it's hard if you can't do it, but for me, comedy was not hard. I could just do it. So I'm like that, I never valued the comedy so much.

JS: But you joked about God and philosophy, addressing serious issues through comedy, no?

WA: Yes, but it was unintentional. I mean, I wrote the comedy that I thought was funny because these were the issues that were on my mind, it's what came out. I did think I won't write about politics or mother-in-laws, but I was thinking about mortality and the meaning of life and it just came out. And that became the basis for my comedy, but it was not forced, it was just what was on my mind. It's who I am. I've been asked: "Do you ever think you might wake up one morning and not be funny?" And honestly, that's never occurred to me. When I talk, when I do some thing, it comes out funny and I've no idea why. It's not something that can go away because it's just what I sound like or look like.

JS: How, then, has film making helped you deal with the big questions in life?

WA: There's no positive answer to the grim reality of life. No matter how much the philosophers or the priests or the psychiatrists talk to you, the bottom line is life has its own agenda and runs right over you, and so we're all gonna wind up in a very bad position one day. It's the same position for everyone, but it's a bad one.

The only way out of it, the only thing you can think of as an artist is to try and come up with something that can explain to people why life is worth living and is a positive thing that has some meaning. Now, you can't do that without conning them, really, because in the end it's a random universe and we're living a meaningless life. Forget everything you create or do in your life: it will vanish and the earth and the sun will burn out and the universe will be gone and it's over and everything that Shakespeare or Beethoven or Michelangelo did, it'll all be gone one day, no matter how much we cherish it. So it's very hard to sell someone a bill of goods that there's any good to this.

Therefore, my conclusion is, that the only possible way you can beat it a little bit is through distraction – you can distract people, so if you turn on the baseball or you watch Fred Astaire dance, you find something that distracts you. So for me, I'm thinking, *Can I get Emma Stone or Joaquin Phoenix to do this scene right?*, like it really means something in life – but it doesn't, it's a trivial problem, I'll solve it. And if I don't solve it, so it'll be a bad movie, but I won't die. So that's what I do, I distract myself.

And movie making is a wonderful distraction. These actresses come and they worry about their part and their character and how they're gonna do it and that's what they're thinking too. If they weren't doing that, they'd be at home or sitting on a beach or something thinking, *My God, what is life about? I'm gonna get old, I'm gonna die, my loved ones are gonna die, I'm gonna get Ebola,* you know …

So the only thing you can do in life is distract yourself so you have some moments when you're not facing reality – all the great thinkers all felt that too much reality was too much to bear. And that's a very grim thing to think about, that you have to keep pushing away reality – so I go into the movie house and watch Fred Astaire dance for an hour and a half and I'm not thinking about my death, my decaying body, that I will be old one day in the very distant future and that's it. Then I come out of the movie house and I'm struck by the problems that hit when I have to face reality again.

And movie making is a nice thing to keep me busy – like they give the inmates in an institution basket weaving to keep them occupied.

JS: You get distracted making the films and then they distract us. You've done it many times, every year, with these 50 or so movies. Can we tell anything about you from your movies? I think we can trace a line from *Take the Money and Run* through to *Irrational Man* and get something of you.

WA: There are recurring themes, certainly, but they're unintentional. It's like psychoanalysis: if you just talk and talk and talk, and the doctor doesn't say anything and then after five years, you notice that the same

subject has come up, it's obviously meaningful to you. So you could see that even with my earliest films, the same subjects were coming up – I mean *Love and Death*, for example, you could think it's a lot of jokes and it is, a million of them one after the other, but the jokes were all about life and death and mortality and choice, but there was no insight to them, they were just jokes, but the subjects were the same.

Similarly, over the years, I've done many things about magic because magic is related to religion, the belief that there is some force beyond what we see with our eyes, whereas in fact this is it, this is all you're gonna get, there's no magic, nobody's gonna save you.

So the same themes just pop up all the time. So yes, you can trace intellectual preoccupations and in the characters that I've played you can trace that I was pessimistic and it's remained that way, nothing has changed to make me feel better. I haven't gotten any more serious, for example. I was ponderously serious at a young age, I was boring to be with when I was young, always very serious then and if I'd have had my way I'd have made one very heavy movie after another my whole life and would not have worked in comedy except very sparingly, so in my case that was not something that came with age, that was with me my entire life.

JS: You don't feel that your films have made us pause and think about life?

WA: I've not succeeded in the job of the artist … to show people that you can at least enjoy life, or why there's a positive side to it somewhere. I find this very hard – in 45 movies I have failed to be able to do it, the most contribution that I could make is to distract people. So I've said, "Come to my movie, see *Bananas* or *Annie Hall*," and for two hours I forget my problems because there's other people up there, and music and maybe laughs, but then you come out of the theatre and you're faced with real life again and I don't like it. It's like a cold drink of water on a hot day – you'll say I've had it, I feel a little refreshed, enough to go on with my day, but then life starts crushing you and I need to watch basketball or go to the park to play with the children, something to distract from the terror …

JS: But many people have been inspired by you and by your films …

WA: Me? I don't say this with any modesty, my feeling is I've inspired nobody. It doesn't bother me at all, but when I look at my contemporaries, I can see the tremendous influence of Martin Scorsese, who I think is great, and I can see his influence every place, Steven Spielberg … but I can't see my influence. Whenever you see young film makers being interviewed, they always say *I grew up watching Spielberg* or *I saw* Star Wars, but my name never comes up. And I understand that, and the proof is on the screen – you don't see my influence up there like you see those others.

I myself was influenced, of course, by Bergman and Fellini and Truffaut and Godard, those icons of cinema who were around when I was a young man becoming interested in the movies, so it's not bad to influence people, but I don't mind if I hadn't have that …

JS: Well, you should see my record collection. I don't think I'd have found Gershwin or Harry James or Ben Webster without your movies.

WA: Oh I may have influenced people's record collection – I will admit that. And that's a great pleasure to me, the best part of making the movie, you know, putting on the music. When you finish a movie and there's no music in it, it's cold as ice, and then I go to the other room and pick out from the many records I keep in the room next to my cutting room, and we pick out Mozart, or Louis Armstrong and we bring 'em in and it can still look terrible, so we try another – quite randomly in some cases. In the case of *Irrational Man*, we put on the Ramsey Lewis, and click, instantly, the whole thing came to life. So if I've influenced people in their record collection, that's fine with me.

JS: You influenced my taste in women too, you made us fall in love with girls like Annie Hall …

WA: Well, you can't go wrong with that and you can't blame me for that. If you get in trouble with women, that's your business, don't take it out on me. I have certainly worked with some of the most lovely women in film. You know, starting way back with Janet Margolin, she was beautiful, and Diane Keaton, just beautiful and Scarlett Johansson now and Emma Stone, you just can't imagine anyone more beautiful, Charlize Theron, Mia Farrow, who I wound up fighting with, OK, but still beautiful as can be – just one after the other … Naomi Watts, all these terrific actresses too, Maureen Stapleton, Geraldine Page, Meryl Streep briefly, Cate Blanchett, Dianne Wiest, Gena Rowlands. I mean, they're great actresses …

I have learned that one of the great pleasures of life is to look at a beautiful woman. It makes you feel good, and one of the great things about show business is you get to work with beautiful women – you know if I worked in a drug store, which my mother wanted me to do, you know maybe once in a great while a beautiful woman might come in, but in the movies, every year, every day I go to work in the morning and eight o'clock in the morning, there's Emma Stone looking like she's a goddess, there's Scarlett or Naomi and you work with them all day and it's just great. And then you come in the next day, and there they are again and this goes on for months – I mean it's a great way to make a living …

Even the guys are charming, you know, some great actors, charismatic to be around – I mean, Colin Firth, he's a charming nice-looking witty man, and Michael Caine … and er, er, for some reason I can't remember the guys as easily as I remember the women, to be honest with you … that's the best part, the beautiful women and the music…

JS: I suppose if you don't feel your movies have had quite the weighty effect you wish they'd had, you could have been a novelist, but then you don't meet so many actresses.

WA: There's certainly a plus and minus to that choice of writing movies. If I see a scene in a movie and I don't like it – well, it's gonna cost me a million dollars to fix it, and I don't always have a million dollars to do that. But if you're writing a novel, you just screw up the paper and start over, nothing to it.

But there's a minus, because I have tried to write a novel and found it too hard. I obsess over every word and days go by and you've got a couple of pages done, it's like lapidary work, like a Fabergé egg or something, and I'm not a perfectionist like that, you know. With my films, I do it, we let the actors say what they want, we change it the next take, try it a different way, but the novel, it was so precise, so tough for me.

JS: But you still have managed great control over your movies and gotten so many great performances out of people.

WA: The secret to that is you hire great people, great actresses and actors, and then get out of their way. I don't play the director, I don't hover over them. You let them change your lines and make their own contributions and do things, because the people I've worked with have had careers and are famous before they met me and they're great in my movies and they're great when they leave me. I've found that's all you have to do – just don't mess them up, you know, it's a very simple thing. And then you get credit, people say, "Oh, you did such a great job," but it isn't that, you're just not screwing them up that's all.

JS: Over all these films, all the plots and stories and actresses, what have you learned in your 80 years?

WA: You become more tolerant of people, less cranky. I think you understand that everyone's got the same problems and fears so that makes you a bit nicer, more aware that everyone suffers when they're alone and you tend to care about that.

In movies you learn nothing. You learn very quickly after two or three movies – I had a great editor in Ralph Rosenblum and then the cinematographer Gordon Willis taught me some things, but after that it's all instinct.

In life, you can learn – I've been in and out of psychoanalysis many times and you learn a little bit, not much, it helps a bit, I wish it was a magical help, but it's not – but you learn that very little fantastic happens. I know people don't want to hear that necessarily because there's births and experiential events and marriages and deaths, but I've found it teaches you very little.

JS: What are doing for your 80th birthday?

WA: I'm hoping to sleep right through it.

Introduction

Director, writer, actor, musician, stand-up comedian, philosopher, author – Woody Allen is all of these things and more.

Over the course of 50 years, he has cemented his position in the history of cinema and, by extension, in both popular and academic culture. Now he is as iconic and instantly recognizable a figure as any of his heroes, from Charlie Chaplin to Groucho Marx and even Louis Armstrong.

He has perhaps exposed himself more than any of these, however, putting himself on the screen in mind and body, heart and soul, presenting generations of fans with stories that seem to offer dramatized versions of his own reality. His personal and private life, his lovers, friends and childhood have all become food for his creativity. They have become the building blocks for a remarkable body of work, a construction of stories and characters acting as both barrier and gateway.

This book aims to find out what we can about Woody Allen by using his films, those parts of his soul that he has let run (or sometimes walk) amok, on cinema screens around the world once a year, every year, since 1969.

What do these films and created characters tell us about the man himself? Just as importantly, what do they tell us about the world – or, at least, the world in which he lives? Vietnam, the first moon landing, the fall of the Berlin Wall, the Internet, 9/11, an African-American president, the dawn of the 21st century – all of this has happened during the years in which Woody Allen has been making films, but you wouldn't know it from watching them.

Could *Sleeper*'s Miles Monroe, the character frozen for 200 years, watch Woody's films to learn anything about what he'd missed? I doubt it. Yet, even so, these films have defined the neuroses, the fears, the loves, the language and the humour of several generations. This suggests that his work avoids contemporary matters to go much deeper, addressing our fundamental human needs and dealing in eternal themes – in much the same way that Shakespeare's plays don't require of their audience any knowledge of Elizabethan or Jacobean current affairs and fashions. Woody Allen's films are the abiding stuff of art – and that goes for the funny ones, the serious ones, the whimsical ones, the brilliant ones and, yes, even the bad ones.

But do these films, one by one and wire to wire, reveal the man to us, showing us how he grows over the years or how his attitudes to life alter? In attempting to trace the imprint of Woody Allen film by film, this book will look at the jokes, the philosophies and the stories that have earned their author 16 Oscar nominations for Best Original Screenplay. That's a record, an indicator that we may be looking at the greatest screenwriter ever, a man who has used the medium of the cinema to ask questions of the universe and who has fallen over, physically and emotionally, trying to answer them. And, thankfully, every year, he's got back up on his feet to try again.

Woody Allen's films capture the absurdity of life and love, the humour and the pain. He can somehow nail what is most modern and evolved about us and yet also skewer our most basic, primal urges. His characters take us to the abyss and yet transport us, in fits of laughter, on flights of fantasy. Alvy Singer, Fielding Mellish, Harry Block, Gil Pender – all these creations with their tics and stammers, their inadequacies, desires and thick glasses, are far removed from most of us, yet in them we see ourselves reflected.

Right "I had an ear for jokes. Without it, who knows what I would have done?" Woody Allen in 1967, New York City.

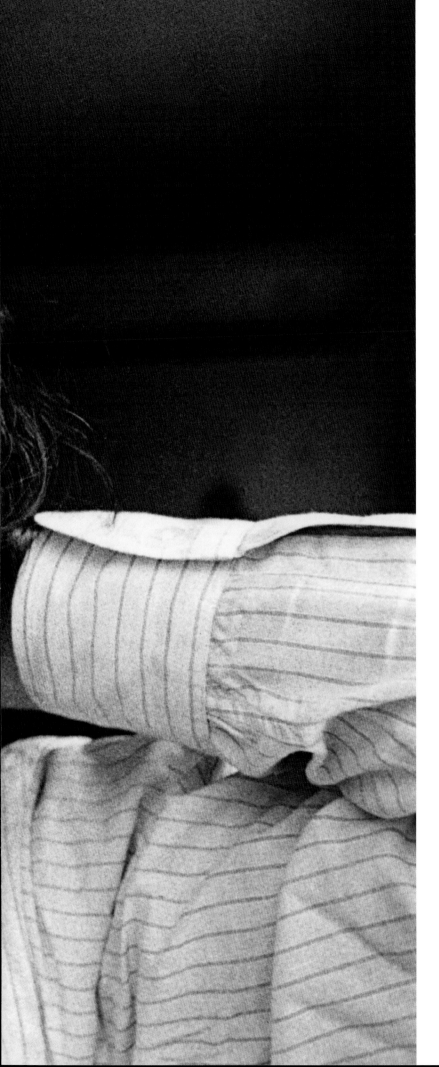

We will meet all of these characters throughout this book, and many more, male and female, all of them prismatic reflections of both us and of their creator, Woody Allen. Can we separate these fictitious folk from his life and our lives? Can he, especially when he plays most of them, or his real-life girlfriend does? As Alvy says of writing his first, rudimentary play in *Annie Hall*: "You know, you always try to get things to come out perfect in art because, uh, it's real difficult in life …" This book will examine the career-long tussle between the two.

I'm not sure Woody believes he ever got either art or life to come out perfect. As he told me recently and as he's often said before: "If I could I would shoot them all again, all my movies. But I don't have that luxury so, knowing that, when I make a film I never ever look at it again, because you always see what you did wrong and how you can improve it. I could very happily take any movie I have and shoot it again, if I could get the cast back and the circumstance by rolling back time, I'd do them all again."

I'm glad, however, that he can't do that. We need his characters to remain where they are, so we can have them as our guide to the universe Woody has created.

So, like Cecilia in *The Purple Rose of Cairo*, we will dive into Woody Allen's film world. Like Isaac in Manhattan, we will romanticize it out of all proportion. Like Sandy Bates in *Stardust Memories*, we will look for meaning. And like Mickey in *Hannah and Her Sisters*, we will probably find it only in the silliness of a Marx Brothers film. But we will keep looking because, well, we need the eggs.

Jason Solomons, 2015

Left "I always wanted to be a serious filmmaker." Woody lies back during a shoot for the *Evening Standard*, London, July 1971.

Woody the Actor, Woody the Writer

Above all else, Woody Allen has always considered himself a writer.
That famous Olympia typewriter, bought for $40 when he was 16 years old,
has tapped out millions of words and formed them into the jokes, stories,
stand-up routines and scripts that have made his name and fortune.

But would those words have had such an impact if he hadn't ended up voicing so many of them himself? As his stand-up career grew, Woody Allen's stage persona became so popular that audiences wanted to see that character in a variety of situations. So when it came to making his first film, Woody was stuck with him, if only for financial reasons. As Foster Hirsch put it in his 1981 book *Love, Sex, Death, and the Meaning of Life*: "*Take the Money and Run* is a mess Woody has been cleaning up ever since."

"You can't believe the problems I encounter writing for myself," Woody Allen told his biographer Eric Lax many years ago. "Because I'm not an actor, I'm not going to write a story where I play a southern sheriff. I'm always going to play within my limited range, and I'm believable as me only as certain things, as an urban, studious-looking twerp my age. I would not be believable, say, as a physical trainer or a Marine."

He does have what he terms a "minuscule" range – but as minuscule ranges go, it's one of the best. The persona, hiding behind thick glasses, has allowed him to articulate many of the absurdist and existential thoughts that have occurred to him as he writes, alone, in his room.

So Woody the writer was engaged in a long struggle to say what he had to say using the mouthpiece of a character only he himself could play – and that character was himself trapped in the body of a silent-era physical comedian but with the verbal wit of a Greenwich village stand-up. To put it another way, the Woody Allen persona is all the Marx Brothers in one. This was a clown who underwent psychoanalysis.

Woody's clowning, all things considered, is pretty good. Perhaps he doesn't have the balletic qualities of Buster Keaton or the athletic prowess of Harold Lloyd, but his physical routines are comic homages to these, if not outright spoofs. The comic urge is the same: to put Woody's character at the mercy of mechanisms.

To that end, he's a hapless product tester in *Bananas*, then a useless guerrilla fighter; in *Play It Again, Sam*, while trying to impress a girl, he falls over the sofa, knocks down shelves and sends a record flying out of its sleeve; he runs riot in a motorized wheelchair in *Sleeper* and dangles from a haywire tape machine; in *Love and Death*, he's fired out of a canon; in *Take the Money and Run*, he plays cello in a marching band and his carefully fashioned soap gun turns to bubbles in the rain. This isn't easy to pull off, but he does have a gift for it and it makes us laugh, if only because we know that we shouldn't be laughing at this kind of stuff any more. We're all more sophisticated than this, more evolved – aren't we?

You could see Woody's out-of-time physical clowning as a corrective to our own assumptions of intellectual superiority, and there's always humour in seeing an inadequate Jewish man trapped within all this mechanical paraphernalia, usually trying to impress a girl. It's a humour tinged with tragedy, of course, a crushing, absurdist comic mechanism.

By the time of *Annie Hall* and *Manhattan*, Woody was content or confident enough to just stand there and open with some gags.

Right Woody Allen tapping away at his trusty Olympia typewriter in his home in New York City, 1976 – a scene repeated almost every day since he was 16 years old.

No falling over was necessary, apart from some lovely comic business involving live shellfish. The characters of Alvy Singer and Isaac Davies presented a more relaxed protagonist, where the humour came from internal mechanisms rather than exterior ones – they still tripped, just not on giant banana skins but on their own neuroses and flaws, their psychological weaknesses. It is in these two performances that we probably see the greatest synthesis between Woody the actor and Woody the writer. Indeed, he's actually playing a writer.

In between, Woody did appear as someone who pretends to be a writer, in Martin Ritt's 1976 film *The Front*, probably his best performance as an actor-for-hire. His own mannerisms as Howard Prince are well tempered here. Firstly, by Michael Murphy, playing the blacklisted writer for whom Howard agrees to act as the titular "front", putting his name to a prolific series of scripts. Secondly, and perhaps most importantly, by the huge performance of Zero Mostel.

It's a great bit of casting and it probably taught Woody, a remarkably quick learner and autodidact, how to dial down his performances from the zaniness of the early comedies to the funny yet movingly tortured lovers of *Annie Hall* and *Manhattan*.

However, the salutary lesson came in *Stardust Memories*, when Woody played Sandy Bates and faced the ire of critics who'd begun to conflate Woody the writer and Woody the actor with Woody the man. "If I'd let Dustin Hoffman or some other actor play the lead, it would have been much less criticized, I think," he said. But the die was cast.

Having laid the ghost of the early, antic comedian, Woody the actor allowed Woody the writer to stretch his range. *Zelig*, a film that's partly about the nature of acting, required a hundred different little performances, which Woody achieves with underappreciated acting skill.

Left "You call your analyst Donny?":
Diane Keaton as Mary and Woody
Allen as Isaac, on the set of
Manhattan in 1979.

After that, during his most amazing run, Woody's writing and directing soared. *Broadway Danny Rose* aside, he appeared only in segments of his films, lightening the mood in those perfect dramas *Hannah and Her Sisters* and *Crimes and Misdemeanors*. In *Radio Days*, he only does the voice-over, reading out his own beautifully written narration – and, by the way, not even appearing in the credits.

And yet, the confusion remained – to the extent that by the time of the film *Husbands and Wives*, and the scandal of his relationship with Mia Farrow's adopted daughter Soon-Yi, viewers could no longer separate the writer/director/actor from the real person. And Woody knew it. In that film, he plays Gabe Roth, but nobody watching it on its release in 1992 could possibly see anything else but Woody Allen and Mia Farrow breaking up, cracking up. It's a raw wound of a film even today, and brilliant for it – but the blurring of, the convergence of, the professional and personal lines will always be one of the most bewildering moments in cinema.

Woody acted and wrote his way all the way through the scandal, even as the public perception of him altered. The delightful *Manhattan Murder Mystery* finds his performance and his writing at its most spry just when his reality was at its heaviest.

Bullets Over Broadway was fascinating because, for the first time, Woody appeared to give away the part he'd usually play himself – and to a younger man. John Cusack took the role of David Shayne, a character who, like Woody himself, was a playwright. "I'm an artist," are his very first words. Who was Woody trying to tell that to as he wrote it?

During the scandal, Woody could have chosen to withdraw the film persona, to retire the actor. Many people couldn't bear to look at him any more, feeling a sense of personal betrayal. New Yorkers even felt he'd let the city down, so bound up in his own screen images had Woody the actor, writer and director become. Yet there he was, in *Mighty Aphrodite* and *Everyone Says I Love You*, still trying to win our affections and still trying to have sex with younger women.

Perhaps his frustration climaxed in *Deconstructing Harry*: Woody played the angriest version of himself ever, in the form of bilious writer Harry Block who leaves a trail of destruction in his personal life as he tries to make his fictions work. "I'm sure everybody will think it's me," he said before he'd even made the film. It's the film in which the writer's creations overtake him, berate him but ultimately applaud him, while the real people he's hurt still hate him. "Our life consists of how we choose to distort it," concludes Harry as he writes another novel, about a man who's "too neurotic to function in life but can only function in art".

Woody the actor could be just another tool for Woody the writer, a way of ensuring that the vision he has at his typewriter comes out as close to the way he envisioned it. Maybe that's why he let Kenneth Branagh do such a close approximation of him in *Celebrity*, publicly praising the British actor for "getting every nuance of what I wrote".

Gradually, Woody the actor got older than Woody the writer. In *Small Time Crooks*, *The Curse of the Jade Scorpion*, *Hollywood Ending* and *Anything Else*, he simply didn't look the part any more. The jokes, the themes, the ideas were still there in the writing, but somehow the actor wasn't connecting with the material and audiences were not connecting back.

Almost in a bid to widen his appeal, Woody began acting in other people's films. *Scenes from a Mall* for Paul Mazursky, opposite Bette Midler, saw him play against type, sporting a ponytail and enjoying LA. I don't think anyone bought it, though.

In the TV version of *The Sunshine Boys* and opposite Peter Falk, Woody played the part for which George Burns had won an Oscar in 1975. It should have been a success – personally, I think they cast it the wrong way round and Woody should have taken the Walter Matthau part. As for Woody, all he has said is: "It was a very significant amount of money for two weeks' work, more than I make on my movies. I went in and I did it. What happened in the end I don't know, I never saw it."

In 1998, he had his biggest ever hit – *Antz*. "When you're the middle child in a family of five million, you don't get a lot of attention," complains Z-4195, a worker ant voiced by Woody. An early DreamWorks animation, the whole film plays out almost like one of the cartoon segments of *Annie Hall* (itself based on the Inside Woody Allen comic strip by Stuart Hample). Smartly, the other voices in *Antz* are provided by actors who have all appeared in Woody Allen films:

Sylvester Stallone, Gene Hackman, Sharon Stone, Christopher Walken and Dan Aykroyd. What's more, the story has some resemblance to the political satires of *Bananas* and *Sleeper*.

Woody's appearances in Stanley Tucci's *The Impostors* and Douglas McGrath's *Company Man* felt like brief turns to help out former collaborators and are little more than cameos. His part as a murderous butcher on the Mexican border in Alfonso Arau's *Picking Up the Pieces* seems plain weird.

In these acting appearances, Woody simply doesn't have the control he's accustomed to, and one can almost feel his contempt for the process. At least his most recent appearance, for John Turturro in *Fading Gigolo*, showed his comic mojo rekindled; he plays the fast-talking manager "pimping" out the initially reluctant gigolo, played by Turturro himself. It's a vaguely distasteful premise rendered funny and charming by the comedy, with Woody feeling very much at home making Jewish gags in the face of heavy enforcers.

In his own work, the gradual fading out of Woody the actor has given the writer a certain freedom. *Match Point* and *Blue Jasmine* do not have characters that might be identified as the Woody "surrogate" – and are all the more remarkable and unusual for it. Owen Wilson's Gil in *Midnight in Paris* is clearly a part Woody might once himself have played, but the Californian actor brings a lovely looseness to it, obliterating the Woody stammers and tics with great success.

Woody the actor – the icon with the glasses, the nasal whine, the hair, the shrugging hands and the verbal tics – will remain in our consciousness, although he will forever be confused – one character with another, and with Woody Allen the man. That was part of his existence, part of his raison d'être, a magician's trick to distract us, a sort of glamorous assistant to the writer.

Woody the writer, however, is likely to endure far longer, with other actors coming along over time to play the parts Woody once did, bringing new nuances and rhythms to the themes. As we have seen, Woody the actor is, in general, lost without a really fine writer; Woody the writer can be even better with other actors speaking his words, as all those Oscar winners from his films will happily attest.

Themes, Styles and Motifs

Wander into any cinema or come across a TV station playing one
of his films, and you will instantly recognize a Woody Allen world.

That is, for me, the very definition of an auteur, and with
Woody it is something pronounced and profound. Of course,
the first giveaway for a casual viewer might be his own appearance
in it; yet even in the 18 films in which he does not appear, his
presence is just as strong.

You will probably hear jazz. Whatever the period or the tone,
Woody Allen usually finds an audio match for his visual images
from interpretations of the Great American Songbook – by
composers such as Cole Porter, Jerome Kern, Rodgers and Hart,
and Gershwin, performed by artists such as Erroll Garner, Lester
Young, Duke Ellington, Coleman Hawkins and Louis Armstrong.
You might hear a bit of classical music (Prokofiev for *Love and
Death*, Mendelssohn in *A Midsummer Night's Sex Comedy*, the tenor
Caruso in *Match Point*), but most likely, the soundtrack will feature
jazz, even 200 years in the future.

As for his visual traits, these have been honed to become almost
a trademark. A character might well wander into a bathroom,
out of shot and keep talking, leaving us listening but watching
an empty hallway or bed. They will most probably return a few
seconds later, maybe with a little brown box of pills to quell the
headache brought on by that same conversation.

We might watch from across a New York street as a couple
emerge in long shot from an opposite building, and we will
probably follow them along the pavement, almost spying on them
as they speak. Or we will be a block away and they will walk
towards us, slowly coming into focus while we listen to their chat.
Then the lead character might directly address the camera.

These stylistic refrains welcome us into the world of the film.
It is most likely that the colour palette will be a familiar shade of
beige mixed with warm autumnal colours (never any blue), just

as Woody's outfits will be brown cords and tweedy Ralph Lauren
jackets over a plain V-neck jumper or unshowy but tailored shirt.
Alternatively, the film might be shot in black and white – starting,
of course, with that familiar, welcoming, white-on-black font
(Windsor Light Condensed) for the opening and closing credits.

Speaking in Bob Weide's definitive filmed portrait *Woody Allen:
A Documentary*, the critic FX Feeney claims that the use of black and
white in *Manhattan* creates "a nostalgia for the present". But Woody
also achieves this when working in colour, using the sorts of earth
tones and sepias which mean that as soon as the image plays in front
of your eyes, it takes on the quality of memory. The story melts
away, into myth, not after it's told but even while it's being told.

What typifies Woody Allen's films is their remarkable facility
for toggling between past and present, slipping into different modes
with a smooth economy and narrative precision. Despite these
huge leaps of logic, the audience are rarely left wondering: "What
just happened?" or "Is this a dream sequence?" or "Wait, how is he
talking to his mother?" There is never any need for wobbly visual
dissolves, special effects or *Twilight Zone*-style music to signal this
alternate mode. And Woody can do it in any genre or tone: *Midnight
in Paris, Annie Hall, Crimes and Misdemeanors, Another Woman* – in all
these films, characters wander the rooms of their past and interact
with other characters to comic, philosophical or tragic effect. The
weird thing is that it never, not for a second, feels weird at all.

Right Fashion icon Woody relaxes,
showing off his typical casual
ensemble of beiges, a costume
he has worn on and off screen.

Just as his characters will interpose in their own backstory, so too will they swap their reality to disappear into fantasies and fictions. Cecilia, the Depression-era heroine of *The Purple Rose of Cairo*, falls in love with a fictional character from a film. He jumps right out of the screen to join her in dowdy New Jersey; later, just as neatly, she will jump into the screen for a breathless night in his glamorous movie world.

Owen Wilson's Gil Pender will fall in love with "a woman from another era" in *Midnight in Paris* and spend nights in the 1920s with the Fitzgeralds and Hemingway as well as an evening in the Belle Époque with Degas. Harry Block in *Deconstructing Harry* takes a standing ovation from the characters he created. In *Play It Again, Sam* Humphrey Bogart is perched on the sofa, advising Alan Felix about "dames". Alec Baldwin advises the younger Jesse Eisenberg after they meet in *To Rome with Love*. And the nondescript Zelig plays jazz in Harlem, tennis in Hollywood with Charlie Chaplin, mixes with presidents and finally puts Adolf Hitler off his oratory.

Whimsical though these elements might seem, the result is often as poignant as it is funny and playful. When the comedy dies down, Cecilia and Gil will have to choose between fantasy and reality; Harry Block will have to exploit some other real-life situation or person to "spin gold out of human misery"; and for Alice the invisibility herbs are great fun, but they will also lead to her discovering her husband's infidelity.

Above "If I only had the nerve to do my own jokes ..." – Woody prepares to direct on the set of *Annie Hall*.

So much of Woody Allen's work is about this tension between art and life, fantasy and reality, but this is not limited to his characters. The possibility always hovers over the work that this is Woody's own life we are watching. More than for any other artist, the temptation is to read these works autobiographically. How can *Annie Hall* not be inspired by the love affair between Woody and Diane Keaton (real name: Diane Hall)? How can we not see Hannah as Mia Farrow herself, when those are her real children, real mother and real apartment up there on the screen? Surely Sandy Bates in *Stardust Memories* and Harry Block are dark embodiments of their creator's true soul? And what of *Husbands and Wives*, in which Mia Farrow tells Woody Allen on screen "we both know it's over" just as the whole world had found out that, in real life, it was over between them, too?

Woody strenuously denies in interviews that his films are autobiographical. His characters, he insists, are just creations, but because he has often chosen to play them himself, audiences

> ## "My one regret in life is that I'm not someone else."
> Woody Allen

think it's really him. The whiny, neurotic, weedy Jewish stand-up comedian – the one who went to a fancy dress party with a moose or who, in the event of war, became a hostage – may not be the real Woody Allen, but it's a likeable, acceptable version of him, and in his presence people are comfortable enough to laugh.

But it is an undeniable marker of the work that this particular artist puts, if not himself, then something of himself or someone sounding very much like himself, into every frame. Such is the conflation of artist and work that even when actors as varied as John Cusack, Kenneth Branagh, Owen Wilson, Will Ferrell, Jason Biggs, Jesse Eisenberg and Larry David (or, for that matter, Gena Rowlands, Mia Farrow or Mary Beth Hurt) play a part, they are viewed by many as Woody Allen "surrogates". This from the man who once said: "My one regret in life is that I'm not someone else." Most of the time, he is.

The other key recurring themes in his work are death and Jewishness. Again, Woody's characters tend to have the same fear of mortality as his stand-up persona ("I am not afraid of death, I just don't want to be there when it happens") and they tend to want answers to the big existential questions. Wondering about God, one character pleads: "If he would just speak to me once. Anything. A sentence. Two words. If he would just cough." Not many knockabout farces are concerned with such things as the meaningless of existence and the expanding universe. As Alvy's mother says to her five-year-old son in *Annie Hall*: "What is that your business?"

I'm not sure that his Jewishness has influenced his view of death ("There is the fear that there is an afterlife but no one will know where it's being held"), but it certainly influences his adult philosophy. His persona, his delivery, has traded on him being Jewish, making for a lifetime of material – on such matters as outsider status, assimilation, sex, anti-Semitism, the folly of religion, and the question of morality.

For many viewers around the world throughout the 1970s and '80s, Woody Allen personified the New York Jew: the neurotic, unsporty, Holocaust-obsessed, urban intellectual who, when faced with sex, the countryside or anything mechanical, becomes a total "schlemiel". "I am at two with nature," he says.

Putting such a Jew into a variety of incongruous situations was a recipe for hilarity. Two hundred years into the future, a Russian during the Napoleonic Wars, in the middle of a Latin American guerrilla revolution – in any of those settings, even dropping a Jewish name or accent was good for a big laugh. There were the robot tailors in *Sleeper*, the enormous deli order in *Bananas*, the soldier in *Love and Death* who declares that "History shall mark my name well: Sidney Applebaum", and promptly collapses, dead.

Once established and with audiences baying for more of it, that humour could be carried over into "a nervous romance" such as *Annie Hall* or *Manhattan*, where the Jew is hopelessly out of his skin at a WASP Thanksgiving table ("It's dynamite ham") or where he lives up to his cultural stereotype while taking a taxi with Mary (and no Jewish girls are called Mary): "You're so beautiful I can barely keep my eyes on the meter."

Zelig plays on questions of identity and acceptance with great ingenuity and it could well be his most Jewish film, except that there is another contender in the form of *Crimes and Misdemeanors*. It also engages in theological debate around the morality stemming from a father's religious teachings: "The eyes of God are on us always," the young Judah is told.

In the exquisitely self-mythologizing memoir *Radio Days*, the family is horrified when Uncle Abe eats with the communist neighbours on Yom Kippur (he's immediately punished by a mild heart attack). They also accept they will always be excluded from the glamour of uptown Manhattan: "They don't take Jews at the Stork Club." And Allen takes his Jewishness to its hilarious limit in "Oedipus Wrecks", his chapter of *New York Stories*, when the Manhattan skyline is dominated by his over bearing Jewish mother urging him not to marry a "shiksa" …

Just as indicative are the times when Woody feels the need to sublimate his Jewishness, such as in his late, European phase or in his "serious" dramas. The three dramas *Interiors*, *September* and *Another Woman* take place among the East Coast elite – a milieu so rarefied that he dare not make an appearance, lest his Jewishness and comedy ruin the atmosphere.

Match Point, too, is set among a London elite – the outsider here is the social-climbing tennis pro. Nor do *Cassandra's Dream*, *You Will Meet a Tall Dark Stranger*, *Vicky Cristina Barcelon*a or *Magic in the Moonlight* have a single Jewish character or even a word of Yiddish. It is odd, but I believe these films do thereby lack a certain something, even when they are grappling with such familiar themes as fate, luck, death, morality, sex, magic and the afterlife.

All his other films contain at least a shrug of Jewishness: even in *Sweet and Lowdown*, the prostitutes joke that business is slow "because it's a Jewish holiday" and *A Midsummer Night's Sex Comedy* may be set before there were many Jews established in the upstate countryside, but it features Woody himself at the mercy of mechanical inventions.

Amid the magic and the nostalgia other themes recur in Woody's work with such regularity you might term them obsessions: sex, neurotic actresses, prostitutes, paranoia, Groucho Marx, antipathy to California, hatred of TV, psychoanalysis, Nazis, novelists, film makers, hypochondriacs, masturbation, celebrity, crime, show business.

Like Clark says in Neil Simon's *The Sunshine Boys* – a play adapted for television in 1996 starring Woody – there are some words that just are funny. For Clark it was words with a "k" – pickle, chicken, Alka-Seltzer. For Woody Allen there are keywords that he will fall back on and from which he will always get a laugh thanks to the way he delivers them: moose, Boy Scouts, shellfish, sinuses, dental hygienists, insurance salesmen, Finklestein, Mandelbaum, Fischbein, tremendous, corned beef, chicken, allergies, New Jersey, penis envy, nauseous, fleeing, masturbation, egg salad, polo mallet.

And if you're not laughing by now, Woody Allen's world probably isn't for you.

Right Woody Allen delivering a classic stand-up routine: "I shot a moose once. I was hunting upstate New York, and I shot a moose …"

Waiting for Woody

Woody Allen's bestselling *Without Feathers* includes a secret diary with instructions that it should be published "posthumously, or after his death, whichever comes first". A mock journal entry reads: "Should I marry W? Not if she won't tell me the other letters in her name."

Just as Woody is wary of this W, so too, perhaps, should we be wary of Woody Allen. This is an artist who, throughout his long career, has seemed willing to show us the other letters in his name – but it's a name that isn't his own.

So, we can know that he was born Allan Stewart Konigsberg on 1 December 1935, in a lower-middle-class area of the Bronx, New York, to parents named Nettie and Martin Konigsberg. Shortly after, the couple moved to Brooklyn, probably after much arguing.

We know it was a happy, well-fed childhood and that Martin did a variety of jobs, from engraving jewellery to driving a cab. We know the young Allan went to Public School 99 and then Midwood Elementary School – and that he hated both and didn't do particularly well. He was also sent to Hebrew school, with similar results.

He would spend days practising magic tricks, mastering a sleight of hand he has maintained all his life. We know he taught himself the clarinet with the help of a well-known jazz musician, Gene Sedric, who visited the family home. He also took tap classes and spent hours listening to radio programmes and disappearing into the several local movie houses – particularly in the heat of the summer because he liked the air-conditioning as much as the films.

At 16, he began to send jokes to newspapers and agents who would use them for their celebrity clients' ghosted columns. As soon as his own name began to appear in print, he changed it. And this "Woody Allen" has been getting cheques for his writing every week since 1952.

I cannot do justice here to the biographical picture already assembled in books by John Baxter or Eric Lax, and brought to life – partly in the company of Woody Allen himself – in Bob Weide's superb documentary. That film is particularly smart on Woody's early years and shows how these youthful days later fed the characters of *Annie Hall* and *Radio Days*, where autobiographical memories were amplified into glorious comic details.

There are the summer days he spent in the Catskill resort Tamiment, honing his comic writing skills with sketch shows for holidaying Jews; his days writing comedy for Sid Caesar alongside Mel Brooks; and his time in LA working for *The NBC Comedy Hour* with Danny Simon, Neil Simon's brother. There is his failed marriage to Harlene Rosen at the age of 19 and his brushes with college education, which kindled an enduring interest in philosophy, literature and smart women.

Then there are the hours spent writing comedy routines and then overcoming his nerves to perform them himself, encouraged by the management of Charles Joffe and Jack Rollins. They put the nervous young comic on to chat shows and TV spots to widen his appeal while he toiled at night in Greenwich Village stand-up clubs or cabaret venues in Chicago.

All this time, Woody Allen was creating himself and his act – the name, the glasses, the persona of the stammering, neurotic weakling with the unfeeling parents and the heartless wife who'd come into the bathroom and sink his boats.

It was this man, this creation, that the world came to know and like – and it is with this creation that we must concern ourselves

Right Blowing hot at the Carlyle, New York, 1996: Allan Stewart Konigsberg took his pen name from jazz clarinettist Woody Herman.

"The theater is for entertainment … There's an old saying, if you want to send a message, call Western Union."

Woody Allen

in this book, a biography through film. This Woody Allen had the same problems with life and love as his audience. He was a bundle of worries and witty observations that chimed with the speed of 1960s urban modernity, and he seemed to symbolize New York's intellectual prowess and sophistication yet also epitomize its street smarts and survival instinct in a philosophically hostile, post-Holocaust universe.

While every joke, every story appeared to let the audience further into the world and mind of Woody Allen, each phrase was in fact taking us further away from Allan Stewart Konigsberg. By the time his film career took off, audiences felt they knew him to the point they cherished him as part of their own family. All the early heroes he played – Virgil Starkwell, Fielding Mellish, Miles Monroe, Victor Shakapopulis, Allan Felix, Boris Grushenko, Alvy Singer and Isaac Davis – looked like Woody Allen.

These were men who kept hiding behind the glasses and under the untameable ginger hair even when camped in the jungle, forming part of a chain gang or beating a man with a giant strawberry – but these men were not one man. Cumulatively, they might have stood for the lonely Jew. Philosophically, these characters appeared to be the only Jew left standing in a world where the brutally efficient system of the Holocaust had succeeded and, but for Woody, there was no one left in the universe capable even of telling jokes, let alone laughing at them. Miles, Boris, Fielding, Virgil are all Jews out on their own, while Alvy feels anti-Semitic paranoia on the New York streets.

What I'm trying to say is that we cannot know Woody the real man from all of these works, despite his constant, teasing invitations for us to do so. This game of non-disclosure deepens the more the work matures, with films such as *Zelig* practically spelling out these problems of identity and the ludic nature of film imagery.

And yet, his films are a truth – he made them, appeared in them and played roles that he had imagined and written for himself, often alongside actors to whom he was close and whose roles he had also imagined. As Jean-Luc Godard points out, film is truth 24 times a second and these 50 Woody Allen films do document what happened when the cameras were rolling and a

man calling himself Woody Allen stood in front of those cameras, often with his lovers, and performed and joked and fretted and gave us a version of truth.

To what extent are these characters his mouthpiece? As Woody once wrote: "The theater is for entertainment. There's an old saying, if you want to send a message, call Western Union." But audiences have found many messages in his films, works in which he has examined, excused and explained his characters' behaviour, and has outlined the ideas, morals and philosophies that he believes make life bearable, liveable, workable.

Woody Allen's characters rarely condemn others, nor are they themselves condemned by anything other than their own behaviours. They assume the moral consequence of their actions, whatever they can get away with. Are they selfish, non-judgemental to the point of amorality? Or do they simply provide an excuse for the artist behind them to be as selfish as he might wish?

Can we even say the "real" Woody Allen is hiding in the work? It all seems pretty simple to me. The stories and characters might not be actually, pedantically, physically autobiographical, but all the jokes and the troubles and the existential despair, all that stuff is emotionally and philosophically biographical. In other words, we can suppose that Woody really thought these thoughts and felt these feelings and then figured out how to express them pithily or bring them to dramatic life on the screen.

Perhaps my suggestion that these characters are his "mouthpiece" is pertinent. Maybe Woody Allen is not like a filmmaker at all, but rather a jazz musician, using his instrument for self-expression. Like some of the jazz artists he so admires, he has lived a creative life, always playing, recording, forming new bands and puffing out new variants on old tunes well into old age, creating new compositions and collaborations, reinventing himself and his music.

Tapping away, he makes his typewriter his keyboard, his piano. In that sense he has outdone his avowed heroes such as Louis Armstrong and Art Tatum. Nor has he lived the drug life or the drunken, dissolute life of the true jazz bohemian such as he imagines in his film *Sweet and Lowdown*. No, he is perhaps more akin to the great survivors and professionals of the bebop era, and

Above Woody directing on the set
of *Melinda and Melinda*, a film split
between comedy and tragedy.

the hard bop era that developed from it, players such as Sonny Rollins, Herbie Hancock and Wayne Shorter. Like Woody, they started work in clubs in the 1950s and have continued issuing new iterations and sounds, experimenting and gigging well into this new century. We can know these men only through their music, through the way they interpret songs both familiar and new. Nevertheless, after so many songs, albums, concerts and tunes, we do feel we know them, and even feel we own a part of them.

It is that sense of familiarity and friendship with a great artist through his work that resulted in what has (and I write this with a certain sadness) come to define the life and image of Woody Allen: the whopping great scandal of his real love life. "The heart wants what it wants," he explained, stealing from Emily Dickinson. Yet so many people felt – and still feel – that his choice to begin a relationship with the young, adopted daughter of his longtime partner Mia Farrow represents some kind of betrayal, as if he were reneging on the contract he signed when they bought their tickets to see his films.

Couldn't Woody have stopped himself, they ask, when he first had feelings for Soon-Yi? He must have known a whole

heap of trouble lay ahead. Is it possible that the artist in him had constructed so many non-judgemental moral universes that this real situation, no matter how toxic, simply seemed to him to be yet another scenario produced from his never-ending stream of creativity?

For all the acts and routines and films and tunes that have created Woody the man, the one choice made by the man himself is this love affair with a much younger girl who had appeared in one of his films and who spent her formative, teenage years living as the daughter of the woman who was then his lover and the biological mother of one of his children.

Many have seen this as indicative of a moral lassitude, even depravity. Critics have, seriously, suggested that all his work since – nearly 25 films – has been tarnished by this one act. That he has, in other words, spent the 25 years since making films that are thinly

veiled, grovelling apologies which have also sought to justify his despicable behaviour – to himself and to us.

Well, he did make those films, and if that is how some choose to interpret them, that is their choice. Audiences can look for autobiography in these later works as much as they like – as much as they do in the early, funny films.

But there is also the incontrovertible fact that Woody Allen the man has spent those 25 years with Soon-Yi, raising a family and finding some kind of happiness. Indeed, the two have been married since 1997. So would it be outrageous to see Woody's love for her as an admirably brave and romantic act? And to suggest that he made the decision to follow his heart despite finding himself cut off from part of his own family and demonized by half the world – the same audience that used to worship him.

Like those many characters he has created, we cannot expect Woody the man to behave in a way that would please everyone all of the time. That is an impossible task for anyone, from a politician to a sports star.

Woody has had to live his life the only way he can make it work for himself. All those who would denigrate him may well be jealous of his freedoms – artistic, financial and moral – but these are freedoms he has never hidden from us, freedoms he has long espoused in his work.

I don't propose that the behaviour in this one aspect of his private life is to be lauded or seen as normal. But that it should tarnish the work – whether made before or after – is ridiculous.

Woody the man and Woody the artist have been engaged in one long tussle during a yearly cycle in which both must necessarily co-exist at the same time. Woody the man is constantly, physically engaged in the many processes of being Woody the artist – the writer, thinker, actor, director and/or musician.

Meetin' WA was what Jean-Luc Godard called the short film about interviewing Woody in 1986. In fact and in fiction, Woody Allen invites us in while also keeping a distance. "WA" are simply two letters in a made-up name, part of a creation that has allowed him many roles. So many that maybe only a typewriter can make sense of them all.

"The heart wants what it wants."

Woody Allen

Left Woody strikes a pose on a visit
in 1964 to Manchester, England,
where he recorded a now legendary
stand-up set for Granada Television.

Below Hard work: Woody Allen
looks strained during an interview,
November 1998.

The Cultural Impact of Woody Allen

He might not have invented the genre of romantic comedy – for argument's sake, let's agree that was Shakespeare in *The Taming of the Shrew* – but Woody Allen certainly reinvented it in *Annie Hall*.

Since 1977, almost every film about relationships has been inescapably in its debt, even down to the inevitable jazz-inflected soundtrack and the dominance of New York as a romantic locus. From Rob Reiner's *When Harry Met Sally* (1989) to Noah Baumbach's *While We're Young* (2015), and every pale imitation in between, neurotic Jewish boys have been smitten by whimsical Gentile girls, trying to get them into bed with jokes rather than animal magnetism.

Although Annie and Alvy ultimately break up, the witty stuff does at least work in the movies. But there must be countless Jewish guys who've tried it in real life, only to lose out to more proactive wooers. (Just me, then?)

Thankfully, Woody's lasting imprint isn't all about Jewishness. *Annie Hall* had a huge impact on fashion, Diane Keaton's self-styled "look" inspiring trends for years to come. But the film also had a formal, visual and verbal influence, changing the way people spoke and what they spoke about, an influence extended and deepened by Woody's repeated capturing of urban mores and foibles in new filmic iterations every year.

Manhattan, Broadway Danny Rose, Hannah and Her Sisters, Radio Days, Another Woman – these films made it OK to feel inadequate and lost, and to question the meaning of existence even while still enjoying sports, sex, Chinese food and the opera. Woody Allen films simultaneously smartened everyone up intellectually and loosened them up emotionally and philosophically. He made us want to improve, and always pricked pomposity for trying to keep us down. Although the people most in his debt are probably psychiatrists, a profession he made publicly acceptable even while satirizing it,

we've all wanted our own Marshall McLuhan moment so we could embarrass some ass who thinks they know better in a cinema queue.

Allen's influence isn't merely cinematic. Hit TV shows such as *Friends*, *Seinfeld*, *Sex and the City*, *Scrubs* and *Girls* owe everything to Alvy and Annie in the way the characters speak and write, work and socialize, kvetching and confessing to each other and to us, the audience. Woody's ability to write such terrific parts for actresses (13 women in his films have been Oscar-nominated) has done a lot to redress perceived gender imbalances in films. Woody's women are often smarter than his men and are certainly more complex.

To label Woody a rom-com writer is grossly reductive, though. Only six or seven of his films can even faintly be described in that way, and he very rarely conforms to any genre. Rather, he takes elements of established genres to create situations in which everyday people get mixed up, as if they'd unwittingly wandered into someone else's plot, as in *Manhattan Murder Mystery*, or *Sleeper*, or *Small Time Crooks*.

But there are countless stand-up comedians today influenced by his albums and routines and many writers and thinkers inspired by his collected writings in *Getting Even* and *Without Feathers*. Not to mention the many jazz collections that must have started with a Woody Allen soundtrack. (My own is pretty extensive, but I still bought Ben Webster and Art Tatum's 1956 collaboration straight after hearing it again when watching *September* for this book.)

Watching Woody Allen makes you want to watch old musicals and films by Bergman, Fellini or the Marx Brothers. They make you want to imagine and think and go against the mainstream. They may well be the work of a depressive, but most of the films themselves err on the side of hope, laughter and having "a little faith in people".

Below "Not only is there no God,
but try finding a plumber on
Sunday": Woody thinks about
life in New York, 1978.

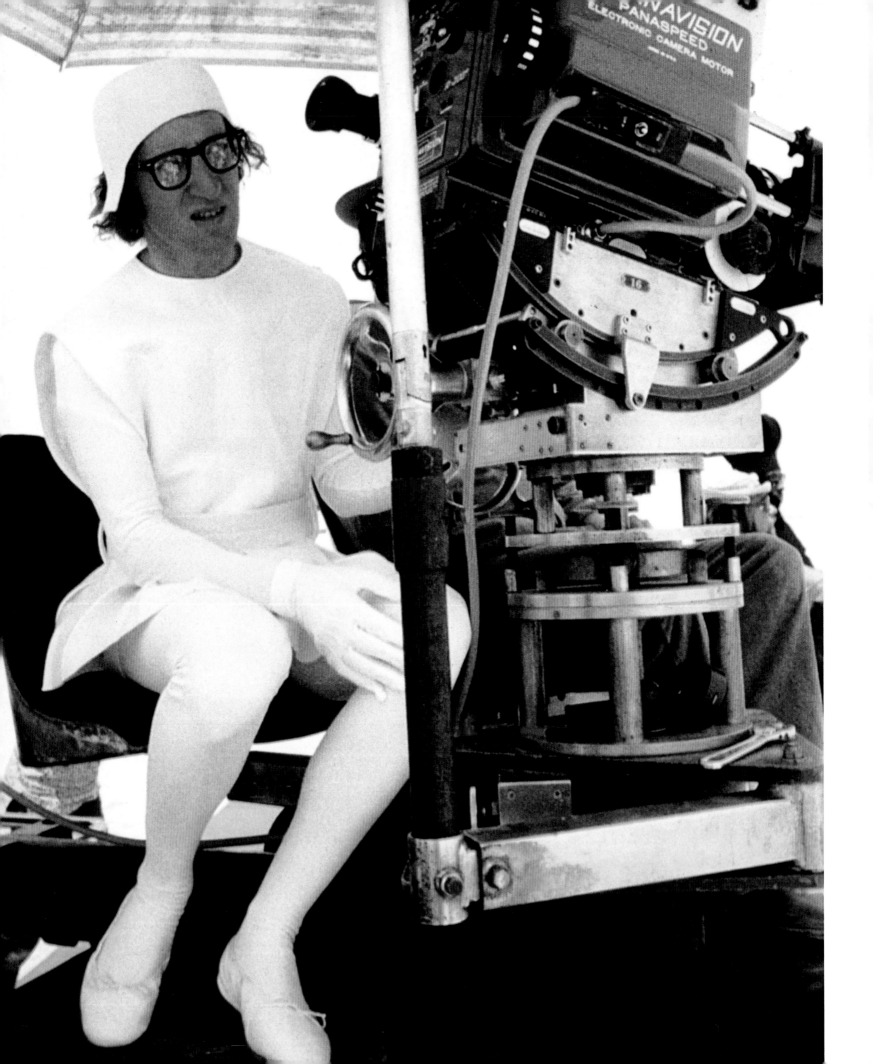

Above Woody's New Year's Eve parties became a fixture of New York society. Here, he leaps into 1968 over some flowers left from the night before.

Left Woody Allen displays the perils of the comic auteur – would you take direction from a sperm?

Outside the confines of what's up on the screen, Woody's methods are equally an inspiration. This guy stuck in the music and romance of the 1930s has somehow been an example to successive generations of independent filmmakers, including Spike Lee, whose debut *She's Gotta Have It* earned him the label of "the black Woody Allen". Chris Rock has now happily taken over that role.

Meanwhile, Nicole Holofcener, a former assistant on *A Midsummer Night's Sex Comedy* and *Hannah and Her Sisters*, has been dubbed "the female Woody Allen" for such films as *Walking and Talking* and *Please Give*.

Woody has inspired independent filmmakers too. His ability to work the way he has wanted; to retain final cut; to experiment with colour, time, tone, genre, comedy or drama from film to film; to write, direct *and* star – all this has been a shining example to filmmakers such as Jim Jarmusch, Hal Hartley, Richard Linklater, Steven Soderbergh and even Quentin Tarantino. True, nobody has quite Woody's power or his ability to do it year after year and to keep attracting such top talent. But the ideal of a distinctive style and voice, as well as the concept of a repertory of actors to execute his ideas, have remained a beacon for aspiring directors.

And what of the careers launched by a Woody Allen film? It's practically a badge of honour to have appeared in one of his films, and it's something for which actors are happy to take massive pay cuts, just as they are to play Shakespeare in the Park. (Just going to take that excuse to quote Tony Roberts delivering one of my favourite lines: "I did Shakespeare in the Park, Max, I got mugged.") And although some of his films may not be as good as others, no actors were ever harmed in the making of them. In fact, they all come out with reputations enhanced.

Many big stars got their first breaks with tiny parts in Woody's films: Sigourney Weaver, Christopher Walken and Jeff Goldblum in *Annie Hall*; Sylvester Stallone in *Bananas*; Sharon Stone in *Stardust Memories*; Julia Louis Dreyfus and John Turturro in *Hannah and Her Sisters*; William H Macy in *Radio Days*. We can go on playing such blink-and-you'll-miss-them games: spot Kirsten Dunst in *New York Stories*, Zach Braff in *Manhattan Murder Mystery*, Paul Giamatti in *Mighty Aphrodite* and *Deconstructing Harry*, Natalie Portman in *Everyone Says I Love You*, JK Simmons in *Celebrity*, and Tom Hiddleston and Léa Seydoux in *Midnight in Paris*.

Woody's consistency – of thought and productivity – has kept his creativity rolling along for 50 years. He's his own mini-studio, his own production line, one blissfully free from much commercial or financial imperative. As he strides into his 80s, his longevity is becoming as admirable as his art, perhaps all part of that famous desire to achieve immortality not through his work but by "not dying".

Watch his films, and you become immersed in the artistic process along with him. It may well be a leftover from his stand-up days, but the audience feels part of the work, as if we are witnessing a step in the creation of a project. Of course, at the basest level, if nobody's watching a film, it doesn't exist, so getting it out to an audience is always a most important step. But you do feel part of a loyal family just by watching. Maybe I'm a weird case, but the familiarity of those recurring names over the end credits is as comforting as the typeface in which they appear, disembodied names such as Scenic Artist James Sorice, or Louis Sabat on Boom and the dependable Transportation Captain called Harold "Whitey" McEvoy – whom I imagine with a shock of grey hair under his captain's hat, shouting at convoys of equipment trucks as they take over some Midtown street.

At the risk of being impolite, watching some of the weaker films even feels sometimes like attending a read-through. If you ask me, though, that's actually a bit of a thrill, one that elevates the action of watching them into an artistic process itself, one in which your own imagination does a few more takes and tightens up some dialogue. You might even feel like shouting your notes out loud – I mean, it worked for Cecilia in *The Purple Rose of Cairo*

and Cheech in *Bullets Over Broadway*, who both left their seats in the stalls to became active participants.

I don't think Woody Allen's intent was ever to become an example or a breeding ground. He wants, above all, to make us think and to question. Through identification with his many characters, these films make us reflect on our own relationships, to each other and to the universe.

Woody's films, as I've already pointed out, don't have much context. You don't need to know much about 1970s politics, '80s fashions or '90s celebrities to understand them – the abiding context lies in the characters' relationship in the wider scheme of things, in their place in a godless and cruel expanding universe. Given that context, the films ask: how on earth do we get by? And then they provide the answer: with love, laughter, music, sex, movies, writing, working – you know, whatever works.

Annie Hall and *Manhattan* caught the zeitgeist of a generation thinking about such things (crystallized in the image of Ike and Mary, soaking wet, pondering infidelity on the lunar surface of the Planetarium). Now, I'm sure, there are younger filmgoers who saw *Midnight in Paris* and were enchanted by the romance, the fantasy, the jazz of Sidney Bechet (which they may well not have heard before) and then inspired to find out more about Zelda Fitzgerald or Gertrude Stein or Hemingway, about Buñuel or Dali or Mondrian.

Maybe because of it, someone is living in Paris right now, bewildered by all the modernity at their fingertips but transported by the history that surrounds them as they browse the booksellers and flea markets for old jazz records. Maybe, they're even falling in love.

Woody may yearn to make a film to take its place alongside the giants he so admires – but he's changed the way we dress, the way we talk, the music we listen to, even our dreams of romance. No filmmaker, no artist, can really ask for more than that.

Right An American in Paris – director
Woody Allen is photographed for
Le Figaro magazine in August 2014.

Woody Allen Film by Film

The 1960s

From hilarious to austere and everywhere in between, the films of Woody Allen capture the soul of modern man and woman as they navigate the absurdities of life, love and death ... without falling over too much along the way.

Left *The Woody Allen Special*, 1969 – on the cusp of his film career, Woody starred in a one-off television show of sketches, music, stand-up and this interview about God with the Reverend Billy Graham.

What's New Pussycat? (1965)

A British magazine editor in Paris seeks psychiatric help to cure his serial infidelities so he can marry the girl he loves.

On his 29th birthday, Woody Allen shot his first scene in the movies. On the surface, this was an auspicious beginning: he was filming a big-budget comedy in Paris with Peter Sellers and Peter O'Toole, having been commissioned to write the script after Charles Feldman, the big Hollywood producer, saw his stand-up routine one night in Greenwich Village and loved it.

While it might have looked like the luckiest of breaks, the end result is so bad you wonder why on earth Woody didn't turn his back on filmmaking forever. The film remains noteworthy today for only two things: the Tom Jones title song and the opening title credit "introducing … Woody Allen".

Perhaps, though, this was how Woody discovered how not to do it. Certainly, out of the rubble, one of the great cinema careers was born.

It was Shirley MacLaine who had brought Feldman to watch Woody's stand-up routine, just at the time the producer was toying with a comic vehicle for her brother, Warren Beatty. His legendary way of answering the phone had already been chosen as the film's title: *What's New Pussycat?*

Seeing Woody's act, Feldman immediately hired him as scriptwriter and promised him a part in the film. According to Peter Biskind's Hollywood history *Easy Riders, Raging Bulls*, Allen's rewrites did not please Beatty, who was angered that the unknown comic was giving himself more lines.

Feldman wielded his power and the film went ahead with Beatty's catchphrase as the title, but without the man himself – a star who, as his sister once put it, "couldn't commit to dinner". It was a decent hit at the time but has dated badly, the sort of romping sex farce that can only be viewed as a historical document now, and even then with something bordering on embarrassment.

Peter O'Toole played the philandering lead, a fashion magazine editor in Paris called Michael. He seeks the help of manic psychiatrist Dr Fassbender, played by Peter Sellers, to help him commit to his girlfriend Carole, played by Romy Schneider.

How does Woody fit in to all this? He plays O'Toole's unlikely – and rather forced – friend Victor Shakapopulis, but what's most remarkable is how well formed the Woody comic persona is already in this first appearance. Victor is a weed, an intellectual and a would-be womanizer. As he explains to Michael, he is pleased with his new job at the Crazy Horse strip club:

Victor: I help the girls dress and undress. Twenty francs a week.

Michael: Not very much.

Victor: It's all I can afford.

And that, ladies and gentlemen, is the first, classic Woody Allen gag on celluloid.

Unfortunately, there's not much else recognizably Woody in the whole picture in terms of jokes, except when Victor later calls hotel room service and asks for "twelve loaves of bread and one Boy Scout uniform".

By his own account, Woody hated the experience. "I was plunged into Hollywood at its most venal," he told Eric Lax. Powerless, he watched his script being misinterpreted and rewritten by the studio, leaving even the British director Clive Donner helpless. "I felt if everyone would get out my way I could

Right Feline groovy? Woody poses with the Croft twins to promote his movie debut.

make a funny movie here. The big lesson from that is if a picture is successful and you're not happy with it, it's an unhappy experience not worth anything."

But still discernible in what's left of his mangled script are what will become familiar Woody Allen tropes: comic psychiatry, incongruous flashbacks, infidelity, unstable but beautiful women and a jazz soundtrack.

If you want to see Woody Allen at the wheel of an uncontrollable sports car or driving a go-kart into some hay, then *What's New Pussycat?* might tickle out a few chuckles, but mostly Woody's own assessment rings true.

Woody is a filmmaker whose work is fertile ground for a constant cross-fertilization and regeneration of jokes and ideas, and two moments will echo later in his work.

On the quayside of the Seine where he and Peter Sellers filmed that very first scene, Woody will one day dance an unforgettably funny and romantic pas de deux with Goldie Hawn in *Everyone Says I Love You.*

And, just before Woody's appearance in the film, we see on the pavement outside a café a table of artists and can make out intended caricatures of Toulouse Lautrec and Vincent Van Gogh (the bandages are a giveaway). It's a gag to which Woody will return with a vengeance in *Midnight in Paris* nearly 45 years later – by which time he would have long been exercising total control, not just of his own material but of the entire art form.

Right The only way is up: Woody Allen and Romy Schneider seek literary inspiration in *What's New Pussycat?*, 1965.

What's Up, Tiger Lily? (1966)

Woody Allen and several chums dub ridiculous comic dialogue over an original Japanese spy comedy to turn it into a spoof about a stolen recipe for the perfect egg salad.

The success of *What's New Pussycat?* is hard to fathom now, but it cemented itself into the popular consciousness to such an extent that Woody's stock was high. His self-esteem, however, wasn't so high that he could refuse another offer from a Hollywood studio, no matter how inane it seemed.

Henry Saperstein at American International Pictures – which distributed a lot of B films for drive-ins – had bought the US rights to a Japanese hit. A comedy-spy picture, it was itself cashing in on the sudden spy mania that had everyone trying to jump on the James Bond bandwagon.

Kokusai himitsu keisatsu: Kagi No Kagi (International Secret Police: Key of Keys) was the original title but Saperstein wasn't really convinced of its crossover potential and had the admittedly bright idea of overdubbing it with spoof dialogue. He hired Woody Allen and changed the name to chime with his new writer's still-fresh hit.

It must be said, nobody in the film utters the title line. And, in what must be one of the biggest surprises in a Woody Allen film, there are two unnecessary appearances by the hippy rock band the Lovin' Spoonful, accompanied by some heavily edited footage of young hipsters dancing in "far out!", 1960s style.

Helping out Allen with the voices in what's billed as a "No Star Cast" are his childhood friend and future co-writer Mickey Rose as well as his wife Louise Lasser, although the film actually starts with a lengthy segment of fight scenes from the Japanese original.

The action is then interrupted by an interviewer talking to Woody Allen – already making his contempt for the interview format clear. Asked to explain what's about to happen, Woody says: "They asked me to supervise the project because, as you know, death is my bread and danger my butter. Or danger is my

bread and death is my butter. No. No wait. Death is my, no, I'm sorry. Death and danger are my various breads and butters."

It's about the only really Allenish moment in the film, although his increasingly familiar image does then feature in the cartoonish opening credits, which mash up Pink Panther and James Bond credit styles to give us an animated Woody in glasses ogling Japanese girls.

In fact, there's much ogling in the film itself. It's odd that, so early in his film career, Woody found himself mixed up in these modish sex comedies. Tiger Lily's outmoded incorrectness is a touch unpalatable these days. These white Jewish actors do numerous crude stereotyped accents as they voice the supporting cast. Meanwhile the camera leers over strippers, bottoms and bikinis. (In his own *A Midsummer Night's Sex Comedy*, Woody will admit, "I look, I leer, I salivate").

One sexy woman in a towel teases our "loveable rogue" hero Phil Moskowitz and asks him to name three Presidents. "Johnson, Kennedy," he says, pausing to unwrap the towel and look down at her naked lower regions, then adding: "Lincoln?"

It doesn't really get better or worse than that. The other comedy default is to throw a smattering of Yiddish into the mouths of Japanese gangsters as they seek "an egg salad so delicious you could plotz". Another is shot and cries: "I'm dying, call my rabbi."

In truth, this film is likely to work now only if you're high – Woody himself would show his disapproval of that in *Annie Hall*. Nowadays *What's Up, Tiger Lily?* acts mainly as a guide to examples of the early Woody comic technique, and the words he frequently uses to get a laugh: sinuses, shellfish, prostitutes, chicken, rabbi and, disappointingly, rape.

To his credit, Woody hated what he later called a "stupid and juvenile" enterprise and wanted to sue the producers and prevent

Below, left What's up, Woody Allen?
Woody hated the first film on which
he was credited as director.

Below, right The poster for *What's Up,
Tiger Lily?*, 1966, tells us very little about
the film itself – probably just as well.

its release after they recut his version and inserted the rock group.
However, the picture was released before any lawsuit could
be settled and it was a surprise, if modest, critical and
commercial success.

It did Woody Allen the comic star no real harm, and it got him
his first directing credit. But it was out of such creatively frustrating
experiences that Woody Allen, the singularly unsullied and
unhindered film artist, was soon to be born.

Casino Royale (1967)

A star-studded, faintly dreadful spy spoof based on Ian Fleming's first James Bond novel. Woody Allen has little screen time playing "evil" Dr Noah, otherwise known as Jimmy Bond, the frustrated nephew of the famous 007.

Producer Charles Feldman showed great instincts when, hearing the positive reactions to a new spy character called James Bond, he took over the film rights to the novel *Casino Royale* in 1960, originally wanting Cary Grant to play Bond.

But Feldman's other projects interfered and, later, he couldn't reach an agreement to team up with producers Albert Broccoli and Harry Saltzman, who had snapped up the rights to the rest of Ian Fleming's Bond novels. By the time Feldman could concentrate on his own investment, the Bond film franchise was already booming.

By 1965, Sean Connery was shooting his fifth Bond film, *You Only Live Twice*. Feldman was determined to at least make some profit from his property, so he went for a parody, utilizing many of the vogueish ingredients that had made *What's New Pussycat?* such a box office hit.

Feldman already had Allen under contract and he admired the performer so much that he offered him even more money just to appear. Instructing Woody to concentrate on writing his own part, he would also hire nine other authors, including Ben Hecht, Terry Southern (one of the writers for Stanley Kubrick's *Dr Strangelove*) and even Billy Wilder.

Feldman also called in five directors, including John Huston (who was also to play M), Val Guest and Joseph McGrath. The production was in London, at Pinewood and Shepperton studios, and Woody was there for nearly eight months, even though ultimately he would appear on screen for only the final 20 minutes of the film. It was a chaotic shoot, of clashing personalities, where Peter Sellers and Orson Welles clashed for supremacy, each commandeering their own writer and director for their sequences.

The end result is, frankly, rubbish, even by the standards of 1960s spy spoof sex romps. The film is incoherent, unfunny and notable only for terrible Scottish accents, the game commitment of David Niven, the shortness of the women's skirts (Jacqueline Bisset plays a spy called Giovanna Goodthighs) and the sheer size of Orson Welles as Le Chiffre.

Thankfully, there is also Burt Bacarach's Oscar-winning song, 'The Look of Love', sung by Dusty Springfield.

Woody says he regards it as "a dreadful film experience" and you can almost see the self-loathing on his face during his scenes, some of which he plays silently, as if in tacit resignation. He plays little Jimmy Bond, a neurotic nephew who becomes twisted and takes over the evil organization SMERSH using the alias Dr Noah. His dastardly plan is to use biological warfare to "make all women beautiful and kill all men over four foot six", leaving Jimmy as the "big man who gets all the girls".

Jimmy captures sexy British secret agent The Detainer (played by Daliah Lavi) and forces her to be his accomplice. Untying her, he says: "Then we can run amok. If you're too tired, we can walk amok." It's about the only recognizably "Woody-ish" moment in the whole picture, apart from an earlier, very brief scene where Jimmy is captured and faces an execution squad. He protests, "I have a very low threshold of death. My doctor says I can't have bullets enter my body at any time."

Jimmy spends the shambles of a finale – during which there is a saloon-style brawl in the titular casino involving Cowboys and Indians and into which wander brief cameos from George Raft and Jean-Paul Belmondo – counting out 300 hiccups after swallowing one of his own atomic pills. When his countdown reaches zero, the pill explodes, blowing up the casino and putting us all out of our misery after a preposterous 2 hours and 15 minutes.

Woody's Jimmy is seen over the closing credits as an angel, strumming a harp but descending to hell.

Allen spent his time in London making a few television appearances, including a now celebrated 30-minute set for Granada Television, which is often said to be the only surviving footage of a complete Woody Allen stand-up routine. It includes many of his most famous jokes – "My grandfather, on his death bed, sold me this watch" – as well as a note-perfect rendition of the genius moose sketch, with what is – for me anyway – a killer line when the moose attends a fancy dress party alongside Woody: "You know the Solomons."

So something good came out of it. And it had another important effect: Woody now determined not to get mixed up in somebody else's film mess ever again.

Above "We can run amok – if you're too tired we can walk amok": Woody's Jimmy Bond releases The Detainer (Daliah Lavi) in *Casino Royale*.

Take the Money and Run (1969)

A mockumentary – perhaps the first ever – following the life and crimes of inept thief Virgil Starkwell, through love, bad prison breaks and the world's worst bank robbery.

Although Woody Allen will always try to distance his real self from his fictional work, we are going to spend much of this book caught between those two personae. He can hardly blame our confusion when, in the opening lines of his very first film as writer/director/actor, he gives the date of birth of his very first fictional character as December 1, 1935 – the same date as a certain Allan Stewart Konigsberg.

Probably, it has more to do with Allen feeling that this was his proper birth in films after the unhappy experiences on *What's New Pussycat* and *Casino Royale*. Finally, he had control of the script and the camera, and the film was going to come out just how he (and his co-writer and childhood friend Mickey Rose) had imagined it.

It must be remembered that Woody Allen himself was pretty famous by now. Although only 33 years old, he was already wealthy and a celebrity through his stand-up comedy, his writing for the *New Yorker*, a hit play, and many TV appearances. People were accustomed to his comic persona and liked that creation's bumbling, nervy inadequacies in the face of the modern world.

But could he put all that into a hit film? Despite the support of the producer and Woody fan Charles Feldman, United Artists had passed on it, and his agents, Jack Rollins and Charles Joffe, looked for financing from start-up company Palomar Pictures.

Allen was given carte blanche to do what he liked, but he was smart enough to give his audience what they wanted.

Virgil Starkwell is a classic Woody creation for whom little goes right – essentially, we will be seeing versions of Virgil all the way up to *Annie Hall* – and Allen, the filmmaker, is obviously borrowing from (or paying tribute to) his comic heroes. Virgil's relationship with the angelically gorgeous Louise (played by Janet Margolin) is straight out of Chaplin films such as *The Gold Rush* and what clearer debt can he acknowledge to the Marx Brothers than having Virgil's parents appear here in full Groucho glasses, complete with nose and moustache? (The parents of his next hero, Fielding Mellish in *Bananas*, will also appear covered up, in surgeons' masks.)

After an initially small release in one Manhattan cinema, word of mouth picked up and the film was a big hit. Particularly so in Greece.

Even today, it is still very funny in places. Playing the cello in a marching band, picking up the chair in between notes, is a brilliant sight gag; so too, the fashioning of a gun out of prison soap only for it to dissolve, on the night of the attempted escape, into bubbles in the rain.

The narration is brilliantly, sternly delivered by Jackson Beck, whose voice announced *The Adventures of Superman* on the radio of Allen's childhood. (Allen would use that voice again in his fond tribute to that era, *Radio Days*.) "A jungle is no place for a cellist," intones Beck. "Unable to fit in with any aspects of his environment, Virgil strikes out on his own." There are foreshadowings here of Woody's later 1983 mockumentary masterpiece *Zelig*, the story of the Human Chameleon who could always blend in.

Starkwell embarks on a life of crime, even if he's no good at it. The mechanisms of jails, courts and robberies allowed Allen plenty of comic business, reworking situations and gags from his stand-up routines, jokes he would return to quite often. When Virgil

Right Prisoner of his own talent: Woody Allen stars as Virgil Starkwell in his debut *Take the Money and Run*.

Right Woody as convict Virgil gets a surprise during a hard stint in the prison laundry.

Left Exit pursued by a gorilla: a robbery at a pet store backfires on hapless Virgil Starkwell.

volunteers for an experimental injection, it has the surreal side effect that "for several hours, he is turned into a rabbi". Cut to Allen in full rabbi regalia in his cell.

The film also features the classic gag: "Is sex dirty? It is if you're doing it right." There's a great routine of Allen getting ready for a date in front of the mirror, which is funny and, just when you think it's finished, is then topped by him returning, realizing he's forgotten his trousers.

Some of it is plain silly but instantly recognizable as Allen's trademark humour of the absurd. Virgil and Louise have a son. Says the narrator: "They name him Jonathan Ralph Starkwell, after Virgil's mother." Virgil recounts the time he held up a butcher's and made away with 116 veal cutlets – "but then I had to go out and rob a tremendous amount of breading".

There are slapstick routines in the prison laundry and a very funny running – make that "shuffling" – gag with the chain gang, eventually culminating when they escape and Virgil suggests they should all split up. When Louise visits him in prison, the voice-over tells us she brings him "home cooked meals" – and we watch as she squishes a hard-boiled egg through the chicken wires.

It's curious that even in this, his first film, Allen's screen romance does not end happily. This is also the first time, I think, that anyone uses the word "schlemiel" about a Woody persona – or more properly, given that Allen wrote this script, that he uses it about himself. Interestingly, the character who describes him thus is an ex-girlfriend, Kay Lewis, played by Woody's wife at the time, Louise Lasser.

Woody already knew funny, and knew too plenty about cinema. But he was about to learn a lot more, and quickly, in the making of *Take the Money and Run*. He'd shown his production team several key films to get across the feel of what he wanted to achieve: *Blow-Up*, *Elvira Madigan*, *I am a Fugitive from a Chain Gang* and the documentary *The Eleanor Roosevelt Story*, the classic style of which he wanted to parody. Subsequently the shoot, in San Francisco, went quickly and cheaply, coming in under the $1.7 million budget and a week ahead of schedule, but Woody found editing it all together a far tougher task.

After test screenings were met with stony silence, he was introduced to Ralph Rosenblum, who had recently cut Mel Brooks's hit *The Producers*. Rosenblum put back a lot of the funny bits Woody had originally cut and taught Woody to edit to music, for which a hot new composer called Marvin Hamlisch had been hired.

Allen now credits Rosenblum, who would edit his next five pictures, with teaching him everything he always wanted to know about filmmaking but was, I guess, afraid to ask. "He had a wonderful sense of humour and was like a burst of fresh air," recalls Woody. "What he did completely saved the picture and turned it from a failure into a success. I learned everything from him. I couldn't have gone to school with a better guy."

Take the Money and Run proved a prophetic title – and it's precisely what Woody Allen did. With his debut film's critical and commercial success, the ground was laid for one of the greatest careers in the history of cinema. Woody hit that ground running and never looked back.

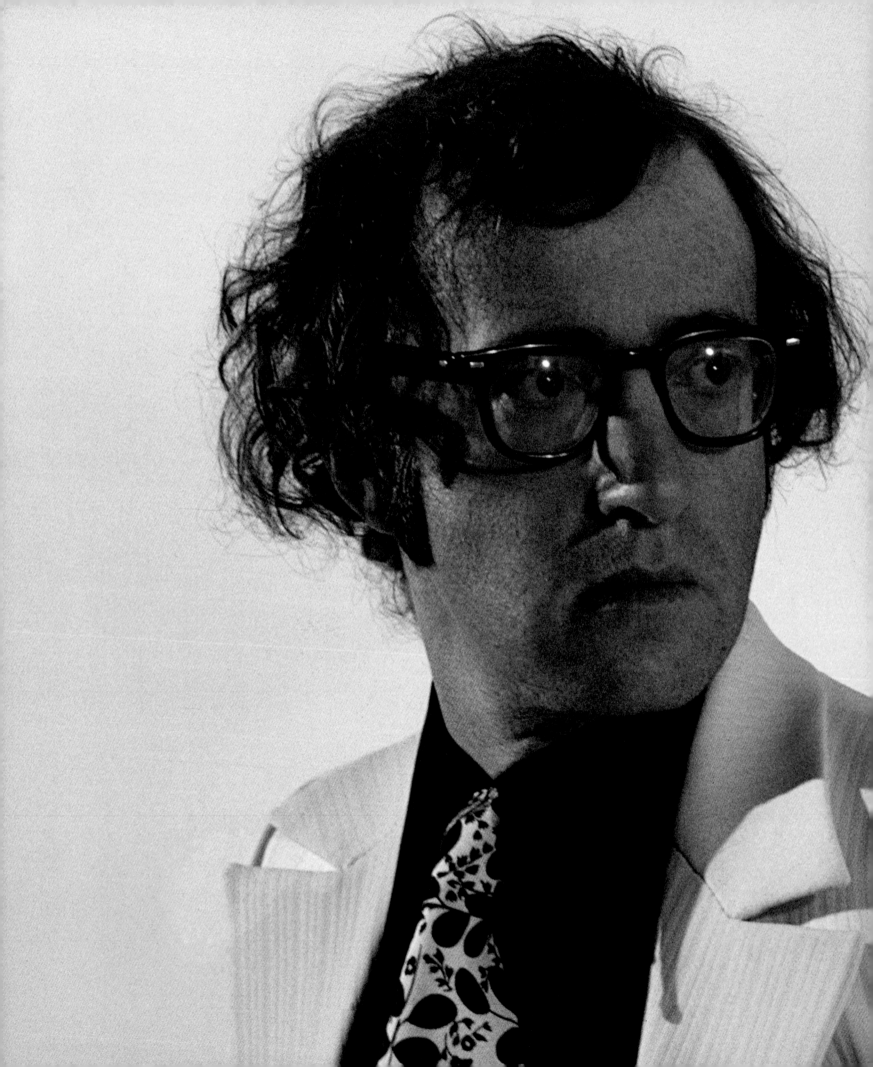

Woody Allen Film by Film

The 1970s

With his comic persona as firmly established as his fan base, Woody Allen launches the most spectacular and prolific film career of the late 20th century, starting with side-splitting comedies and building to neurotically funny, heartbreaking studies of modern relationships, mostly with the sparkling Diane Keaton.

Left Smart comedy: Woody Allen copies European style in a sketch from the farce *Everything You Always Wanted to Know About Sex*, 1972.

Men of Crisis: The Harvey Wallinger Story (1971)

This fake TV news documentary, about President Richard Nixon's fictitious political advisor Harvey Wallinger (Woody Allen), sent up the administration, politicians and the media. It was pulled from transmission and never shown.

For many years, this episode of the never-commissioned TV series *Men of Crisis* remained locked in a library vault. Only visitors to Manhattan's Paley Centre for Media were able to see it. However, it was recently posted (with Spanish subtitles and no great quality) on the Internet, on YouTube, allowing one of the great "lost" Woody Allen works to be widely viewed.

According to the film's producer, Jack Kuney, it was shot at Columbia University. He told the *New York Times* back in 1997: "Mr. Allen had a few weeks of free time after making *Everything You Always Wanted to Know About Sex (But were Afraid to Ask)*. He had a hiatus and wrote it in 10 days."

Perhaps most significant for Woody completists is the fact that the film marks the first appearance of Diane Keaton on screen with the director, whom she was dating at the time. Keaton had gained some publicity after appearing in the New York production of *Hair*, because she'd been the only cast member to appear clothed in the musical's famous nude finale. She also auditioned, successfully, for a part in Woody's Broadway hit theatre production of *Play It Again, Sam* in which they then appeared together every night.

Keaton's appearance as Renata Baldwin in *Wallinger* is brief, though sweetly funny and performed throughout as cross-eyed. She leaves him, she says, because he had an affair with a Democrat "and there's nothing worse than that – they're lascivious people".

Allen's second wife, Louise Lasser, whom he'd recently divorced, also makes a brief contribution as a former lover. As in *Take the Money and Run*, though, her character is less enamoured of Wallinger, calling their affair, "a mistake, a bad first experience". She does, however, recall: "We used to double date a lot with the Nixons, Pat and Dick. Harvey would often dance with Dick." She

ends her contribution remembering that, ultimately, Harvey was a generous soul: "I guess he used his influence in Washington, and got me drafted. I did six months in Korea."

In what is an obvious forerunner of the techniques he later employed, with far more maturity in *Zelig*, Allen plays with news clips, documentary formats and, one of his favourite filmic devices, voice-over. Narration is by Reed Hadley, who had played radio cowboy Red Ryder in the 1940s and was also employed by the Department of Defense on information films. His tone is key to the comedy, and it is in all seriousness that he tells us: "Born to parents of German Jewish extraction, Harvey Wallinger is named after Rabbi Harold Weinstock, who will later be wanted by police for passing counterfeit matzo."

The film amounts to a profile of Harvey Wallinger, who has somehow become very close to President Nixon and various White House officials, including Spiro Agnew. One aide suggests Wallinger was chosen as he was "the only person who could make the President laugh. He'd come up behind him and just tickle him."

Although Woody's character here is clearly and comically ridiculous, it is clear that Allen is vaguely riffing on the political giant Henry Kissinger. If the names and personalities involved are very much of their time, the skit's themes and jokes are timeless and remain valuable. Indeed, many people will recognize in *The Harvey Wallinger Story* the juxtapositions employed by documentary maker Michael Moore in the more playful parts of his Palme d'Or-winning *Fahrenheit 911*. Nixon, for instance, is shown to be a guest at Harvey and Renata's wedding, delivering a speech about corn blight as Allen and Keaton fall asleep.

Why was this satire banned? It is likely that the Public Broadcasting Service feared they would lose political favour and their public funding status in the run-up to an election – one that Nixon

was to win by a landslide. There's one scabrous scene featuring Wallinger and a plastic surgeon looking at Nixon (played in obscured profile by the popular impersonator Richard M Dixon). The two men are criticizing Nixon's face: "It's like looking at a cement wall," says Wallinger. "Can't you do anything? It doesn't spell trust, you know. It puts people off. Can you do maybe blackface?" Eventually the suggestion is made to cover up Nixon's face with a flag. "Hmmm," cogitates the surgeon. "What country?"

According to the same article, previously mentioned, from the *New York Times*, station officials particularly objected to one gibe directed at the First Lady. Wallinger tells the camera: "Pat Nixon occasionally calls me, you know, and says, you know: 'Dick's not home. Come on over. He's on a European trip or something.' But I try to discourage that kind of thing, because I just don't think it's right."

The newspaper itself gets a mention, when Wallinger is shown calling for an injunction against the paper on the grounds that: "It's a New York Jewish communist left-wing homosexual newspaper, and that's just the Sports section."

Men of Crisis is rough and scrappy but still funny and certainly bears all the hallmarks of classic, early, funny Woody Allen. There's a wonderfully silly moment too: after Wallinger has extolled the intellectual prowess of Nixon and Agnew ("they, um, sometimes read and they know, er, all the numbers in sequence") the narrator tells us that, under their administration, the White House is a "cultural Mecca". Cut to an audience with Nixon in the front row applauding, while we see an old and terrible Yiddishe comedian introduce his slide flute version of the Spanish standard 'Cielito Lindo', and then warble to a big finish: "How'd you like that? Where'd you ever see that?"

Only in a Woody Allen movie.

Bananas (1971)

Woody Allen's second film as co-writer, director and star takes
parody and pastiche and turns them into potent political satire.
The zany, gag-filled farce confirmed Allen's commercial appeal but
also established him as a filmmaker with serious directing credentials.

Following up the surprise hit *Take the Money and Run* needed careful planning and Allen sensibly gave his audience more of the same comic style in *Bananas*.

Playing with format and media, he begins with a skit in which ABC's *Wide World of Sports* covers an assassination live in the tiny Latin American country of San Marcos. The legendary commentator Howard Cosell, more usually seen ringside during Muhammad Ali's fights, provides the colour and conducts interviews impressively deadpan: "This is tremendous, just tremendous … This reporter is going to get to him through this mob for one last word before he expires …"

Back in New York, Woody extends his clownish persona playing Fielding Mellish, a (rather hopeless) product tester for a large corporation. "Why did I become a product tester?" he whines after machines have yet again got the better of him. "I should be working at a job I have some kinda aptitude for, like donating sperm to an artificial insemination lab."

One of his most finely named creations, Mellish (echoing the Yiddish word *nebbish*, meaning a pitiable, timidly ineffectual person) is a perfect, early Allen comic creation – sexually hopeless, nerdy, weak but thrust into the unstoppable mechanism of actions to which he is entirely unsuited.

Recently dumped by Nancy, an earnest political activist (played by Woody's second wife, Louise Lasser), Mellish tries to impress her by travelling to San Marcos. Captured by rebels, he then becomes President, and dons a hilariously ginger Castro-style beard (which makes him look more rabbi than rebel) to revisit New York and raise funds.

Although it doesn't acknowledge it in the credits, *Bananas* was loosely adapted from the 1966 satirical novel *Don Quixote, U.S.A.* by Richard Powell. Woody wrote the film with his childhood friend Mickey Rose and it contains several gags that the pair had previously worked into Woody's stand-up routines. While the film strains to maintain comic momentum, it retains considerable value as a series of funny sketches with some great lines. Making love to Nancy, he says, "I love you." She begs him: "Please, say it in French. Oh say it in French." "I don't know French," he counters. "What about Hebrew?"

When Nancy breaks up with him, he wants to know why. "You're immature," she tells him. "Immature? How am I immature?" "Emotionally, sexually, intellectually …" "Yes, but in what other ways?"

Bananas smartly satirizes the volatile societies of banana republics while always conscious of the huge influence of American policies. The CIA is depicted as the chief instigator of such revolutions, and Allen the dictator is somewhat confused. Proudly he announces: "I have made a deal for reinforcements with the UJA." "You mean the CIA, your excellency? The UJA is the United Jewish Appeal." "Uh oh."

Left She's latex, but you can't have everything: this publicity image of Woody and a blow-up doll became a popular postcard in the early 1970s. Contrary to rumour, he and the doll never married.

"Immature? How am I immature?"
"Emotionally, sexually, intellectually…"
"Yes, but in what other ways?"

Woody Allen as *Fielding Mellish*

Allen ridicules dictators and rebels alike. When a new President seizes power, he proclaims: "From now, the official language of San Marcos is Swedish. In addition, all citizens will be required to wash their underwear every half-hour. Underwear will be worn on the outside, so we can check."

Meanwhile, there are great comic sequences of the rebels training in the jungle. One gag, they're starving, so some are sent out of hiding to collect an improbably deli-style lunch from a café in a small local village: "1,000 grilled cheese, 300 tuna, 200 BLT, mayo on the side, and coleslaw." Each lunch is brought back to the jungle in individual take-out bags. These bags were sourced from Allen's local deli back in New York and brought out to Puerto Rico where the filming was taking place.

Aside from the Howard Cosell cameo – the sportscaster reappears at the film's finale, to commentate on the wedding night of Fielding and Nancy – *Bananas* marks the first film appearance of a young Sylvester Stallone, playing a thug on the subway train. Allen initially sent him away, saying he didn't look "tough enough". Stallone begged him to reconsider and came back a minute later in different make-up that changed the director's mind.

This was Allen's third film collaboration with Louise Lasser, even though they had recently divorced. By this time, Allen had already begun a relationship with Diane Keaton, who accompanied him in Puerto Rico throughout that portion of the shoot.

Bananas was a success on release and brought in $11 million at the box office, pleasing backers United Artists for whom it was the first in a three-picture deal. Initially, Allen had pitched them a film called *The Jazz Baby*, which they rejected but which he reconfigured many years later as *Sweet and Lowdown*.

One famous gag, hailed as a masterstroke of surrealism, features a string quartet playing with no instruments on a balcony at the presidential palace. It's a joke that happened simply because on the day of the shoot the instruments hadn't yet arrived and Woody couldn't be bothered to wait.

Asked if he enjoyed making *Bananas*, Woody told Eric Lax: "It was boring being in Puerto Rico. There was nothing to do. The food was not good, the weather was hot and humid. The movie house leaked and I found a dead mouse in my room. I don't like to dwell on the past."

Play It Again, Sam (1972)

Woody Allen plays neurotic film critic Allan Felix, who takes dating advice from an imaginary Humphrey Bogart. After a series of disastrous dates, he falls for the wife of his best friend but uses *Casablanca* as his moral guide.

Play It Again, Sam was the second stage play written by Woody Allen after *Don't Drink the Water* had enjoyed a successful Broadway run at the Morosco Theatre in 1966–67.

He'd written it during a lengthy stand-up stint in Chicago. It opened, with him starring, at the Broadhurst Theatre on Broadway in February 1969, lasting for 453 performances, to March 1970.

It was a hit, and it was also how he met and fell in love with Diane Keaton, the pair performing together every night alongside soon-to-be Allen regular Tony Roberts.

"There's no easier job than being in a play," he told Stig Bjorkmann years later. "You have the whole day off, you can write, relax, whatever you want. You just drop into the theatre at eight o'clock. I lived nearby, so Diane and I would stroll down Broadway. You're on stage with your friends and two hours later, you're in a restaurant. It was very pleasurable."

Woody sold the film rights to the play early on, having little interest in making it himself since he had already started work on his next film scripts. When the plans for *Play It Again, Sam*, finally kicked into gear three years later, he agreed to whip up a quick screenplay (it took two weeks) with the designated director Herb Ross. This classic Hollywood filmmaker had become a regular director for Neil Simon (*California Suite*, *The Sunshine Boys*, *The Goodbye Girl*) and also worked with Barbra Streisand (*Funny Lady*).

Ross's direction is elegant, accessible and uncluttered, and it allowed the increasingly familiar Allen screen persona to flourish and find an even wider audience. Sure enough, it was a hit comedy and bears all the traits of classic, early, funny Woody Allen.

Of his character Allan Felix, Woody has said: "It seemed to me like a very standard film persona for a comedian. Someone who is a physical coward, who lusts after women, who is good-hearted but ineffectual and clumsy and nervous. All standard things that you've seen in different various disguises. In Charlie Chaplin, or WC Fields or Groucho Marx, there's the same things."

The blend of slapstick and verbal wit is often hilarious here: a scene such as Allan preparing his flat to impress a date is an almost canonical piece of Woody. Indeed, jazz pianist Oscar Peterson even composed 'Blues for Allan Felix' just for the scene.

There are many fine jokes in the film, and Keaton looks fabulous in various outfits. Because of an impending strike in New York, the action was moved to San Francisco (where Woody had shot *Take the Money and Run* and where he would later return for *Blue Jasmine*), letting in a hippy vibe to the fashion and a funky feel to the film.

Playing a fashion model, Keaton stuns in a variety of outfits: hats, furs, hot pants with long socks, tartan slacks, a knitted dress, a backless satin night gown. "She was an eccentric dresser. And wonderfully funny. She has flawless instincts," said Woody, who would always let her choose her own styles, most notably and influentially later on *Annie Hall*.

The pair's chemistry is delightful and Keaton as Linda has a way of making her laughter and enjoyment of Woody's jokes seem absolutely genuine, never forced or fawning – and remember, the spark we're seeing on screen comes after 450 performances of this stuff on stage together.

Right "That's quite a lovely Jackson Pollock": Woody's Allan Felix flirts with a suicidal art lover, played by Diana Davila, in *Play It Again, Sam*, 1972.

"Allen . . . understands that humour can be based on pathos as well as sadism."
Roger Ebert

"I can never be like that. That
stuff is strictly movies."
Woody Allen as *Allan Felix*

Left "You have the most eyes I've ever seen": Woody fumbles advice from Jerry Lacy's Bogart as he woos Diane Keaton's Linda.

Right "I've waited my whole life to say it" – Woody Allen gets his Bogie moment in a publicity still for *Play It Again, Sam*, 1972.

Thematically – and this was the film's big advance in terms of having a story arc and some meaning – Woody deals with his frequent struggle to get real life to match up to the life seen in the films. "I can never be like that," wails Allan after seeing *Casablanca*. "That stuff is strictly movies."

Allan's flat is covered in film posters, many of which buffs will enjoy spotting – some bits of memorabilia were very rare and the production could afford only to rent them. It all comes to a cinephilic head at the film's climax, at a foggy airport, where Allan wows Linda with a speech. "That's beautiful," she says. "It's from *Casablanca*," he says, adding excitedly: "I've waited my whole life to say it."

In a device that will be used again in *The Purple Rose of Cairo* years later, Bogart leaves the screen and reappears, haunting Allan. Played by Jerry Lacy, who'd also followed from the Broadway show, Bogart gives out macho advice on how to behave with women, sorry, dames. Some of these attitudes come over as hideously out-dated now and that's part of their comic appeal. However, there's a jokey discussion between Allan and Linda about rape that would, I very much hope, shame both Woody and Diane these days.

The rest of the film is very neatly made and constructed. Tony Roberts gets a great running gag of leaving his phone number every place – a gag that, of course, is now also out of date, but still funny.

Play It Again, Sam was a fashionable, fairly mainstream hit and made Woody a good deal of money because he had a percentage of the profits. Audiences took it – and therefore the Woody and Keaton pairing – further to their hearts, laying the ground all the way up to *Annie Hall*.

Critics were also satisfied with the film's steady maturation of Woody's comedy into something more coherent. Roger Ebert wrote in the *Chicago Sun Times*: "Woody Allen is one of those rare comedians who understands that humour can be based on pathos as well as sadism. While the high-pressure comics overwhelm us with aggressive humour, Woody is off in the bathroom somewhere being attacked by a hairdryer."

And this film contains one of my all-time favourite Allen moments when, on Linda's encouragement, he approaches a cute girl in an art gallery to discuss the painting she's staring at.

Felix: That's quite a lovely Jackson Pollock, isn't it?

Girl: Yes, it is.

Felix: What does it say to you?

Girl: It restates the negativeness of the universe. The hideous lonely emptiness of existence. Nothingness. The predicament of man forced to live in a barren, godless eternity like a tiny flame flickering in an immense void with nothing but waste, horror and degradation, forming a useless bleak straitjacket in a black absurd cosmos.

Felix: What are you doing Saturday night?

Girl: Committing suicide.

Felix: What about Friday night?

Everything You Always Wanted to Know About Sex* (*But were Afraid to Ask) (1972)

Although he stars in only four of these pastiches, Woody writes and directs all seven sketches dealing comically with various sexual questions. Each is based on a chapter of a bestselling sex manual.

Coming home from a basketball game one evening, Woody was in bed with Diane Keaton, watching TV. He saw a chat show interview with Dr David Reuben, who was answering questions from his popular sex guide.

Woody immediately saw in his head the outline for a film consisting of funny sketches that would answer the questions. When he inquired about the rights to film the book, he discovered that the star Elliot Gould already owned them but wasn't planning on taking them anywhere. Woody bought them and, indulged by Arthur Krim at United Artists, was given a large budget to make his comedy.

The film was a big hit, ending in the Top 10 of 1972 in terms of box office and proving Krim's instincts correct. It also cemented Allen's ability to attract top acting talent to guest on his projects: Gene Wilder, Burt Reynolds, Lou Jacobi, even Anthony Quayle and Lynn Redgrave.

Viewed now, the comedy is only patchily inspired, but there are familiar recurrences of punchlines and themes, including the opening credits set in a typewriter font and underscored by a jazz standard, Cole Porter's 'Let's Misbehave'.

The first sketch, "Do Aphrodisiacs Work?", has Allen as the Fool in the court of a mediaeval English king, played by British Shakespearean actor Anthony Quayle.

Glibly riffing on *Hamlet* ("Rosencrantz and Guildenstern are dead and their tailor's shop is shut"), it's a silly sketch but gamely played. Woody's Fool is under threat for not being funny. He is further endangered when he gets his hand caught trying to get into the Queen's chastity belt: "Think of something quickly or before you know it the Renaissance will be here and we'll all be painting."

Interestingly, this image of Woody as court jester, must have been what, many years later, inspired Jean-Luc Godard to ask Woody to play the Fool in his bizarre version of *King Lear*.

The second sketch is much better. "What is Sodomy?" features a great comic performance by Gene Wilder, who falls in love with Daisy the sheep. He starts by stroking a lambswool sweater at home and then, smitten, steals Daisy from the Armenian shepherd who first brought her in.

Wilder plays it all so straight and serious. Who else could deliver so sweetly from his hotel room the following room service order: "A chilled white burgundy, some caviar, and some plain, green grass." His fall from grace is also brilliantly done: he goes slowly insane as a waiter, and ends dishevelled and bereft on the streets, drinking from a can of Woolite.

Lou Jacobi, who starred on Broadway in Allen's first play, *Don't Drink the Water*, has fun in the next sketch, as a secret transvestite caught while visiting his son's prospective in-laws.

Next is a skit on the modish Italian films of Antonioni. Woody and his ex-wife Louise Lasser talk Italian (they learned their words phonetically) and are able to have sex only in public places. It's the one time, I think, we ever see Woody wearing unfamiliar glasses – and, you know, he looks very, very different.

Right "It's great to be back at the palace" – Woody opens in *Everything You Always Wanted to Know About Sex*.

Below Woody Allen and Louise Lasser in an eventually deleted sketch about the sex life of a female spider.

"What if he's masturbating? I'm liable to end up on the ceiling."

Woody Allen in *Everything You Always Wanted to Know About Sex*

Right Woody Allen and Louise Lasser play with a vibrator in a scene from *Everything You Wanted to Know About Sex*.

Below "What Happens During Ejaculation?": Woody is seen in reflection directing a scene of the seminal sketch.

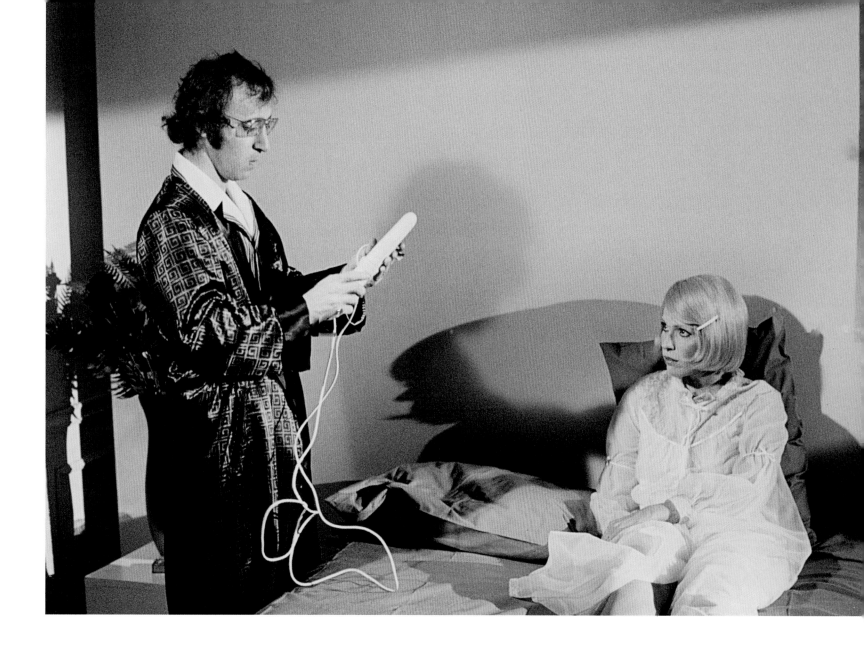

The spoof black-and-white TV game show "What's My Perversion" is crass, unimaginative and not funny at all, making jokes out of rapists and child molesting, then ending with a rabbi tied up and whipped while his wife eats pork ribs at his feet.

Spoofing B-movies and gothic horror, the sixth film is better, as Woody plays a young scientist and author of a new book: *Advanced Sexual Positions (and How to Achieve Them without Laughing)*. He and a pretty reporter visit mad Dr Bernardo, who is experimenting with various captives in his basement, and who has proven "the connection between excessive masturbation and entering into politics".

When the lab blows up, it gives birth to the famously enormous single breast ("they usually come in pairs"), which moves like the B-movie monster the Blob, terrorizing the American countryside. The girl reporter utters the great line: "What are we gonna do to stop this fiendish tit?"

The seventh and final vignette is the film's most, er, seminal: "What Happens During Ejaculation?" stars Woody as a sperm waiting to be ejaculated. In a spoof of submarine and sci-fi films (most probably

Fantastic Voyage, with which this film shared a set designer), the man's brain is run by Captain Tony Randall and First Mate Burt Reynolds, both giving orders to various body parts. The penis and its erection, for example, is operated by men winching away in the engine room.

Woody is wearing the now iconic white sperm suit, and his trademark glasses are back in place – that's partly what makes it funny, right? When intercourse is in full flow, the brain echoes a gag from *Play It Again, Sam* by repeating the names of baseball players to delay climax while the sperm line up like parachutists to jump out.

A reluctant and doubtful sperm ("What if he's masturbating? I'm liable to end up on the ceiling"), Woody eventually gets shuffled up to the launch position, looks up and around briefly, and shrugs to camera: "Oh well, at least he's Jewish."

The film's commercial success, coming just months after *Play It Again, Sam*, meant that Woody was now a bankable name in cinema. It also secured his future as an artist in whom his backers at United Artists – the home of independent cinema – had absolute trust and whose contract they would honour by never interfering.

Sleeper (1973)

Frozen in 1973, health-food store owner Miles Monroe wakes up 200 years in the future and is reluctantly enlisted by the Resistance to thwart the cloning of the president from his only remaining body part – his nose.

Technology and modern gadgetry are hardly instrumental to the work of Woody Allen. In fact, such things are sent to torture him, particularly in the early comedies, where he is often to be found at the mercy of machines.

The sewing machines in *Take the Money and Run*, the executive desk exerciser that Fielding tests in *Bananas*, and even a hairdryer in *Play It Again, Sam* – all of these modern aids get the better of Woody Allen on screen.

The sequences involved allowed him to indulge in some beautiful slapstick routines that pay homage to silent comedians such as Charlie Chaplin, Buster Keaton and France's Jacques Tati. All of them, apart from being very funny, also encapsulate an absurdist response to the infernal machines of the universe, emblematic of man trapped in mechanisms beyond his control.

Complete with its very own giant banana-skin gag, *Sleeper* would take the comic, if not the cosmic, potential of this to its limits. Originally, Woody Allen got together with a new co-writer Marshall Brickman (both were managed by Charles Joffe and Jack Rollins) to work on an epically long comedy that would have an intermission, just like Stanley Kubrick's *2001: A Space Odyssey*. So, the first half would be set in contemporary New York and, when the audience returned from the interval break, the second would be set 200 years in the future in a white dystopia where nobody spoke.

Backers at United Artists were keen on the idea, but Allen then decided it was too ambitious and, more practically, too much like writing two films in one. So he and Brickman condensed the first half into the backstory of Miles Monroe owning the Happy Carrot health food store in Greenwich Village and using then-faddish health products for occasional jokes. When Miles is woken up and told that all his friends from New York are long dead, he cries: "But they all ate organic rice."

Typically, Allen's most futuristic work also becomes his most old-fashioned – it was eventually advertised as "a nostalgic look at the future" – with its slapstick comedy and trad jazz on the soundtrack. This features Woody himself playing clarinet with his own New Orleans Funeral Ragtime Orchestra alongside the prestigious Preservation Hall Jazz Band. They recorded the tracks both at Preservation Hall in New Orleans and at Michael's Pub in New York. Woody has since said that laying down the music was the best part of making the whole film for him.

Allen originally had the idea of shooting in Brasilia, the futuristic city designed by Oscar Niemeyer. However, budgetary concerns limited filming to Colorado and the Mojave Desert. The two main houses are designed by architect Charles Deaton and are still visible today in the Genesse Mountains near Denver. The main set designs are by Dale Hennesy, who constructed the sets of the sperm sequence in *Everything You Always Wanted to Know About Sex*.

Right "My God, I beat a man insensible with a strawberry." Woody creates havoc with giant fruit in *Sleeper*.

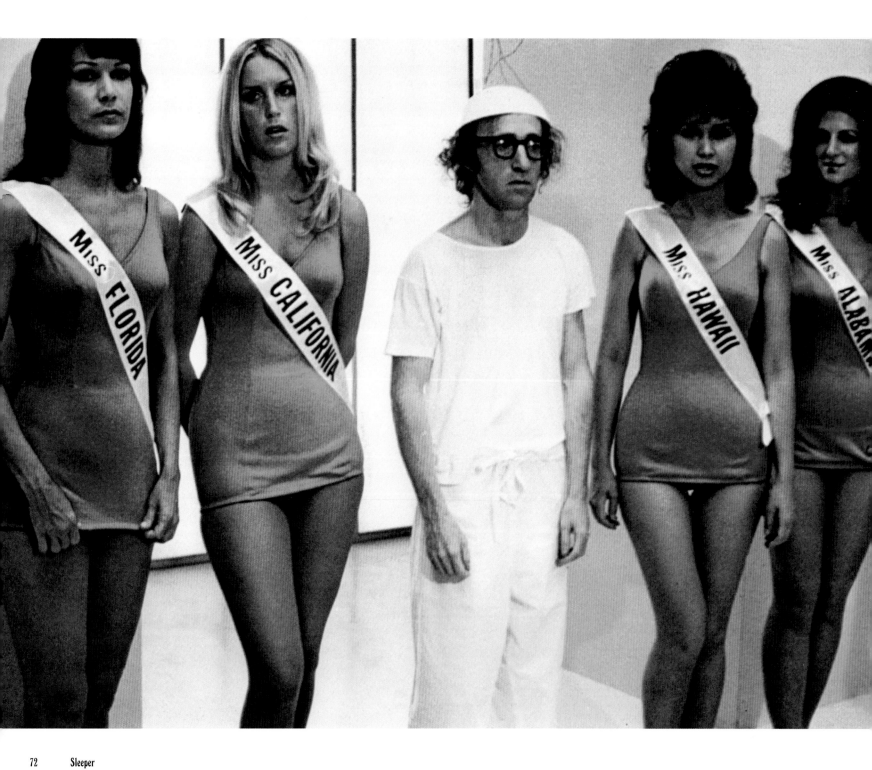

And, yes, the computer during the cloning operation is voiced by Douglas Rain, best-known as HAL in *2001: A Space Odyssey*.

Yet the best element of *Sleeper* now is to reflect on the growing comic skills of Diane Keaton in the part of Luna. Not only is she beautiful, cool and sexy in those white robes (the costume designer was Joel Schumacher, who went on to direct huge Hollywood hits such as *The Lost Boys* and *Flatliners*), but she becomes a sparkling comedy partner for Woody in the film's final third. It's now clear that this helped his swift progress from mere sketch-maker to director of more developed narratives and characters.

Audiences in 1973 would have roared at the scene where Woody regresses into being Blanche Dubois, only for Keaton to top him with her own impression of Stanley Kowalski – as performed by Marlon Brando, with whom she had just appeared in *The Godfather*. But there are countless other moments too, where the pair play off each other like a long-practised vaudeville team. "Miles, you're biting my nails," she complains. "That's because you're tense," he gnaws in reply.

I used to giggle like a fool to *Sleeper* when I first saw it as a teenager, and it remains very funny and very silly, although I have noticed that in film, nothing dates as quickly as the future. "I bought Polaroid at seven, it's probably worth millions now," says Miles, a gag that has passed from funny anachronism to obsolete reference even during this film's relatively short life.

Scientists in the film use Miles to confirm theories about history using what few artefacts they have. He is shown photographs that include Charles de Gaulle ("a famous French

Left "I would bring peace to all nations": Miles undergoes regression therapy as Miss Montana in *Sleeper*.

Right Loving the Alien: Woody in a hydrovac suit makes his escape in *Sleeper*.

Above A comedy dream team: Woody and Diane Keaton seek the Aries Project on the set of *Sleeper*, 1973.

Right A robot could have directed this film: Woody Allen sets up a shot on the set of *Sleeper*.

chef on television who'd show you how to make soufflés and omelettes") and Norman Mailer ("he donated his ego to Harvard University"). Will future generations, or even younger viewers now, get these references?

Of course, some things remain just about as funny now as they must have been in 1973, including the jokes about President Nixon, McDonald's and, maybe, the Jewish robot tailors. Even these will fade, though, which may explain why there are so few references to current politics or modern-day devices throughout the rest of Allen's work.

Sleeper seems to have made him aware how quickly such referential laughs fade away, leading him to decide that only the enduring human condition is forever funny. Though, actually, so is a robot wearing glasses. And a talking robot dog called Rags: "Is he house trained or will he be leaving little batteries all over the floor?"

For a gag-fuelled slapstick caper, *Sleeper* was a big hit in 1973, extending Allen's bankability. Crucially, it isn't without its thought-provoking satire on religion and belief systems. There's the confession machine that gives out a plastic toy while flashing

up "Absolved"; a comment on the futility of politics and leaders – "Don't you realize in six months we'll be stealing Erno's nose, or someone else's?"; and, of course, there's Luna's profound observation that "God spelt backwards is Dog."

Miles wins over Luna by telling her he believes not in political systems, nor God, nor science but only – and Woody might simply have been cueing up his next film title – in Sex and Death.

"I'm a teleological existential atheist," he says. "I believe that there's an intelligence to the universe, except for certain parts of New Jersey." That's still pretty funny today.

"I believe that there's an intelligence to the universe, except for certain parts of New Jersey."

Woody Allen as *Miles Monroe*

Love and Death (1975)

A cinematic pastiche invoking Russian literature, *Love and Death* follows Boris Grushenko from snivelling coward to inadvertent war hero. He fights for the heart of cousin Sonja and plots to assassinate Napoleon before dancing off through the trees with Death.

Allen's films often open with a great piece of music. Gershwin's *Rhapsody in Blue* at the start of *Manhattan* is probably his most famous choice, but the first moments of *Love and Death* are similarly arresting.

It opens with the fabulous troika motif from Prokofiev's *Lieutenant Kijé*, music written by the composer for a comic Soviet film of the same name – I wouldn't call it a barrel of laughs, not even a bucket, a thimble maybe. Released in America in 1934 as *The Czar Wants to Sleep*, it is the "story of a spelling mistake" that creates a fictitious soldier, who is then erroneously accorded heroic status by the despotic Czar Paul.

It's unclear if Woody had seen this film before he dashed off the script for *Love and Death*, in which the coward Boris unwittingly becomes a war hero after being fired out of the cannon where he was hiding and landing on a tent of French generals.

The story Allen tells is that he was unhappy with his current script – from which he would later develop both *Annie Hall* and *Manhattan Murder Mystery* – and was panicking about delivering his next film to his studio's deadline. He was pacing his penthouse when a tome on Russian history caught his eye and he thought of doing a funny take on *War and Peace*, changing the title to two of his favourite subjects, *Love and Death* (lucky he left out the third, masturbation).

He wrote the spoof in a little over two weeks and gave it to his producer Charles Joffe, who loved it and passed it on to the studio. United Artists were expecting a film about modern New Yorkers, but they trusted Woody's track record and were prepared to green-light the project, insisting only that the war scenes be shot in Budapest to save money.

Conditions were difficult. It was cold and Woody would eat only the tinned food he'd brought with him from America. He recalls trying to play the clarinet between takes, and finding his hands too cold to move over the keys. He had to take 20-minute hot showers to thaw out each night back at the hotel.

What's more, as he recalled in an interview with *Esquire*, shooting in Hungary came with its own problems. "When good weather was needed, it rained. When rain was needed, it was sunny. Each shot was chaos by the time my directions were translated. The cameraman was Belgian, his crew French, the underlings were Hungarian, the extras were Russian. I speak only English – and not really all that well."

Things improved when Woody returned to shoot in Paris, the city he'd been in love with since that fateful shoot for *What's New Pussycat?* Whatever his complaints, the end product is glorious, easily his most polished work to date. Much of this was to do with hiring the French cinematographer Ghislain Cloquet, who had shot Alain Resnais's documentary *Night and Fog*, about the Nazi concentration camps, and had made Jacques Demy's musical *The*

Right A still contact sheet detailing Woody Allen shooting the human cannonball sequence from the set of *Love and Death*, November 1974.

Left "If God's gonna test us,
why doesn't He give us a written?"
Woody soldiers to the front in
Love and Death.

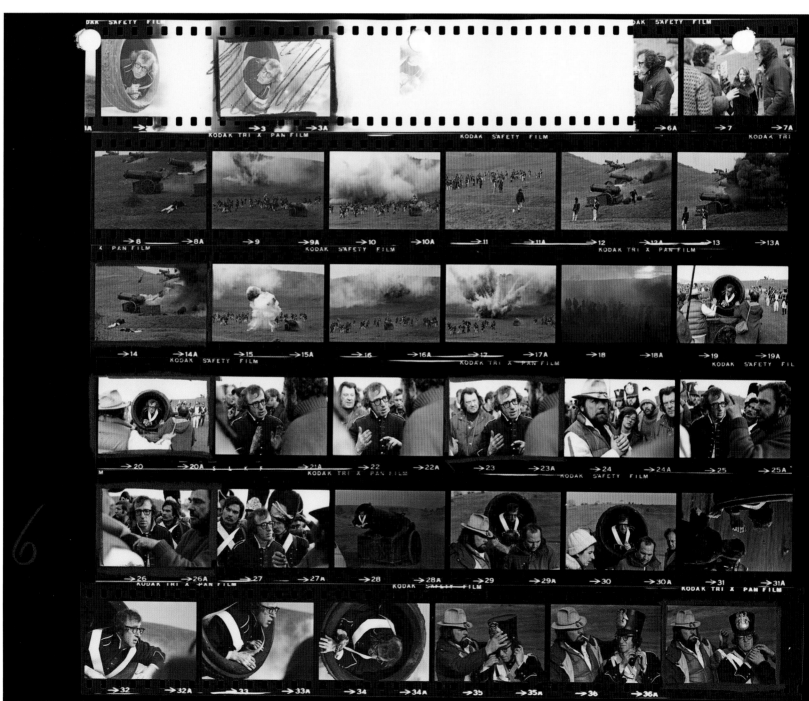

Young Girls of Rochefort so beautiful (a few years later Cloquet would win an Oscar for Roman Polanski's *Tess*).

Love and Death is a very funny film, visually and verbally. If this were to come out now, it would make Woody a huge star and he'd have a hit on his hands, just as happened to Ben Stiller and Will Ferrell with their films *Zoolander* and *Anchorman*. And yet Woody tops all of those parodies here, delivering a comedy that not only looks classy and delivers laugh-out-loud jokes but which also weaves them around hefty themes such as the meaninglessness of existence, the futility of war and the life of herring.

As Woody told *Time* critic Richard Schickel: "I had always loved the Russian classics and I was trying to do a film with philosophical content, if you can believe it. And I learned that it's hard to do a film with philosophical content if you're too broad. It's just like people can't see the structure of a film in a broad film, they also don't take seriously anything you might be wanting to deal with, or little comments you want to make – not desperately profound or original, but any little serious pretensions you might have in the film go unnoticed, because what gets noticed are always the jokes, the snappers, the one-liners and the sight gags."

It's true that Woody's Bergman gags here – the aping of a shot from *Persona*, the figure of Death from *The Seventh Seal* – and the quotation from *Battleship Potemkin* (he'd already done that in *Bananas*) don't actually mean much, except to reveal a cineaste's eye. So, too, the philosophical discussions between Woody's Boris

and Diane Keaton's Sonja can't be taken seriously on their own:

"So who is to say what is moral?"

"Morality is subjective."

"Subjectivity is objective."

"Moral notions imply attributes to substances which exist only in relational duality."

"Not as an essential extension of ontological existence."

But, thank God, Woody still can't resist deflating pomposity with a gag. Sonja invokes Voltaire and sighs, "This is truly the best of all possible worlds." Boris adds, "And also the most expensive." It's a joke, yes, but one that dares to top Voltaire and certainly adds to the philosophical richness.

"God is testing us," says a soldier as they march into battle. "If he's gonna test us," shouts back Boris, "why doesn't he give us a written?" He has a point.

Love and Death is where Woody takes his existential preoccupations and starts to work them in with his sense of anarchy and humour, finding a visual, cinematic equivalent for his conception of the absurd. The shouting black drill sergeant is funny because of its anachronistic incongruity, but it's also a gag that points out the ridiculous clichés of films. The same could be said of his child avatar asking questions of Death: "What happens after you die? Is there a heaven? Is there a hell? Are there girls?"

He also breaks the fourth wall with his gags, looking to camera for several punchlines, including his reply to the pious observation

that "sex without love is an empty experience". "Yes," he retorts, "but as empty experiences go, it's one of the best." We're one step away from a drum roll here.

Love and Death is full of these classic Woody jokes ("I've been in the mood since the late 1700s"; "I can't do anything 'til death, doctor's orders"; "If only God would give me a sign ... if he would just cough".) With Shakespeare, we quote from the tragedies; with Woody Allen, we quote the one-liners.

Above all, the real joy of *Love and Death* is the blossoming of Keaton as an inimitable comic actress. She's wonderful here, preparing the world for the massive crush it would soon develop on her as *Annie Hall*. She only has to narrow those darting eyes and nearly stumble over the word "epistemological" to have you in pieces.

Sonja isn't exactly a fully rounded character as written, but Keaton gives her soul, complexity and a beguilingly determined confusion to match Boris's crisis of thought and action. There's her famous, brilliantly bizarre "To love is to suffer" speech and her despair when bemoaning her marriage to Voskovec, the herring merchant: "This is a man who has reduced all the beauty of this world to a small pickled fish."

Later, she wails an apology to his dead body: "I could have made love to you more often ... or once, even." And she's capable of nailing great Woody gags. When a guard overhears her and Boris having a conversation and bursts in, Sonja says she was praying to God. "But I heard two voices," says the guard. "I do both parts," she bats back, without a beat.

Above "I was Men's Freestyle Fleeing Champion, two years in a row": Woody the coward in *Love and Death*.

Above left "I've been in the mood since the late 1700s": Boris tries to convince Sonja that to love is not to suffer.

Love and Death is a hilarious treat for Woody aficionados. He's very good himself here, too, as the weedy comic objector, the poetic, intellectual wimp at a loss in a macho world, where his brother Ivan should "cut down on his raw meat". But it's a role we've seen him play before and in some scenes his acting limitations are shown up. In the scene where Boris and Sonja agonize over the future, Woody is reduced to mere mugging. Meanwhile, Keaton argues herself into a tortuous quasi-logical thesis that concludes with Swiss cheese. It's far funnier than anything Woody's doing – and he comes out looking a bit desperate beside her.

More than jazz, more than jokes, more than New York, more than Love, more than Death, real Woody Allen fans are smitten by Diane Keaton. And in the very next film they made together, she'd capture the world's hearts forever.

Annie Hall (1977)

One of the greatest romantic comedies of all time, *Annie Hall* remains Woody Allen's most beloved film and the one that marked his arrival among the most instantly recognizable auteurs in cinema. It is the film that invented the "relationship movie" and has had a lasting influence on the style, delivery and vernacular of comedy on the big – and small – screen ever since.

Through the eyes and mind of neurotic New York comedian Alvy Singer, the film looks back over the failed relationship between Alvy (played by Allen) and the beautiful aspiring jazz singer Annie Hall (Diane Keaton). It takes the viewer on a scattered tour of the highs and lows of their time together: from their meeting at an indoor tennis club, through moving in together, an ill-fated stay in Los Angeles, to their poignant final goodbyes, outside a New York café after a visit to a cinema.

Key to the film's success is the almost personal relationship the viewer has with the hero, the doleful, wound-licking Alvy Singer. In the first shot, he addresses the audience directly (the first of many such shots) and launches into a classic to-camera stand-up routine:

"There's an old joke. Two elderly women at a Catskills mountain resort and one of them says, 'Boy, the food at this place is really terrible.' The other one says, 'Yeah, I know, and such small portions.' That's essentially how I feel about life: full of loneliness, misery, suffering and unhappiness and it's all over much too quickly."

Allen's genius in this film is to use his character's job, Jewishness and neuroses as the springboard for comedy and also as a way to inveigle his way into our affections. There isn't much plot, but rather a series of situations and sketches that unfurl naturally, reflecting the characters of both Alvy and Annie.

The film, co-written with Marshall Brickman (whom Allen has often said resembles Alvy far more than Allen does), flits back over Alvy's childhood and schooldays several times. The adult Alvy super-imposes himself on the action, interacting with the other fictional, incidental characters, such as the six-year-old girl classmate who berates him about Freud's latency period.

At one stage, Alvy even takes Annie on a tour of the old neighbourhood. She reciprocates by taking him on an imagined tour of past dates and a party where she flirted with a pretentious actor called Jerry. "You know how I'd like to die?" offers Jerry. "I want to be torn apart by wild animals." Looking on at the scene with detached sarcasm, Alvy interjects: "Heavy! Eaten by some squirrels."

The film is peppered with such little trips, either down memory lane, or on the road.

During a tour performing routines in college campuses, Alvy visits Annie's uptight WASPish parents for Easter, a scene brilliantly intercut and contrasted with the Singers having a chaotic Jewish family meal back in Brooklyn. It eventually dissolves into the two sets of parents conversing across the split screen:

How do you celebrate the holidays, Mrs Singer?
– We fast. No food, to atone for our sins.
Your sins, I don't understand?
– To tell you the truth, neither do we.

Right Diane Keaton gives Woody Allen some encouragement before a day's filming on the set of *Annie Hall*, 1977.

Left Woody's Alvy Singer recoils
from putting a lobster in the pot
during the first scene shot for *Annie
Hall*, Long Island, New York, 1977.

This is one of Allen's most overtly Jewish films – he even appears in Hasidic dress for one shot from the imagined point of view of Annie's grandmother, "a classic Jew hater" – and it's clear he finds Annie's peachy WASPness the big attraction. Similarly, she is fascinated by Alvy's pseudo-intellectual pretensions and his obsession with books about death, which he finds flattering.

By contrast, Alvy played up his non-intellectual side during his previous marriages, glimpsed in flashbacks. At a pretentious literary party, his wife Robin points out:

"There's Henry Drucker. He has a chair in history at Princeton. That short man is Hershel Kaminsky. He has a chair in philosophy at Cornell."

"Yeah," says Alvy. "Two more chairs and they got a dining-room set."

Part of the film's enduring appeal is its constant playfulness with cinematic form and convention, which make it look modern even today. It owes something to Allen's admiration for the French cinema of the Nouvelle Vague (Godard, Truffaut) as well as his love of Italian directors such as Federico Fellini. Yet entirely original is the way he, as Alvy, breaks the "fourth wall" (by addressing the audience directly) or drops in an animated sketch or, in an all-time classic Allen moment, brings in real-life cultural theorist Marshall McLuhan from off-screen to help settle an argument he's having in a cinema queue.

Another obvious homage to foreign-language cinema occurs in a now-famous scene when Alvy goes back to Annie's apartment for the first time. The two begin to discuss her photography work, standing on her roof terrace, and suddenly the screen shows us subtitles. As both characters spout pretentious comments to each other, their true thoughts are revealed underneath. "I wonder what she looks like naked"; "God, I hope he doesn't turn out to be a schmuck like the others."

Left "She senses I'm shallow":
Alvy and Annie and the famous
subtitles scene on a New York rooftop.

"… that's how I feel about relationships – they're totally irrational and crazy and absurd … "

Woody Allen as *Alvy Singer*

There are so many now-iconic comic moments and phrases in *Annie Hall* – the lobster scene, the "dead shark", the sneezing-into-a-pile-of-cocaine gag – that you marvel at the intensity of the laughs and how they're sustained all the way through the film by the complexity of these two characters, Alvy and Annie.

It's as a result of this naturally occurring humour that Allen can offer us one of the loveliest endings in all cinema, establishing *Annie Hall* as one of the most comic and most romantic of films. "We kicked around old times," says Alvy after running into Annie a few years after they broke up. The closing montage – of previous scenes from the film – is ripe with regret yet suffused with warmth, aided by the strains of Diane Keaton herself singing a wistful version of 'Seems Like Old Times' underneath.

Just as the film begins with Allen quoting an old joke, so it ends. Alvy concludes:

I realized what a terrific person she was and how much fun it was just knowing her and I thought of that old joke about the guy who goes to the psychiatrist and says, "Doc, I'm worried my brother's crazy, he thinks he's a chicken." And the Doctor says, "Well, why don't you turn him in?" And the guy says, "I would, but I need the eggs." And that's how I feel about relationships – they're totally irrational and crazy and absurd, but I guess we keep going through it because, uh, most of us need the eggs.

Annie Hall was nominated for five Oscars at the 1978 ceremony and won four, including Best Actress for Diane Keaton, Best Original Screenplay, Best Director and Best Picture. The only category it did not win was Best Actor, where Woody Allen lost to Richard Dreyfuss in *Goodbye Girl*, which was directed by Herbert Ross who had previously directed Allen in 1972's *Play It Again, Sam*. It should also be noted that *Annie Hall* won Best Picture over *Star Wars* that year.

Allen was not present to collect his award, offering the excuse that he was playing his regular Monday-night gig with his jazz band in New York. Although the Oscars are no longer held on a Monday night, Allen still refuses to attend when nominated (that's 23 times now), saying he can't bear to see films in a competitive light.

It's possible to watch *Annie Hall* many times and always get something new from it, be it a gag or a previously unnoticed pun. But there's plenty of extraneous material to chew over too. Cameos to spot include: Christopher Walken as Annie's psycho brother Duane; Jeff Goldblum as man on phone at Hollywood party, saying, "I forgot my mantra"; Sigourney Weaver as the date accompanying Alvy to the cinema when he bumps into Annie at the end; Beverly d'Angelo playing Tony Roberts's wife in the sitcom he's recording in LA; and, as Annie and Alvy sit out of shot on a bench in Central Park remarking on the passers-by, we see a fleeting Truman Capote as "winner of the Truman Capote lookalike contest".

Woody initially wanted Federico Fellini to appear as the cameo in the cinema foyer, since the man behind was irritating Alvy with his remarks about the maestro's films. However, Fellini declined, as did surrealist director Luis Buñuel. Marshall McLuhan stepped in, although he later complained about his treatment on set, saying Allen hardly spoke to him.

Keaton wore her own clothes to create that Annie Hall "la-di-da look" that went on to inspire so many women in the 1970s. Costume designer Ruth Morley wanted to change her style, but Allen insisted that Keaton was "a genius, let her wear what she wants."

Although they had previously been together, Keaton and Allen were no longer a couple during the filming of *Annie Hall*. Theirs had deepened into a long-lasting, mutually respectful friendship that lasts to this day, rather like that of Alvy and Annie by the end. And though often denied, autobiographical interpretations of the movie are also inevitable, particularly as Keaton's real name is: Diane Hall.

The film was originally titled *Anhedonia*, after the psychological condition for one who cannot experience pleasure. Other titles considered were: *Me and My Goy*, *It Had to be Jew* and *A Rollercoaster Named Desire*.

It is the first film to use what became Allen's signature title sequence style, the simple Windsor Light Condensed typeface, a style he has used in every film since.

The cinematographer on *Annie Hall* was Gordon Willis, dubbed the Prince of Darkness after his work on *The Godfather* films. His collaboration with Woody Allen was therefore unlikely yet incredibly fruitful, lasting for the next seven films, up to *Purple*

Rose of Cairo in 1985. Woody readily credits Willis for deepening his own understanding of the art of film and for making him a far more accomplished filmmaker.

Most of us, as Alvy says, need the eggs, but the success of *Annie Hall* allowed Woody Allen to continue working in the often absurd world of filmmaking entirely in his own way. From here he kept going forwards, unlike that dead shark, to create one of the most distinguished and artistically rewarding careers in the history of film.

Above Woody Allen's Oscar-winning success with *Annie Hall* established him as a singular talent in American cinema, for whom directing, writing and performing seemed effortless.

Interiors (1978)

Three sisters deal with the dramatic repercussions of their parents' divorce after a long marriage, including their fragile mother's nervous breakdown and the arrival of their father's spirited new girlfriend, Pearl.

Imagine the shock. After years of clowning around, boxing kangaroos, telling jokes and having hit films dressed as a robot, a sperm or a reluctant revolutionary, your favourite comedy film maker, fresh from making the funniest ever Oscar-winner, delivers a sober blast of miserabilism that arrives like an icy Viking wind from across the north Atlantic.

Even with hindsight, I can't see there were any clues to what was about to come. So when United Artists gave Woody Allen carte blanche to make whatever film he wanted after his Oscar-night triumph with *Annie Hall*, they can't have predicted *Interiors*. Imagine the nerves at the studio when it arrived.

Audiences, keen to champion the comic king of their newly identified urban neuroses, must have been numb in front of this austerely beautiful, emotionally fraught, upscale family soap. And what other reaction could Woody himself seriously have expected?

After all, he'd laid the ground for the success of his comic persona so carefully over the previous 20 years that he couldn't possibly seek to erase it in one bold stroke, not without having first shown even the tiniest glimpses of what lay within.

No wonder the reviews were scathing and the box office probably the worst ever for the follow-up to a Best Picture Oscar winner. "A handbook of art-film mannerisms," complained Pauline Kael. John Simon thundered: "A disaster perpetrated on a gullible public by a man with a Bergman complex." Stanley Kaufman called it a "tour of the Ingmar Bergman Room at the Madame Tussaud's wax work museum".

They're all wrong, of course. *Interiors* may not be quite the masterpiece its director was aiming for, but we can look back now and see that it is a beautiful, moving and often brilliant dissection of family secrets quite unlike anything else made in one of American cinema's most dazzling decades.

It may have been a pity for Woody that, at the same time, his film idol and inspiration Ingmar Bergman was making *Autumn Sonata* with Liv Ullman and Ingrid Bergman (who had to turn down Allen's offer to play the mother in *Interiors* because she was committed to filming in Sweden). The two films share eerie resemblances.

Yet it still must have been the bravest – or most arrogant – act to make something this high-minded after so much successful comedy. The Woody Allen that comes through in *Interiors* is a serious artist, and a director to be considered at the highest level.

Testament to the film's enduring worth must be that, viewed now, it still feels very much like a Woody Allen film. What then must have looked like an insane U-turn now feels like a cornerstone of his filmic output, the serious drama in which neurotic New York intellectuals are desperately trying to find meaning in their well-designed, evolved lives.

The dynamic of siblings is also a recurring theme in his serious dramas, most notably in *Hannah and Her Sisters*, but also in *Crimes and Misdemeanors*, *Cassandra's Dream* and *September*. In particular, the character of Joey (Mary Beth Hurt) is very much an Allen type, struggling to find an artistic voice to express her self-proclaimed deep sensitivity. Her search is so anguished it borders on the comic, even while we pity her.

The sisters' bickering and snippy resentments are subtly managed in the scheme. Their mother (the outstanding Geraldine Page) creates tasteful interiors with everything in its place in a harmony of earth tones, while these tortured souls are seething inside like the sea outside the windows of their gorgeous Hamptons beach house.

Diane Keaton had made such a comic joy of *Annie Hall* (and Luna and Sonja before her) that it must have been tough to accept her as Renata the poet, yet her performance seems to me all the better for it. Seriousness seems to have settled over her like a blanket of depression, a sadness so heavy it can repress even that famous comic spirit, squeezing out and crushing the la-di-dah.

It must also be noted that the last half-hour of the film is unquestionably masterful. Maureen Stapleton's energy as the blowsy, colourful Pearl has something to do with it, giving the sisters a new focal point for their resentments, some sort of common ground again at last.

Her sudden marriage to their father is brilliantly done and the wedding party scene is astoundingly directed in a long unbroken take, fluidly moving around the room while people dance and cutting looks are exchanged. All this is underscored by Tommy Dorsey's 'Keepin' Out of Mischief Now', which pulses with joy and excitement yet seems to bring everyone to the edge of the abyss.

Noteworthy, too, is a shocking attempted rape scene featuring the terrible, self-loathing writer Frederick and the pretty sister Flyn, played by Kristin Griffith. It is quite unlike anything else in Woody's work, while a superbly handled, heart-in-mouth action sequence in the ocean waves creates a tension which I don't think Woody ever matched again.

The film's beautiful final shot is probably its most iconic and the most obvious nod to Bergman – which again can't have helped the

film's cause at the time. I can't help thinking there's some part of Woody Allen that could have spoofed this sort of self-consciously arty shot, as he had done recently in *Love and Death*.

Yet here he was, repressing the urge to laugh and also, for the first time in his films, repressing any hint of Jewishness. Of course, it was also the first time he repressed himself, his entire persona, clearly aware that the mere sight of himself on screen now precluded and punctured any attempt at seriousness.

He and cinematographer Gordon Willis had initially wanted to call the film "Windows" (indeed, this was the title Willis chose when he made his own film as director two years later). However, this was not a film in which Allen – to quote his own line about cheating in the metaphysics final – looked into the soul of the boy sitting next to him. Rather it was a film in which he looked deep inside himself.

It was what he sincerely wanted to do and he nearly pulled it off, right off the bat, without any practice or dry run. Accordingly, *Interiors* might just be the most honest and authentic insight into his mind as an artist. It is Woody Allen at his most raw.

Manhattan (1979)

Against the backdrop of a monochrome but modern New York City, television comedy writer Isaac Davies has a crisis. He can't commit to Tracy, the beautiful but 17-year-old girl he's dating, and he falls for neurotic journalist Mary, with whom his married best friend Yale is having a troubled affair.

Sometimes I watch *Manhattan* and it seems to me one of the finest films ever made. Other times, it just fades away, an ethereal will-o'-the-wisp that fails to penetrate my particular mood. Could it be that this undoubted masterpiece of 1970s cinema (a decade of many masterpieces, let it be said) is like a dream? Something that's conjured up by that rising clarinet solo which opens it, and over which Isaac begins his story: "Chapter One. He adored New York City. He romanticized it all out of proportion."

With Gordon Willis's iconic black and white photography and George Gershwin's sumptuous music, lots of the best bits of the film are not really Woody Allen's. "Borrowed grandeur" is what Woody's co-writer Marshall Brickman calls it. Nor is Woody, or Diane Keaton, even the real star. That role is taken by New York itself, to which the film remains an unashamed valentine, perhaps the greatest cinematic love letter ever addressed to any city. I guess that's why they called it *Manhattan*.

And if the city is both backdrop and metaphor, then the people in the film behave like islands unto themselves. The story centres on an emotional and existential crisis in the life of Isaac Davies, who quits his well-paying job as a writer on a TV sketch show.

From the brief look we get of the show, it looks a lot like *Saturday Night Live*, which is the show where Woody's friend – and, later, producer – Jean Doumanian worked, and took charge of for one notoriously unloved season in 1980.

Isaac is in turmoil due to his failure to admit his happiness with his new girlfriend, Tracy, stunningly played by Mariel Hemingway. This relationship, over which Ike tortures himself despite his moments of great emotional connection, has been giving Woody Allen's eager detractors fodder for years. In the opening scene at Elaine's restaurant, Ike tells his friends Yale and Emily: "I'm 42 and she's 17. I'm older than her father."

Although Woody mitigates the situation with some humour – "I'm dating a girl wherein I can beat up her father" – few viewers now find this comfortable given the scandal that would later engulf Woody when he began his relationship with Soon-Yi, the 21-year-old adopted daughter of his long-term partner Mia Farrow.

There's a particularly queasy moment for attentive viewers at Ike's flat, where he says that they're having great sex and "provided the cops don't burst in, we're gonna break a couple of records". Allen, however, and Hemingway, who gives an extraordinary performance, present Tracy as an almost other-worldly presence, an embodiment of uncorrupted purity, something beyond the mere confines of age and the law.

More crucially, she's also the only smart one, happily at one remove from the agonized intellectual maelstrom surrounding Ike, Yale and Mary and Ike's ex-wife who is writing a tell-all book about their marriage and break-up.

"I don't think Woody even remembers me... I went to see *Manhattan* and I felt like I wasn't even in it."

Meryl Streep

Jill, the ex-wife, is played by Meryl Streep, hot off her Oscar nominations for *The Deer Hunter* and *Kramer vs. Kramer*. Only in a Woody Allen film would a star as luminous as her (and she is even more striking in black and white) be reduced to a bit part. "I don't think Woody even remembers me," said Streep of filming her role. "I went to see *Manhattan* and I felt like I wasn't even in it."

Still, hers is a very skilful contribution and adds a crucial shade to the palette of New York romances contained here. Indeed, her

Below "Nothing I wrote was untrue": Meryl Streep plays Ike's ex-wife Jill in *Manhattan*, writing a tell-all book about their failed marriage.

character's words provide one of the most self-revealing moments in the Allen filmography. Here's how a passage from her book describes Isaac:

> He was given to fits of rage, Jewish, liberal paranoia, male chauvinism, self-righteous misanthropy, and nihilistic moods of despair. He had complaints about life, but never solutions. He longed to be an artist, but balked at the necessary sacrifices. In his most private moments, he spoke of his fear of death which he elevated to tragic heights when, in fact, it was mere narcissism.

Essentially, that's Woody writing about himself, getting out all that self-loathing on the page and in the voice of another character. You have to admire the honesty.

In its black and white, twilight state, *Manhattan* has the ability to conjure an immediate and melancholy sense of nostalgia, as if the moment has disappeared as soon as it has happened. It captures a profound moment in these characters' lives.

Woody is painfully aware of history and time throughout *Manhattan*, of the impermanence of buildings, life and, especially, love. It's why one of the key climactic scenes is played out in front of a class-room skeleton. "What are the future generations gonna say about us? Someday, we're gonna be like him," he tells Yale. "And … I wanna make sure that when I thin out, I'm w-w-ell thought of."

It's why the shot of Isaac and Mary (and her dog Waffles) watching the sunrise next to the Queensboro Bridge (or the 59th Street Bridge, the same one as in the Simon and Garfunkel song) has become such a key signifier of Allen's work. It's a beautiful moment, fragile as mist, and it too will pass.

A word on the much-discussed shot: it was taken at 5 a.m. and you can go there today to watch the lights on the bridge flicker off.

Right Diane Keaton and actor, director and screenwriter Woody Allen on the set of his film *Manhattan*.

The setting is Sutton Square but, like Woody, who thought it was a "pain in the neck" to do, you'll have to bring your own bench.

While Woody wanted to capture the New York he'd seen in the old films on the screens of his Brooklyn movie houses, the cinematography of Gordon Willis is more about the beauty of the moment, a "romantic reality" he has called it, which takes its inspiration from the great street photography of the 1940s and 1950s. And, for those future generations about whom Isaac is so concerned, we get a snapshot of how the city itself dictated, pressurized and shaped New Yorkers' lives in 1979 – or, at least, a certain demographic of them.

This is, of course, itself a film that ends with a famous list, as Isaac compiles the things that make life worth living.

On the list he includes the crabs at Sam Wo's (a Chinese restaurant on Mott Street, which he and co-writer Marshall Brickman would often dine in while talking through this very script). Also making the final cut are Groucho Marx, Frank Sinatra, Louis Armstrong, Flaubert, "those incredible apples and pears by Cézanne" and Swedish films. But the only real element for Isaac, and one that stings him into action, is "Tracy's face".

He leaps up and, to the sounds of 'Strike Up the Band', embarks on a now-classic cross-town dash, only to find Tracy loading up a taxi and ready to leave. Isaac can't stop her. We focus on her face, fresh and hurt and confused, beautiful and full of hope. "You have to have a little faith in people," she tells him. And the rhapsodic dream that is *Manhattan* vanishes into the air.

Right Perhaps the most famous shot in Woody's work: Ike and Mary watch the sun come up. Gordon Willis's cinematography glows with romance – but they had to bring their own bench.

Woody Allen Film by Film

The 1980s

Adored and garlanded, Woody Allen deepens his artistic repertoire with a remarkable yet constantly risky series of films. Inspired by the acting range of Mia Farrow, it results in one of the greatest runs in cinema history, films which effortlessly blend bittersweet comedy with deep philosophical inquiry.

Left Floored after the hostile reception to *Stardust Memories* in 1980, Woody Allen picked himself up and found his career-best form.

Stardust Memories (1980)

Revered comic filmmaker Sandy Bates attends a retrospective festival of his work, held at the seaside Stardust Hotel. But Sandy's producers fret over his new direction into "serious" films, fans besiege him and his love life closes in on his increasingly fevered mind.

"I think *Stardust Memories* will be viewed over the years and there will be much less resistance to it," said Woody Allen after the film met with scathing reviews and a level of backlash almost unimaginable today.

Manhattan had made Woody a hero. It was also one of the year's Top 10 grossing films at the American box office and its sophisticated, comic take on urban life had cemented Woody's following into a loyal and sizeable band. "His fans were prepared to follow him anywhere," notes the critic FX Feeney. "Anywhere, it turns out, except *Stardust Memories*."

The film was a commercial flop. With its cavalcade of grotesque fans, sycophants, groupies and hangers-on, it was seen as an insult to the very admirers who had taken Woody to their hearts and made him widely admired as both an artist and a box office draw. Here, it seemed, was a case of biting the hand that feeds you – though given that so many of his fans stayed away from the film, I'm not sure how they recognized it as such.

Here's what the influential critic Pauline Kael wrote of the character of Sandy Bates: "He is superior to all those who talk about his work; if they like his comedies … he shows them up as poseurs and phonies, and if they don't like his serious work, it's because they're too stupid to understand it. He anticipates almost anything that you might say about *Stardust Memories* and ridicules you for it. If Woody Allen finds success so very upsetting and wishes the public would go away, this picture should help him stop worrying."

That vicious review brought Allen's friendship with the famous critic to an end.

Yet the film does seem to be both an end and a new beginning. In fact, it's probably one of the most crucial films in the Allen canon. Viewed now, it's clearly a minor masterpiece as well as one of the great films about filmmaking, in the mould of its obvious model, Federico Fellini's *8½*. (As Tony Roberts's character says at an after-screening Q & A: "An homage? Not exactly. We just stole the idea outright.")

Yes, it does bring out the snobbery inherent in many of Woody's characters, their self-loathing as well as their desire to be taken seriously and their need to be constantly loved by women.

But *Stardust Memories* is also very funny, full of witty lines: "Suicide was not an alternative, you know? My mother was too busy running the boiled chicken through a deflavourizing machine to think about shooting herself." It's also stunningly beautiful. The black and white cinematography, again by Gordon Willis, may not have the romance of the shots in *Manhattan*, but it has many moods and shades, from a harsh glare to a crepuscular stillness.

Sandy Bates is clearly experiencing a mental breakdown. He sees a white rabbit that his housekeeper intends to prepare for dinner. "I don't eat rodent," he says, "it's fur bearing."

We're reminded, perhaps, of the many white rabbits in the credits sequence of *Everything You Always Wanted to Know About Sex*. But this dead white rabbit plunges Sandy, like Alice, down into another world, where the festival guests are distorted as if through a looking glass or hall of mirrors. They assail Sandy from all sides, leering, peering, sneering and cheering. They're a funny bunch, and to be honest, Sandy tries his best with them, signing autographs and accepting scripts and "suggestive items of food" thrust into his hands, snapping

Below Woody Allen levitates actress Jessica Harper during a scene from his film *Stardust Memories*, New Jersey, 1980.

"I don't want to make funny movies anymore. I don't feel funny."

Woody Allen as *Sandy Bates*

him with Polaroids (the "selfie" of the era) and smiling as they approach him to support charities or to eat at local restaurants.

I've personally seen Woody try and move around at various seaside film festivals since – San Sebastian, Cannes, Venice – and he is surrounded and filmed every step of the way. It always makes me think of *Stardust Memories*. He is unfailingly polite and gracious, but having strangers think they know you because of your work must be very odd and distorting and it's also very much the life of the successful modern artist. It's a spotlight from which Woody himself never escapes, at least for very long.

Woody will return regularly to explore the tussle between art and life, particularly in *Celebrity* and *Deconstructing Harry*, and also in *The Purple Rose of Cairo*. But here is the clearest portrait of the actual artist in meltdown, physically and mentally torn between lovers (Charlotte Rampling's haunting, haunted Dorrie and Marie Christine Barrault's more grounded Isobel, even though she's still married) and equally torn between comedy and tragedy.

Sandy says: "I don't want to make funny movies anymore. I don't feel funny. I look around the world and all I see is human suffering." His manager responds: "Human suffering doesn't sell tickets in Kansas City."

Maybe his fans at the time really did believe that Woody was saying goodbye to comedy, to the "early, funny films" that had made his career. *Interiors* had given them a glimpse into what life with only his serious intentions might be like, but *Manhattan* should surely have settled their nerves.

Stardust Memories, inspired by the Tarrytown weekend festivals held by critic Judith Crist – who has a cameo in his film – was an obvious riposte to that reaction, and it now looks like a very legitimate contribution to Woody's ongoing examination of the tussle between life and art and how to live functionally between the two, while also keeping a mindful eye on your own image.

Left "I didn't know you did magic tricks": Woody Allen as Sandy Bates flirts with Jessica Harper's Daisy on the set of *Stardust Memories*.

Maybe the aliens have the answer? Here, they famously tell him: "You want to do mankind a real service? Tell funnier jokes."

It's a film bursting with surprises, clues and observations. Firstly there are the cameos, including most famously Sharon Stone in her first film role, as Pretty Girl on Train, clutching some kind of film award and blowing Woody a kiss as her carriage pulls past in the opposite direction.

John Doumanian, the first husband of Woody's future producer Jean Doumanian, appears as the man whose brother runs an Armenian restaurant. Also making a cameo is Jacqui Safra, who later becomes Jean Doumanian's partner and financial backer in Sweetland Films.

Andy Albeck, then the head of United Artists, plays one of the film moguls concerned at Sandy's new seriousness. This would prove to be Woody's last picture with United, as he followed the executives – including his longtime champion Arthur Krim – who broke away to form Orion Pictures following the box office calamity of UA's *Heaven's Gate*.

Woody's character Isaac listed Louis Armstrong's "Potato Head Blues" as one of the things that make life worth living at the end of *Manhattan*; here, his Sandy fondly recalls being briefly happy on a perfect afternoon with Dorrie when they listened to Armstrong's fabulous recording of Hoagy Carmichael's 'Stardust'.

In an unsettlingly prescient theme, Sandy Bates is gunned down by a man who earlier asks for his autograph and who claims to be his biggest fan. Just 10 weeks after *Stardust Memories* opened in New York, and just half a mile from Woody's own apartment, John Lennon was gunned down by Mark Chapman, a fan who'd asked for an autograph.

Whatever he wanted to achieve with *Stardust Memories* at the time, Woody Allen's romance with films continues. At the end, Sandy is a lone figure, walking back in to the dimmed yet romantically deserted movie theatre. He reclaims his sunglasses, then walks off as the lights fade to black.

Does it suggest a new direction, a new disguise, a new outlook, for our famous spectacle wearer now that's he's got this artistic anger off his chest? As one woman says after the festival screening of Sandy's film: "What do you think the significance of the Rolls Royce was?" Replies her husband: "I think that's … uh, uh it represents his car."

A Midsummer Night's Sex Comedy (1982)

Three couples gather for a summer weekend in a country house.
Old passions rekindle and new loves arise and partners swap,
resulting in a criss-cross blend of bedroom farce and magical pastoral.

After the formal experimentalism and brutal reception that engulfed *Stardust Memories*, Woody Allen softens the mood with the palate-cleansing comedy *A Midsummer Night's Sex Comedy*.

As Sandy Bates in *Stardust Memories*, he seemed vaguely to have threatened to abandon comedy for serious films, so this new project was hardly what anyone was expecting. The film is light, airy and dotted with gags. Charming, but to be truthful, not one of his best.

When Woody left United Artists to join Orion Pictures, he arrived with two scripts: this one and *Zelig*, which he had written first but which was taking an age to prepare. Almost to fill in time, he dashed off *Midsummer* in two weeks and rushed it into production in the summer of 1981, to make the most of the weather just before beginning the filming of *Zelig*.

"I thought it would be fun to get some people in a country house and just celebrate summer, make it very beautiful, with butterfly nets and badminton courts and picnicking. Just this simple story, like a-day-in-the-country for fun. And I thought, Why should I wait? I'll do them both at the same time. What's the difference? And I did."

While making *Stardust Memories*, Woody had met Mia Farrow (legend has it that it was Michael Caine who introduced the pair) and the two began to go out.

Now, he persuaded her to take the part of Ariel, her first role under his direction. He had written it for Diane Keaton, but she was working on *Reds* with Warren Beatty (by then, her lover). He also enrolled his friend Tony Roberts; persuaded 1950s Hollywood star José Ferrer to return to the screen after a long absence to play Leopold, the pompous rationalist philosopher; and cast Julie Hagerty, whose performance he had loved in *Airplane!*, a film he still cites as one of the best-ever American comedies.

The cast gathered in a purpose-built house in Pocantico Hills on land belonging to the Rockefeller estate. Woody saw a magazine photograph of a house built around 1910, and asked for a similar one to be made from scratch. The interiors had to be constructed too. It was also used for filming in *Zelig*, and although the house didn't conform to building regulations, the producers then sold it – the purchaser modified and improved it and lived in it as a private home.

The film was to be the rural equivalent of *Manhattan*. The music was by Felix Mendelssohn rather than Gershwin, and Gordon Willis indulged in photographing owls, fish, flowers and lakes. The result is beautiful, if you like that sort of thing, echoing the work of filmmaker Jean Renoir (and his father, the Impressionist Pierre Auguste Renoir).

I can never get out of my mind how often characters in Woody's films say they hate the country. In *Annie Hall*, Alvy tells his second wife Robin he can't leave New York for the countryside: "You've got crickets, there's no place to walk after dinner and there's the screens with the dead moths behind them and the Manson family possibly ..."

However, he seems quite happy here, mucking about with his silly inventions such as a flying bicycle and an apple peeler while playing Andrew, whose marriage to Adrian (Mary Steenburgen) is in crisis. "I pour all my energy into my inventions now," he tells her. "Because of our lack of sex, I can now fly."

It turns out it was Mia who was miserable during filming. In her autobiography, *What Falls Away*, she wrote: "Our days were spent waiting for moments of perfect light. Meanwhile I was in the camper (Woody and I shared one throughout thirteen films), wearing a robe, with my hair tightly wrapped around cone-shaped curlers, my torso compressed into a killer corset. Bleary-eyed from a pulverizing

Left In *A Midsummer Night's Sex Comedy*, Woody Allen plays an inventor whose marriage has stalled.

Below "Because of our lack of sex, I can now fly": Woody buckles up with the help of Mary Steenburgen.

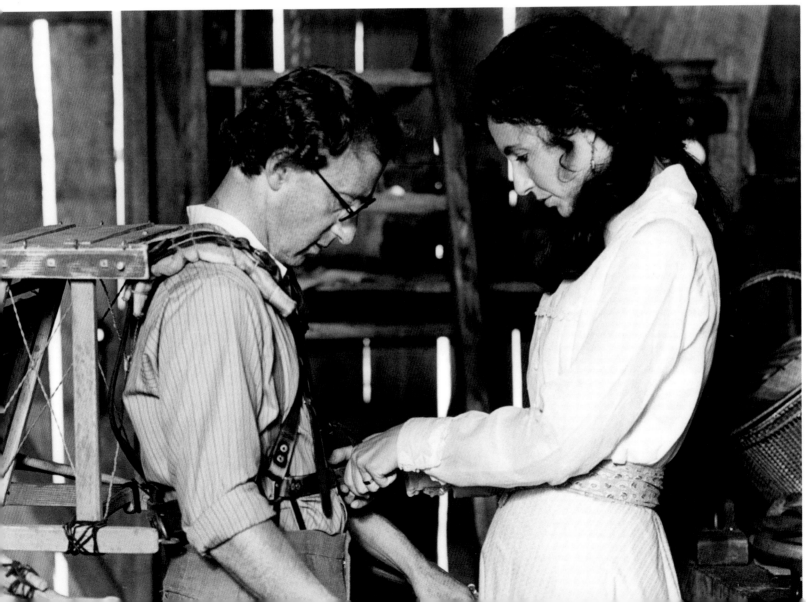

headache (the curlers, the corset, the heat, the humidity, the nerves),
I just wished I could be my sister [Stephanie, who acted as Farrow's
stand-in] out there looking adorable in her jeans and baseball cap
and straight hair, lounging in the tall grass, strolling under the trees,
talking and laughing with Woody.'"

Filming with Allen brought out Farrow's insecurities, which was
not helped by her boyfriend's reticence with his actors and the fact
that he seemed to be flirting with her sister.

"At times during shooting, I was overpowered by such a paralysis.
Woody, now my director, was a stranger to me. His icy sternness
pushed my apprehension toward raw fear. I was no artist, only the most
inept poseur. By mid-movie I had an ulcer and was taking Tagamet four
times a day. I was so apprehensive, dispirited, and humiliated, and so
convinced I had failed Woody, that I asked if in the future, if there was
a future, I could be his assistant, so I wouldn't have to act. He looked at
me doubtfully and said, 'It's hard work being an assistant.'"

It is true that Farrow's performance, in which she often actually
sounds like she's delivering lines in a Diane Keaton style, is probably
her weakest in all Allen's films. It even earned her a Razzie Award
(Golden Raspberry) for worst actress, which may have been cruel but
demonstrates just how little love there was for the film.

Looking back, Allen told filmmaker and critic Stig Bjorkman:
"Nobody came to see *A Midsummer Night's Sex Comedy*. But I
wanted it to be light. I just wanted it to be a small intermezzo with a
few laughs. I don't say this was any great picture at all, but in general
this atmosphere is something that nobody cares about here in the
United States. For me it was fine. I had a great time doing it. I thought
it was good when I wrote it, and I thought it was good when I made
it. But it was not appreciated at all. This one and *September* [1987] are
my two biggest financial disasters."

It was his second flop in a row and while *Stardust Memories* retains
a nightmarish and cutting-edge relevance today, *Midsummer* simply
fades away, like a dream you can't quite remember.

Right Woody Allen walks with Mia
Farrow in a field in a scene from
A Midsummer Night's Sex Comedy.

Zelig (1983)

Zelig marked a return to the fake documentary format Woody Allen used for his debut movie *Take the Money and Run*. Leonard Zelig is the "Human Chameleon", a man so desperate to fit in he takes on the characteristics of whoever is around him. It is one of Allen's cleverest films, visually and thematically. It is also one of his shortest.

An example of Allen's remarkable work rate and mental restlessness, *Zelig* was made at the same time he was shooting *A Midsummer Night's Sex Comedy*. Only the tricky post-production process resulted in *Zelig* being released later.

You can see why. It's not often that you marvel at special effects in a Woody Allen movie – often the reverse is true and, in fact, you're wondering at just how rudimentary they are, and even non-existent in *Midnight in Paris* – but in Zelig the technique is key to the film's success.

Using archive newsreel, photographs and stock footage, Allen literally inserts himself into history – and does so many years before the invention of computer programs made the process relatively easy. The result is what we now call a "mockumentary", although I don't believe that term was widely used until director Rob Reiner used it to describe his film *This is Spinal Tap* in 1984.

The film thus becomes a delightful parody of American history and yet manages to maintain at its core a rather sweet love story between Zelig and the psychiatrist who treats him, Dr Eudora Fletcher, played by Mia Farrow in the first role Allen wrote specifically for her. Interestingly, Eudora Fletcher was also the name of the high school principal Woody hated.

Left Actor and film director Woody Allen dressed in costume as a Native American in a promotional portrait for his film *Zelig*.

In the film, Zelig becomes a cultural phenomenon, generating spinning newspaper headlines that allowed Allen both to pay homage to Orson Welles's *Citizen Kane* and to revisit the Jazz Age and delve into his music library. And with his regular music collaborator Dick Hyman, he created some brilliant parodies, such as 'Do The Chameleon', which were sung by Mae Questel – she's the inimitable voice of Betty Boop and Olive Oyl in the cartoons.

Zelig is very funny. Some jokes are pure sight gags, such as Zelig morphing into both a "tough-looking hombre" in a Chicago speakeasy and a black trumpet player. Or there's the sight of Woody Allen, as Zelig, dressed in full Scottish highland regalia – now that's just funny. As are the photographs of Zelig's father, a Yiddish actor "whose performance of Puck in the Orthodox version of *A Midsummer Night's Dream* was coolly received".

Through the course of the film, the Jewish second-generation immigrant Zelig becomes, variously, black, fat, Native American, Chinese, Greek and even French. So there's obviously a salient theme in the film about assimilation and the Jewish experience, but there is also much on psychiatry and analysis (something for which Allen is, of course, renowned) as well as on fame and the nature of celebrity, another of Allen's recurring themes.

Zelig becomes famous, offering Allen the ultimate wish fulfilment of hanging out with Clara Bow, Eugene O'Neill, Jack Dempsey and Josephine Baker. He even incorporates some of the only existing footage of F Scott Fitzgerald.

Below Taking it on the chin: Zelig clowns with heavyweight champ Jack Dempsey at a training camp in Chicago.

"He tells me the meaning of life ... in Hebrew. I don't understand Hebrew. "

Woody Allen as *Leonard Zelig*

There are also testimonies from some real "talking heads", including literary theorist Susan Sontag, psychoanalyst Bruno Bettelheim and Nobel Prize-winning author Saul Bellow. According to Woody, Bellow initially refused to speak the script when he was given it because it was full of grammatical errors, which he insisted on changing.

Yet Zelig also manages to make points about individuality and fascism. Such is the character's desire to fit in that he eventually becomes the "ultimate conformist" and is spotted at a Nazi rally in 1930s Munich. It leads to the film's major gag, in which Woody Allen appears behind Hitler delivering his famous speech, the bespectacled Jew disrupting the Führer in full flow. Ah, what delicious revenge one can take in the cinema.

Zelig is constantly playful yet cleverly builds plot, momentum and emotion, so the audience really cares about the fate of Zelig and the heart of the brilliant, generous Dr Fletcher, played so skilfully by Farrow. "I have an interesting case," says Zelig while pretending to be a doctor. "I'm treating two sets of Siamese twins with split personalities. I'm getting paid by eight people."

It is also one of Allen's films to feature a narrator. British legend John Gielgud was Allen's original choice and recorded the entire script, but it was felt his voice was too recognizable and "too grand" and he was replaced by the lesser-known British actor Patrick Horgan. Another legend who didn't make the final cut of the film was silent star Lillian Gish, who is said to have berated cinematographer Gordon Willis on set about his lighting.

Zelig is probably not one of Allen's best-known films, but it is one of his most instantly likeable and richest works, as well as being visually groundbreaking. It has even entered the psychological lexicon: in 2007, Italian doctors observed that a patient after a stroke had been affected by an "environmental dependency", which manifested as personality disorders and role playing. At various times, the patient claimed to be a solicitor and a bartender, and even assumed the role of a doctor. The psychologists named the condition Zelig-like Syndrome.

Left Mia Farrow's Dr Eudora Fletcher takes on the case of Human Chameleon Leonard Zelig, and falls in love with his personalities.

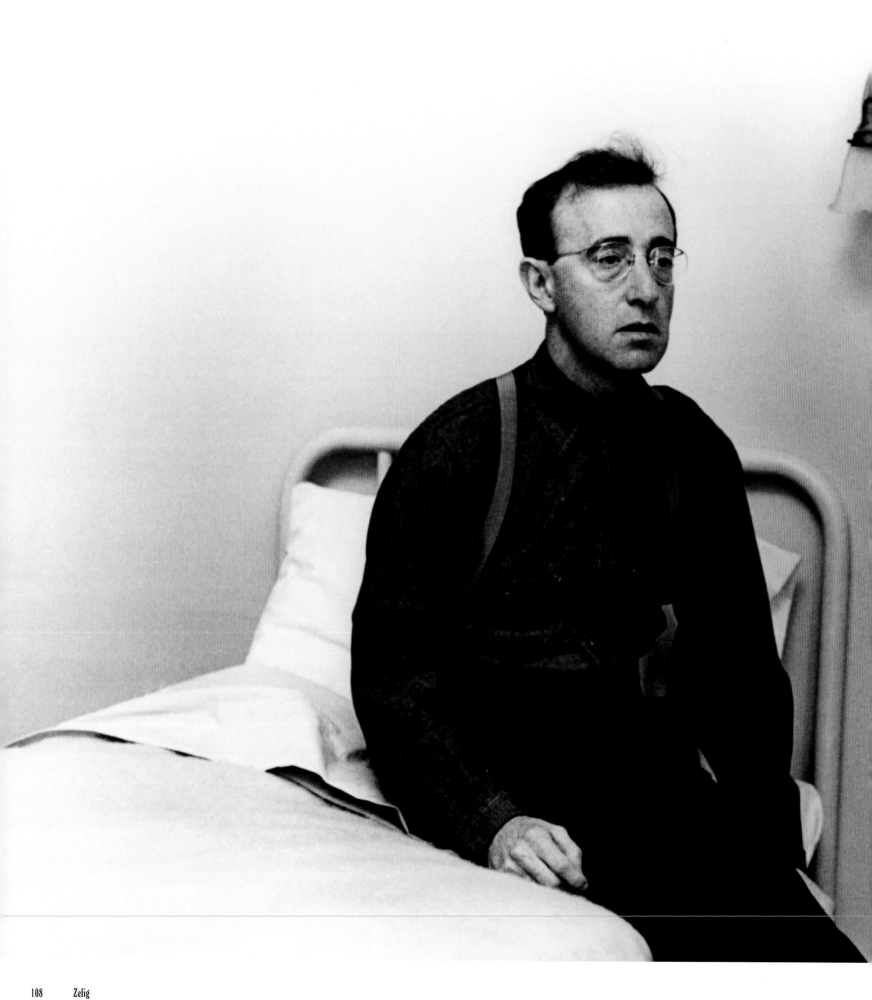

Above The Polish film poster for *Zelig*, 1983.

Left Zelig's multiple personality condition baffles medical science and leads to lawsuits for "plagiarism, property damages, negligence and performing unnecessary dental extractions".

Broadway Danny Rose (1984)

A bunch of old-time New York comedians sit in a deli and tell
the story of legendary theatrical agent Danny Rose, his bizarre variety
acts and how he fell in unlikely love with a gangster's moll named Tina.

For a while, it must have seemed that all Woody Allen films, no matter what the subject, existed, like the *Manhattan* of his imagination, in black and white. *Broadway Danny Rose* was his fifth in a run of six films since *Annie Hall* to use monochrome despite the fact that it's one of his most colourful tales.

Woody always bats off any distinctions: "Hundreds of the films you've loved have been in black and white and hundreds have been in colour – if black and white is inferior, don't look at *Citizen Kane* or *The Maltese Falcon* or *Grand Illusion* or *The Bicycle Thieves* …"

Again he worked with Gordon Willis, and they both saw this as their own version of Italian films from the 1950s. However, for many it will be forever associated with the Carnegie Deli on Seventh Avenue, between 54th and 55th. That's where the story unfolds, like the layers of a corned beef on rye.

Allen has often used a narration to give his films a framework, but this is his most inventive, as a gaggle of comedians sit around to listen to the story of Danny Rose. These guys were real stand-ups: Sandy Baron tells most of the tale, while Corbett Monica, Will Jordan, Howie Storm, Jackie Gayle and Morty Gunty pitch in. Also present is Jack Rollins, Woody's long time manager and in some sense the inspiration for Danny Rose – Rollins and his client spent many nights at that deli dissecting Woody's performances and chatting about comedy.

The Deli's own Leo Steiner has a brief cameo, and Danny has a sandwich named after him: cream cheese on bagel with marinara sauce. In real life this no longer exists, but for $29.99 you can still get the Woody Allen – "lotsa corned beef plus lotsa pastrami". I doubt he actually orders this there – and if he did, he certainly couldn't finish it.

Sandwiches aside, the film is a jewel of comic clash and New York fable. Danny Rose's clients are a wonderful throwback to the variety days of the Borscht Belt summer camps, where Woody himself cut his comic teeth: a one-legged tap dancer, a one-armed juggler, an ice-skating penguin who performs the finale dressed like a rabbi.

It's a milieu Woody knew well and for which he clearly has much affection. The woman playing wine glasses; the husband and wife balloon-folding act; Barney Dunn, the world's worst ventriloquist act ("when he does kids' parties, five-year-olds boo him") – Danny Rose respects them all and gives them his all. None more than Lou Canova, his Italian singing star whose last big hit was as a kid back in the 1950s with 'Agita', a bouncy song about indigestion.

Danny runs into comedy legend Milton Berle (playing himself in a silent cameo) and, ever with an eye for the chance, gets Lou a slot at a nostalgia night. This is their chance at the big time, but Lou feels he needs his latest girlfriend Tina Vitale there on the night or he won't be able to perform at his best.

Playing Lou is an unknown cabaret act and dedicated fisherman Nick Apollo Forte, cast after Woody dug up some of his discs at the famous Colony Records store. He beat to the part such stars as Robert de Niro, Tony Bennett, Nic Cage and Danny Aiello, and gives a great performance despite never having acted before. Nor has he done so since,

Right Comedians at the Carnegie Deli narrate the story of *Broadway Danny Rose*. Sandy Baron gesticulates in the centre; Woody's manager Jack Rollins is on the far right of the picture.

despite subsequent appearances on *The Tonight Show* and a residency in Atlantic City (of which the live recording is still available on CD).

It turns out that Nick was not much of a Woody fan at the time: "I never saw one of his movies before. As a matter of fact, I don't really go nuts on a lot of his movies, especially the first one I really saw was a thing called *Zelig*. I went to the screening of it and I sat back and I said, 'Oh, my god, this is like a joke.' This thing was just a terrible movie."

Extending the film's restaurant connections, Mia Farrow's character is based on Annie Rao, a beehived, dark-glasses-wearing figure who used to chat to the clientele at the famous Italian eatery Rao's in East Harlem. It's still there and is known as one of the toughest places in New York to get a table – there are only ten of them.

"One night Mia says to me she'd love to play a character like Annie Rao," says Woody. "And I wanted to play a different kind of character, not a neurotic, literate type of New Yorker, but more of a lowlife, for which I always think I'm particularly suited as an actor. So I wrote it for us."

Farrow performs most of the film behind her dark glasses, taking them off for only one scene when she is pictured coming out of the shower. "It was a tough job because she had to act without using her eyes, but look at the one shot without the glasses and she's incredibly beautiful, one of the prettiest shots of Mia."

Allen's incarnation of Rose is loquacious and funny, always talking himself out of tight spots – "If I may interject one statement …?" – and often bringing up deceased relatives: "My Aunt Rose, God rest her, not a pretty woman, like something you'd see in a live bait store …"

Danny and Tina end up on the run from Italian gangsters, hiding in the long grasses in New Jersey. "I never saw so many reeds in my life … I feel like Moses." This clash of fast-talking, badly dressed Jewish guy and tough, bombshell Italian broad is terrific and somehow works, probably better than the cream cheese bagel with marinara sauce they spawned. The realization that he's with a mafia moll takes a while to dawn on Danny: "What? Lay low? My whole life I ate the right foods and now I gotta lay low?"

Broadway Danny Rose may not be a major Allen, but it's terrific, New York food, and in just the right portions.

"My whole life I ate the right foods and now I gotta lay low?"

Woody Allen as *Danny Rose*

Above Nick Apollo Forte plays Lou Canova singing his hit 'Agita', about a cure for indigestion.

Left Woody and Mia as Danny Rose and Tina Vitale, an odd couple on the run.

Overleaf Woody's showbiz agent Danny Rose contemplates falling in love with his best client's girlfriend over a coffee in the Carnegie Deli, 1984.

The Purple Rose of Cairo (1985)

A charming Depression-era romance between a girl and her idol who steps
out of the silver screen and into New Jersey, *The Purple Rose of Cairo* is
the Woody Allen film that Woody himself most often admits to liking.
It is, without doubt, one of his very finest and most playful works.

It sounds depressing, but his inspiration for writing *The Purple Rose of Cairo* was to show just how disappointing real life is. "My view of reality is that it's a grim place to be," Woody has said, "but it's the only place you can get Chinese food."

And yet, this film soars and enchants. He presents us with Cecilia (Mia Farrow), a girl trapped in a bad marriage to a brute (Danny Aiello) and fired from her job at a diner, whose only escape is to the local cinema, the Jewel Theatre. There she gazes at images of people having a more exotic and glamorous time.

For the fifth time she watches a movie featuring "Tom Baxter", played by Jeff Daniels. Recognizing her in the stalls, the self-professed "poet, adventurer, explorer" now steps out of the movie and runs off with her, to the fairground (filmed at the recently closed Bertrand Island Amusement Park). "So that's what popcorn tastes like," is one of the first things he says, having watched people munching it for so long.

Baxter's departure prompts unscripted chaos on the screen as well as outrage in the stalls. "We're all so lost up here on the screen,

we don't know what to do," cry the characters in the movie Tom has left in the lurch. "I'm a dramatic character, I need forward motion." And a disgruntled lady leaves the Jewel in a huff, complaining to the manager: "I want what happened in the movie last week to happen this week. Otherwise, what's life all about anyway?"

All this is wonderfully playful and surreal, yet Allen plays it as straight as possible. There are certainly elements of Buñuel's *The Discreet Charm of the Bourgeoisie* here, but the spell is more magical, with disbelief suspended on several levels. When the movie's director Raoul Hirsch, back in Hollywood, hears about his character's elopement, he says: "But that's not physically possible." One of his producers points out: "It's New Jersey, anything's possible."

On one level of comedy, a movie character is on the loose, behaving chivalrously and true to his character as written, the only way he knows how. There's a lovely scene where Tom takes Cecilia to a plush restaurant and swaggeringly picks up the bill, only for his money to be fake movie money. When they make a run for it, Tom can't believe the car they jump into won't just drive.

All along, Allen crashes fantasy up against reality, like a two-way mirror. Cecilia dreams of being one side, while Tom, the character, desires freedom of choice – the one thing humans certainly do have, even if they feel, like Cecilia, that they are trapped by circumstance.

Another layer is added when Gil Sheperd, the Hollywood actor who plays Tom, comes to town to persuade his character to get back in the movie lest his burgeoning career be derailed or tarnished by Tom's behaviour. The pair – both played by Daniels,

Above left Jeff Daniels as the naïve Tom Baxter,
lured to his first brothel by Dianne Wiest.

Left *The Purple Rose of Cairo* is the film
playing at the Jewel – a picture house
based on one of Woody's childhood
haunts, the Kent Theatre in Brooklyn.

of course – become rivals for Cecilia and both their courtships are miles away from the rough treatment she's received at the hands of her drunken husband Monk.

In the scene where Cecilia and Gil perform a duet – he singing, she on the ukulele – Mia Farrow is at her all-time loveliest, enraptured by the magic that's happening to her. But there's a remarkable fragility contained in Mia's performance, like that of the silent movie heroine, tightrope walking between comedy and tragedy – she makes us laugh but also cry, almost in the same frame.

Such a wonderful performance earns her the just reward of delivering, perfectly, one of the greatest, sweetest, funniest lines in all Woody's work: "I just met a wonderful new man," she breathes, before giving the most delicate of little shrugs. "He's fictional, but you can't have everything."

In another delightful pastiche sequence, Tom takes her on a whirlwind night out in "madcap Manhattan", transporting her into the movie, into his world, to the neon lights, to Club Harlem and Club Morocco.

Of course, the end is cruel. Cecilia can't live in the movies. Woody is building up the fantasy so that reality bites harder and, when she is finally forced to choose Gil over Tom, reality over fiction, he'll leave her stranded in front of the Jewel Theatre.

Commentators have found this finale very sad, Woody denying his characters and his audience any happy ending. Yet have we learned nothing? If he does endings at all, Woody doesn't do happy ones. Cecilia reacts how only she could, by retreating into the dark comforts of the stalls again.

This time she dives in – oh for the days when you could dip in at the middle of a film and wait for the bit you missed to swing around again – just as Fred Astaire swirls Ginger Rogers around in *Top Hat*, singing 'Cheek to Cheek'.

Right Cecilia finds solace in the escapism of films and watches *The Purple Rose of Cairo* for the fifth time.

"My view of reality is that it's
a grim place to be ... but it's
the only place you can get
Chinese food."

Woody Allen

For all the Hollywood glamour, it's her face that becomes the real picture. Tears drying on her cheeks, she gazes up and a smile forms on her lips once more. Cecilia is, at last, transported into the movies – but only for as long as the movie lasts.

Then both movies end.

Just as Woody's suicidal character Mickey in *Hannah and Her Sisters* realizes the meaning of life when he ducks into a cinema and catches the Marx Brothers in *Duck Soup*, here is a character who finds happiness in the fleeting escape of the movies.

If we believe – and after watching this film in particular, why shouldn't we? – that Cecilia gets up, leaves the cinema and walks off into a happier or at least more self-determined life, then we can draw great strength and joy from the film. She has learned freedom from the character of Tom and resilience from her bitter brush with eternal fantasy.

The Purple Rose of Cairo doesn't feature Woody as a performer. But he is, of course, omnipresent. And not just when Tom Baxter responds to a question about believing in God by assuming that Cecilia is referring to the writers of the movie. The interior of the Jewel was actually one of Woody's childhood haunts, the Kent Theatre on Coney Island Avenue in Brooklyn. "You could always hear the freight train in the Kent," he once told his biographer Eric Lax. "You'd be watching a movie and you'd hear the freight train going by for about five minutes."

Exteriors were shot in the village of Piermont, up the Hudson River, where an entire street was covered with false Depression-era façades.

The film also enables cinematographer Gordon Willis to display some of his most skilful work with Allen, creating the warm interiors as well as the black and white film within the film (the eponymous *The Purple Rose of Cairo*) and getting the two to blend. He also worked on creating the harsh light of the exteriors to capture both the grey of the Depression but also the contrast that comes when exiting any cinema into the cold light of day, a contrast that heightens the clash of reality with the retreat into fantasy.

"I remember being influenced by Fellini's *Amarcord*," Allen has said. "I remember the feeling of this small town with this movie house and larger than life characters and I wanted that feeling of nostalgia and melancholy."

Despite its exquisite charms, *The Purple Rose of Cairo* earned only one Oscar nomination, for Woody's almost customary category of Best Original Screenplay. Maybe this was just an unlucky year for purple: Steven Spielberg's *The Color Purple* was nominated for 11 Oscars – and won none. Mia Farrow's beautifully skilled, light comic playing surely deserved wider recognition.

It was not one of Allen's more commercially successful pictures, earning just over $10.5 million at the US box office. Perhaps it would have had more earning potential if the original star had stayed in the film. Michael Keaton was let go after eight days of shooting and replaced with the fresh-faced Jeff Daniels. Allen has said that when he looked at Keaton in the first dailies, he was just "too hip" to be from the 1930s.

One of the best things, for Allen, about making *The Purple Rose of Cairo* was that he was able to work with one of his childhood idols, the actor Van Johnson, who had featured in many of the wartime films on which Allen grew up during the 1940s and who went on to star in *Brigadoon* and *The Caine Mutiny*. Van Johnson plays Larry Wilde, one of the wealthy Manhattanites in the film within the film.

Left Script notes: Woody directs Mia Farrow on the set of *The Purple Rose of Cairo*.

Hannah and Her Sisters (1986)

Three sisters – their husbands, lovers, exes and parents – are subjected to the vagaries of the human heart and the agonies of existence over the course of three Thanksgiving dinners in New York.

Woody Allen is at his best when cramming all his favourite things into one film. Ike's list at the end of *Manhattan* of "certain things that make it worthwhile" are all present in *Hannah and Her Sisters*: jazz, novels, art, a beautiful woman's face, Groucho Marx, classical music … Only Willie Mays and the crabs at Sam Wo's are missing.

Hannah and Her Sisters is about as perfect as Woody Allen gets. It's funny, sexy and sad but remains agile enough to ponder religion, philosophy, poetry and, above all, family life without ever feeling, not for an instant, mired in self-pity. Or, at least, no more than any neurotic, pseudo-intellectual New Yorker in a Woody Allen film can hope to be.

In fact, the prismatic nature of the film's construction is what makes it a masterpiece, something reflected in the film's use of novelistic chapter headings and on its official soundtrack album, which contains a panoply of different musical styles: Harry James, JS Bach and New York cabaret lounge legend Bobby Short.

If the film is centred around anyone, it must be Hannah, played by Mia Farrow. However, in one of the film's most celebrated scenes, Hannah is having lunch with her sisters Holly (Dianne Wiest) and Lee (Barbara Hershey) and the camera circles around them, never finding a centre. All the major characters get their moments and none of the storylines is left unfulfilled.

And as far as the continuing palimpsest of Woody Allen's creative and personal life goes, *Hannah and Her Sisters* is a grade-A artefact, a moment in time where the fusion of his influences feeds the power of the film. Mia Farrow plays Hannah, and her character's apartment, for example, is Farrow's own, her character's mother is played by her own (Maureen O'Sullivan), and the children in the film are hers too, including a brief appearance from Soon-Yi Previn who would, just six years later, become Woody's lover.

How accurate a portrait of Farrow, then, is Woody's creation of Hannah? In her autobiography, Farrow recalled the filming: "The place was pandemonium. The rooms were clogged … the kitchen was an active set for weeks. It was strange to be shooting scenes in my own rooms – my kitchen, my pots, my own kids saying lines, Michael Caine in my bathroom, wearing a robe, rummaging through my medicine cabinet. Or me lying in my own bed kissing Michael, with Woody watching …"

Farrow also says some elements of the script hit "a little close to home". She continues: "He had taken many of the circumstances and themes in our lives and … distorted them into cartoonish characterizations. At the same time … this is what writers do. He had taken the ordinary stuff of our lives and lifted it into art. We were honoured and outraged."

Yet it is this conflation between art and life that always makes for the central tussle in Woody's best work. All this extraneous detail will fade, though. Only the film will abide. And what a lasting testament it will prove – to its actors, to its writer and director, and to (a part of) the city itself.

Woody has joked he doesn't want to live on through his work, he'd rather live on in his apartment. Yet, perhaps through its very

specificity, *Hannah and Her Sisters* has an enduring universality, which made it one of his biggest hits, commercially and critically, as well as earning him another Oscar for Best Original Screenplay.

The spread of connected characters allows the director to explore facets of human behaviour, from stupidity to selfishness, vanity and recklessness as well as probing different aspects of love. "The heart is a very resilient little muscle," says Allen's character Mickey at the end, striking a note of hopefulness.

Yet earlier, Michael Caine's character Elliot is in considerable pain, torn between two sisters, when he, in one of the many internal monologues that distinguish the film, says: "For all my so-called accomplishments, I can't fathom my own heart."

What a fine performance Caine's is, leagues away from his usual roles. Woody originally wanted Jack Nicholson, who was committed to filming *Prizzi's Honour* with John Huston. Caine is unafraid to make a dizzy fool of himself as he runs after the alluring Lee. "God, she's beautiful," he says gazing at her in the very first line of the film, before quickly telling himself: "Stop it, you idiot, she's your wife's sister. But I can't help it …"

A standout in a film of many sublime sequences – one of my favourite in all Allen's work in fact – is when Elliot pretends to bump into Lee, engineering for himself a dash around a downtown block in a ridiculous fur-collared mackintosh coat so he can catch her up. Allen beautifully offsets the essential silliness of this exercise and, indeed, even makes it romantic by playing Harry James's magnificent 'I've Heard That Song Before' underneath it.

When Caine does get his kiss from Lee, he breathes, "I have my answer, I have my answer. I'm walking on air." He's like a little boy, and we feel for him and the success of his almost-heroic efforts, despite the villainy of simultaneously betraying Hannah – something this film makes seem curiously inevitable.

Left Woody Allen and Mia Farrow take a break from shooting *Hannah and Her Sisters* for the fresh, cold air of Central Park, New York, 1986.

In a film of such beauty and precision, it's invidious to leave out any scene. But we can't ignore Allen's own contribution as Mickey. He plays Hannah's ex-husband, who is a TV producer on a top-rating comedy show – similar, one supposes, to *Saturday Night Live*, a job very much like the one Isaac quits in *Manhattan*. And, am I dreaming this, or does Mickey's flat here look suspiciously like Ike's, with the spiral staircase?

Mickey's health crises and religious explorations provide (would you believe?) comic relief and crystallize many of the director's favourite themes, with some of his sharpest comedy. Asking a Hare Krishna in the park about reincarnation, he wonders: "Does that mean I come back as a moose?" As any fans of Woody's stand-up know, moose is always funny.

When he threatens to become a Catholic, Mickey's mother locks herself in the bathroom (possibly to take an overdose of mahjong tiles) rather than face her son's atheistic thoughts and questions about Nazis. "Ask your father," she shouts. The father counters, "Me? How the hell do I know why there were Nazis? I don't know how the can opener works."

Surviving a suicide attempt as well as a possible brain tumour (I did say he was the comic relief, right?), Mickey seeks solace on the New York streets and the shelter of a cinema "to be logical and to put the world back into rational perspective." Cut to: the Marx Brothers playing the xylophone on soldiers' helmets in *Duck Soup*.

Through comic absurdity, and amid the private tortures of Hannah and of her sisters, Allen still manages to find reason for living. "What if there is no God and you only go around once and that's it? Well, ya know, don't you wanna be part of the experience? You know, what the hell, it's not all a drag. And I'm thinking to myself, Jeez, I should stop ruining my life searching for answers I'm never gonna get, and just enjoy it while it lasts."

Philosophically speaking, it's one of his most positive on-screen moments. We can contrast it with the awesome Max von Sydow, the star of so many Bergman films and now appearing for Woody Allen as Frederick, an uncompromising artist and lover/mentor of Lee. His monologue about an evening spent watching TV is a minor classic on its own: "You see the whole culture – Nazis, deodorant salesmen,

wrestlers, beauty contests, a talk show. Can you imagine the level of a mind that watches wrestling? But the worst are the fundamentalist preachers." Yet his reaction to Lee's admission that she wants to leave him is even more magnificent. I can't dispel the image of him sitting on the bed, hands joined in front of him, shaking them up and down in a barely contained rage that finally comes out as a simple yet almost threatening: "Why?" According to Allen, the crew gave the Swedish actor a round of applause after that scene.

There is so much else that is fabulous in *Hannah and Her Sisters*. I've barely mentioned Dianne Wiest, whose performance as Holly the frustrated actress and recovering coke addict earned her an Oscar for Supporting Actress.

Holly and her friend April (Carrie Fisher) compete for the affections of an architect (Sam Waterston) who takes them – after their debut as the deliciously named Stanislavski Catering Company – on an architectural tour of his favourite Manhattan buildings, a sequence with obvious resonance in Woody's work.

He was working for the first time with Antonioni's cameraman Carlo Di Palma (having originally tried to get him for *Take the Money and Run*) and it's as if he was setting the renowned cinematographer the task of matching Gordon Willis's famous Manhattan montage. Capturing a memorable array of shots that include the Graybar Building, Pomander Walk, the New York Yacht Club, the Fifth Avenue Synagogue and the Chrysler Building, Carlo obviously passed the test and went on to work with Woody another 11 times.

Woody has always maintained he was too soft on his characters at the end of this film, finishing on too neat and too hopeful a note. He even presents Mickey with a pregnancy, an issue discussed earlier in the film and one that had eventually led to the split from Hannah.

But these notes of warmth are what allowed audiences to take the picture to their hearts and make *Hannah and Her Sisters* one to savour and treasure.

Left "I cannot fathom my own heart": Michael Caine as Elliot with Mia Farrow's Hannah. It was Caine who first introduced Woody to Mia.

Below Woody Allen's Mickey looks forward to the worst as he calls his doctor.

Radio Days (1987)

Woody Allen's own voice provides the warmly humorous narration to a romanticized version of his own 1940s childhood, interspersed with fictionalized stories of glamorous radio personalities and peppered with glorious popular music and songs.

Every time I see *Radio Days*, it creeps higher up my chart of favourite things. The film may lack existential philosophy, but it has wit, warmth and a knowing wisdom that elevates it to the lofty position of being one of its director's finest works of art.

Indeed such is the beauty of Carlo Di Palma's cinematography and Santo Loquasto's Oscar-nominated art direction that many of the tableaux look just like paintings. The film is about the colour and quality of memory, and how we choose to remember it, and distort it through mythology, legend, gossip and music.

An entire sequence of *Radio Days* concerns individual songs and how their tunes spark very specific memories. 'Paper Doll' plays during his parents' anniversary: "It was the only time I saw them kiss." The nonsense ditty 'Mairzy Doats' by the Merry Macs reminds our narrator of the time Mr Zlipsky had a nervous breakdown and ran through the neighbourhood in his underwear brandishing a meat cleaver.

As well as being one of his funniest, *Radio Days* is Allen's most sensory film, a piece intimately concerned with the immediate tangibility of film, radio and music and yet also – typically – aware of their impermanence.

You can't like Woody Allen or even understand him without loving *Radio Days*. The parents depicted here (played by Michael Tucker and Julie Kavner) echo the stories he tells of his own parents, Martin and Nettie Konigsberg: his father's various but secret jobs, the threat of a beating with a belt, the arguments about anything ("The Pacific is a better ocean than the Atlantic"), the extended family members staying in the house.

Yet it is so much more than autobiography. "Forgive me if I tend to romanticize the past," says the voice-over. This is an exploration of nostalgia and acts as a bridge between the comic flashbacks of *Annie Hall* – the rollercoaster here is Rockaway's now defunct Playland amusement park – and the post-modern musical of *Everyone Says I Love You*. The 43 songs included make it as much a film to listen to as to watch, like putting on an album of expertly chosen gems redolent of a particular place and era. As a Woody Allen mix album, it's hard to beat.

The individual vignettes are rather glorious too, from the "urban legend" beginning of the two burglars who win the "Guess That Tune" competition by answering their victims' phone mid break-in, to the connecting stories of Sally the cigarette girl, delightfully played by Mia Farrow. (Later, at the New Year's Eve finale, Diane Keaton will sing Cole Porter's 'You'd Be So Nice to Come Home to', making this the only film in which Woody's two most famous ex-partners appear together.)

The stories of Farrow's Sally – partly based on gossip queen Hedda Hopper – subtly chart the march of time as she works her way up and changes her diction ("Hark, I hear the cannons roar") to make her ambitions come true. Of course, it is all done with the lightest of touches, but in some ways her journey from working-class neighbourhood to Manhattan rooftop is the very dream Woody

Right Familiar faces: Woody regular Tony Roberts quizzes Dianne Wiest at Radio City Music Hall in *Radio Days*.

"Forgive me if I tend to
romanticize the past."
Woody Allen as *Joe*

himself had while listening to the radio and escaping into the picture houses of his youth. Perhaps the radio success of Farrow's Sally is recompense for the dashed hopes of her movie-dreamer Cecila in *The Purple Rose of Cairo*.

Meanwhile, the episode in which helium-voiced Sally is captured by Danny Aiello's gangster ("I don't meet nobody from the old neighbourhood in years. I finally do, and I gotta kill her") prefigures Olive and Cheech in *Bullets Over Broadway*.

Other characters are mere sketches, recalling the "early, funny" films but perhaps more in tone with Woody's *New Yorker* stories. There is the legend of the one-armed, one-legged blind baseball pitcher Kirby Kyle (inspired, perhaps, by the story of Monty Stratton, played by Jimmy Stewart in a biopic in 1949). And there's the fond memory, brilliantly woven in and out of the film, of spying on a voluptuous woman who later turns up as the kid's stand-in teacher Miss Gordon. It may not mean much in the scheme of things – except, as Woody observes, "I can tell you that it's a wonderful feeling having a school teacher you've seen dance naked in front of a mirror."

Woody also imbues these memories with great pathos. In one episode, Woody's child character (played by Seth Green and called Joe in the credits, but never actually called that on screen) is carrying back a wireless from the repair shop. He hails a cab, only to discover his father driving. It's beautifully done, a gorgeous example of when a pay-off gag can deepen the wistful tone: "He seemed ashamed that he drove a cab ... but I didn't mind what my father did, I loved him anyway. Besides, I gave him the biggest tip he got all day."

Left Bearing bad news: Seth Green as young Woody avatar Joe gets a consoling hug from Dad (Michael Tucker) while Mom (Julie Kavner) looks on.

Overleaf Woody Allen talks to Italian cinematographer Carlo Di Palma and other film crew members during the shooting of *Radio Days*, New York City.

The film's bravura sequence comes near the end, when Aunt Bea (the fabulous Dianne Wiest) turns on the radio to hear a conga and begins leading the family in a conga line around the house. At the same time, little Joe is being chased around the room by his father with a belt for ruining his mother's coat with dye from a chemistry set bought for him by Aunt Bea on a trip to Manhattan.

In this little miniature, the themes and storylines of the family unit all come together while the conga itself is interrupted by a newsflash, a story which, on a much larger scale, brings all of America together. The nation listens to the story of a girl trapped down a well (based on the true events of Kathy Fiscus) and everyone holds each other tighter. It stands out for me as one of the finest achievements of writing and film making in Woody Allen's entire career.

Perhaps there is a touch of philosophy after all. "I'll never forget the chills that ran through me every time I heard his sign off," recalls the narrator of his radio hero the Masked Avenger. And we hear Wallace Shawn utter: "Beware evil-doers, wherever you are." This warning is also the final line of the film, imbuing the words with a lasting, incantatory power that reminds me of the line haunting Judah Rosenthal in *Crimes and Misdemeanors*, a phrase his religious father would instil in the young Judah: "The eyes of God are on us always."

It's as if, faced by a Godless universe, the young Woody used the stories of radio (and, by extension, films) as his religion, his escape, his morality and his faith. The rabbi at the Hebrew School in *Radio Days* warns the young kid, caught stealing from the Israel charity boxes, that nothing good will come of listening to the radio. But the boy quickly realizes he's safer with the Masked Avenger than he is with God. This film gently suggests that there is no God save that of the author who, if he can't control anything in life, can shape his characters' destinies, or at least choose to remember them how he wishes.

Radio Days is a film to cherish and revisit, a trove of stories and songs to hum along to, the sort of thing that gives nostalgia a very good name. Woody may fear he has never made a truly great film, but I believe that in *Radio Days* he has fused memoir and myth to create one of the very greatest films about childhood.

September (1987)

In a straight, theatrical drama, family secrets, friendships and fidelity
are all tested to breaking point during a storm at the end of a hot
summer in a Vermont country house.

Aware that his loyal audience might be wary of this latest homage to his hero Ingmar Bergman, Woody Allen told the *New York Times* magazine in 1987: "Tragedy is a form to which I would ultimately like to aspire. I tend to prefer it to comedy. Comedy is easier for me. There's not the same level of pain in its creation, or the confrontation with issues, or with oneself, or the working through of ideas."

The last time he tried it, with *Interiors*, he'd just won Best Picture at the Academy Awards for *Annie Hall*, and he was given carte blanche by his bankrollers at United Artists. Few can doubt that Woody had earned the right to try again, coming off the back of a breathtaking run of five consecutive outstanding films.

However, it wasn't only himself he "stretched" when trying to get it right for *September*. The film is perhaps most notorious for its off-screen story: how Woody cast it and shot it, only to then recast and reshoot the entire thing from scratch. He did reuse one element, the set built by Santo Loquasto at Kauffman Astoria studios in Queens and loosely based on Mia Farrow's own country house in Frog Hollow, Connecticut.

The original cast included Charles Durning as the kindly neighbour and Maureen O'Sullivan playing Mia Farrow's blowsy 1950s starlet mother (as she was, of course, in real life, and a role she had just played in *Hannah and Her Sisters*). Christopher Walken had initially played the writer Peter, but he was soon replaced by actor and playwright Sam Shepard – who, it is rumoured, argued with Allen about certain improvisations in which he kept mentioning "Montana".

For the second filming, Woody drafted in Sam Waterston as the writer, Denholm Elliott as the lovelorn neighbour, Elaine Stritch as the mother and Jack Warden as her new husband and a most unlikely physicist.

Who knows if this worked better or worse? Woody destroyed all evidence of the first print and, according to Mia Farrow's autobiography, he would actually have liked to have filmed it for a third time.

All this off-screen drama does is to show Woody struggling to attain the perfection he perceives in Bergman, even though the story itself is closer in spirit to Chekhov, with characters pining for New York instead of Moscow. The travails of *September* also betray his technique of filming, one that is so close to his writing – what the French critics might term "le caméra stylo", whereby his actual shooting is like scribbling down and rubbing out. His later films, in fact, would be criticized for not having a bit more polish and drafting – Woody the filmmaker would not always be quite so indulged.

But let's concentrate on what we do have, the film of *September* itself: it's nowhere near as disastrous as its reputation suggests, although it does remain his lowest-ever grossing film at the box office. What I like is that, even if he's not in it and it's not funny, it's decidedly still a Woody Allen film, gently buoyed by the sounds coming from the record player – Art Tatum and Ben Webster's legendary 1956 collaboration.

The camerawork within the set is superb, too. Carlo Di Palma's gentle zooms and glides make the audience feel they are part of a chilly, late-summer breeze wafting in and out of rooms.

And then there are the performances. Dianne Wiest, Mia Farrow, Elaine Stritch are all magnificent and there are moments when you forget what they're saying – and just watch their faces and hear their voices, like jazz improvisations. It's no wonder so many actors want to work with Woody Allen, because they really get to show their stuff.

Above Mia Farrow and Sam Waterston in Woody Allen's drama *September*, set in a country house during a late-summer storm.

"Tragedy is a form to which I would ultimately like to aspire."
Woody Allen

You might not like these self-pitying, selfish, overthinking characters, but you have to admire the way they're played.

I like *September* very much. Even the title is evocative and, of course, it connects neatly with Woody's previous film, *Radio Days*, which is bookended by a mournful version of Kurt Weill's 'September Song', in whose lyrics the "days dwindle down, to a precious few".

Amid the storm, the blackout and the alcohol of *September*, you really get a sense of passions and hopes, of long-harboured resentments and sadness; of time passing and people never attaining the clarity of expression they so keenly desire; of a mood that is – as Jack Warden's physicist says about the expanding universe – "evocative of a deep truth that somehow just keeps slipping away".

Another Woman (1988)

Marion Post, a philosophy professor just turning 50, rents an apartment to write her next book but is fatally distracted by the conversations she overhears through the air vent from the psychoanalyst's office next door.

Although this was only Woody Allen's third "serious" film, it made clear that he had already established a style and voice in this register as unique and distinctive as his comedies.

Having worked with Max von Sydow in *Hannah and Her Sisters*, Woody took his worship of Ingmar Bergman to new heights by finally securing the Swede's cinematographer Sven Nykvist to shoot this "intimist" drama that takes place as much in the head of its protagonist as it does in the rooms and streets of Manhattan.

Woody's serious dramas also share a colour palette of beiges, earth tones and tans. Perhaps the intention is for the images to fade into the sepia of memory, to look as if they are artefacts from the past given how much the characters' pasts inform their actions in these dramas. Indeed, it is one of the subtlest skills in all his filmmaking, the way characters shift into their own pasts with no need for any corny visual dissolve or eerie music. Whether it be comically in *Annie Hall* or *Midnight in Paris*, or more tragically with Judah Rosenthal in *Crimes and Misdemeanors* or Cate Blanchett's Jasmine in *Blue Jasmine*, Allen simply lets us slide into a different mode and I can't think of one instance where it ever becomes confusing for the viewer.

Certainly, Gena Rowlands's Marion finds herself reassessing her own life in response to what she overhears from next door. (Woody will reuse this device to comic effect in *Everyone Says I Love You*.) The anguish of a pregnant woman called Hope (played by Mia Farrow) piques her most, sparking memories of her first husband and of her own childhood under a stentorian father and distant mother. In this regard, Marion is not far from the characters in *Interiors*, imprisoned by her own intellect and the mores of the cultural elite to which she belongs.

This is a deadly serious and heartbreaking film that brazenly quotes poetry. Where *Hannah and Her Sisters* had quoted from e e cummings, this film quotes Rilke's "Archaic Torso of Apollo": "For here there is no place that does not see you. You must change your life." It is a film that demands rigour from its audience as it plays with layers of time, interior monologue and imagination – at one stage, Marion reads to herself an extract from an admirer's novel while the images underneath show her and Gene Hackman acting out the romantic fantasy in Central Park.

Marion's is a confused mind, overflowing with regrets, and this all comes together in a magnificently directed dream sequence that merely has a certain theatricality to signal that it's a fantasy. It is full of tears and agony, not least in the character of Marion's father (John Houseman) who lists his regrets – "Despite achieving a certain eminence in my field, I asked too little of myself." This shattering monologue was to be Houseman's final performance before his death. (Curiously the same was true of other actors in Woody's work at this time: Lloyd Nolan in *Hannah and Her Sisters* and Keye Luke in *Alice*.)

Unpopular with audiences and critics in America, it was highly regarded in Europe, particularly in France, where it continues to enjoy masterpiece status. It's a brilliantly poised and controlled work, an unrelentingly sad picture about our ability to lie to ourselves and to others and in the uncontrollable ways we cause pain.

Woody Allen himself may not be present, but he is definitely there in the detail, in the hurt, and absolutely in the character of Marion. The part was intended for Mia Farrow until her pregnancy made it impossible, and the magnificent Rowlands, who is so synonymous with the grittier work of another New York independent filmmaker John Cassavetes, gives perhaps the finest lead performance in any Allen film – at least until Cate Blanchett's Jasmine comes along to match it over 30 years later.

Right Woody Allen holds adopted daughter Dylan while shooting a street scene for *Another Woman*, New York, 1988.

Below Gena Rowlands's Marion (right) with her stepdaughter Laura, played by Martha Plimpton.

New York Stories: "Oedipus Wrecks" (1989)

In the final episode of this triptych, successful lawyer Sheldon finds himself – and
the whole of New York City – still hounded by his overbearing Jewish mother.

Although it's one of his shortest pieces, "Oedipus Wrecks" is one of
the funniest and most revealing comedies Woody Allen ever made.

Directing the final part of a three-story anthology, Woody was
sharing the billing with Martin Scorsese – whose "Life Lessons" was
about a turbulent artist and his assistant in a Soho loft – and Francis
Ford Coppola – whose "Life Without Zoë" concerned a little girl
who lives in a luxury hotel.

Scorsese's piece was the most intense, Coppola's the most insipid.
Woody found himself being the comic turn, striking very welcome
notes of Jewish angst in a city he'd made famous for it and taking the
joke to its absurdist visual extreme: the image of a giant Jewish mother
dominating the Manhattan skyline.

"I'm nearly 50 years old, I'm a successful lawyer, but I still haven't
resolved my issues with my mother," whines Sheldon to his analyst,
plunging us right into the narrative crux at the start. This story (a
prime example of how to tell a good short story, by the way) would
have fitted well in Woody's own anthology film, *Everything You
Always Wanted to Know About Sex*. At the time, however, he'd just
come off the back of two very serious films, so it was cheering to
know that his jokes – and his Jewishness – were still in full flow when
he wanted them to be.

Indeed, the film can be seen as a tussle between Woody's Jewish
background and his desire to mix in with the New York elite. Sheldon
Mills (he changed it from Millstein) takes his fiancée Lisa to have
dinner with his mother. She, although happy to show Lisa (Mia
Farrow) embarrassing photos of Sheldon as a baby, is not impressed
with this "shiksa", this non-Jewish woman.

Embarrassing Sheldon further, she then appears with one of her
friends at his office. Woody tells a wonderful anecdote about this to

Stig Bjorkman: by a coincidence of casting, the friend is played by a
woman who used to be Woody's biology teacher at high school, Jesse
Keosian. Allen says on set he could never address her as anything but
"Mrs Keosian", just as he had at school.

The mother is played by Mae Questel, who used to be the voice
of the cartoon Betty Boop and who sang the spoof song 'Do the
Chameleon' in *Zelig*, a job for which Woody never met actually met her.

One day, Sheldon takes his mother and Lisa and her kids (one of whom
is played by a very young Kirsten Dunst) to a magic show. To his delight,
his mother is called upon as a volunteer. The look on Sheldon's face as the
magician's swords are thrust into the magic box is pricelessly comic.

Panic follows, however, when Mrs Millstein does not reappear.
In a brief scene backstage, you can see producer Larry David (later
to play the lead for Woody in *Whatever Works*) offering free tickets
to any show as compensation for "the loss of your mother".

Although upset, Sheldon suddenly finds that, free of his mother at
last, he is emboldened and happy and can make love to Lisa like never
before. Except soon enough, his mother reappears, floating in the sky
and berating and embarrassing Sheldon for all of New York to see.
She's even got the baby photos with her.

Lisa cannot take the public humiliation of hearing Sheldon
shouldn't marry her, hounded by the overwhelming Jewishness of
this matriarchal kibitzing from on high. "She's out there calling me
all these names," she complains. "What is a 'koorvah' anyway?"

Sheldon explains it's Yiddish for "whore" and they break up. God
only knows how Farrow must have felt, off-screen, about being used
as the butt of such Jewish "humour".

Getting no help from his analyst, Sheldon resorts to the folk
psychology of the shtetl and seeks the advice of a Jewish mystic

Above Eat your shiksa – Woody Allen, Mae Questel and Mia Farrow break bread in "Oedipus Wrecks".

called Treva. Played with comic relish by Julie Kavner, Treva is warm and blunt. When Sheldon tells her he is a sceptic, she replies with one of the greatest, New York-iest one-liners in all Woody Allen's work: "Yeah, meanwhile, your mother is hovering over the Chrysler Building."

Treva is a woman to his mother's taste – she even cooks terrible chicken that looks like it's been "put through the deflavourizing machine" (to use an old Woody joke about his own mother's culinary skills). Sheldon somehow falls in love with Treva, which finally brings his mother and those baby photos down out of the sky.

Short as it may be at just 37 minutes, "Oedipus Wrecks" certainly hits the funny notes. Any Jewish boy will recognize this blown-up Freudian nightmare with a mix of laughter and cringe. They'll probably call their mother right after seeing it.

The Yiddish folk tale writer Isaac Bashevis Singer couldn't have done a better job. But in Woody's own canon, the film takes on key significance when we finally do meet his real mother Nettie in the 1997 documentary *Wild Man Blues*. In her 90s but vital as anything, she tells us all about Woody as a little boy taking tap dancing classes and she wishes, right in front of Soon-Yi, that he'd "marry a nice Jewish girl".

So maybe the moral of this *New York Story* is: you couldn't make it up, not if you don't have to.

"If you want a happy ending, you
should see a Hollywood movie."
Martin Landau as *Judah Rosenthal*

Crimes and Misdemeanors (1989)

A wealthy ophthalmologist is wracked with guilt over a heinous crime; an impoverished but principled documentary maker ruins his marriage and career. The parallel storylines – one tragic, one comic – converge at a wedding.

Woody Allen had a flourishing film career, and balancing comedy and tragedy had become his preoccupation. He'd started out making either funny films or serious dramas, but fusing the two masks had, he always felt, eluded him: he believed that his hit *Hannah and Her Sisters* had erred too far towards comedy and happiness at the end.

Crimes and Misdemeanors would change all that. It is perhaps the most skilful and soulful picture of his career, an unquestionable masterpiece of considerable philosophical gravity. A film with a cold-blooded murder is also a film about family, love and fidelity, infused with laughs and warmth.

After the commercial failure of *September* and *Another Woman*, Woody needed to get his audience back on side. That usually meant he had to appear in the picture, so this may be a rare instance of him responding to outside pressures. Financing was being provided by Touchstone Pictures, a division of Disney then run by Jeffrey Katzenberg. (Years later, after co-founding DreamWorks studio, Katzenberg would go to considerable lengths to re-establish Woody's commercial appeal, first in the animated hit *Antz* and then with a three-picture deal for comedies in which Woody also had to star.)

The film was written in unusual circumstances: on vacation, while touring Europe in the summer of 1988 with his family.

Handwritten drafts for the screenplay appear on headed paper from some of Europe's grandest hotels – the Villa d'Este on Lake Como, the Gritti Palace in Venice, Claridge's in London. He would work on these in the morning in his room, and then fold them into his coat pocket as he went sightseeing in the afternoon. "By the time he reached London," notes Eric Lax in *Conversations with Woody Allen*, "the pocket bulged as if he had a loaf of bread in it."

At that stage, the script was titled Brothers, perhaps in response to *Hannah and Her Sisters*, and told a story of another extended family's connections, but this time through the male line. The eventual title took some time to reach, with permutations including *The Eyes of God*, *Dark Vision*, *Crimes and Vanity* and *Choices in the Dark*.

Even when he finally shot the film, Woody made several large changes on the reshoots, including a whole section featuring Mia Farrow's character. She runs a nursing home for ageing vaudevillians, about whom Woody's character Cliff is making a documentary. The character of Lester, played by Alan Alda, was in only one scene originally, but Woody was taken with Alda's work and extended his role.

(Lester himself is said to be loosely based on Larry Gelbart, the TV and film producer with whom Woody worked as a writer in the late 1950s and with whom Alda had worked on the long-running hit series M*A*S*H. Woody and Alda would work together again on *Manhattan Murder Mystery* and *Everyone Says I Love You*.)

Whatever the contortions of its creation, *Crimes and Misdemeanors* ended up a perfect cocktail, with each of the

Left "The eyes of God are on us always" – Woody directs Martin Landau on the set of *Crimes and Misdemeanors*.

elements in just the right measure. It is one of the greatest films of the 1980s, up there on a list that would probably include at least another two Woody Allen films. And although Woody rarely reflects outside influences in his work, there is a certain *fin de siècle* air about *Crimes and Misdemeanors*, coming as it does right at the end of a most extraordinary decade in this filmmaker's output.

Woody would try to make comedy and tragedy co-exist again, most obviously in *Melinda and Melinda*, but seldom can a film have been made that contains enduring comic lines alongside existential aphorisms. Indeed, each genre amplifies the other, in a perfect symbiosis. When Woody delivers one of his great zingers, "The last time I was inside a woman was when I visited the Statue of Liberty", it has added import because he's deadly serious and we feel for his character as his marriage collapses.

Similarly, when Martin Landau's Judah flashes back to eavesdrop on an family seder, it's a comic technique Woody used before in *Annie Hall*, only this time it's replayed as a deeply inquiring conversation about the nature of sin and God. "The eyes of God are on us always," says Judah's religiously observant father.

In one scene, Lester says: "Comedy is tragedy plus time." We laugh as Cliff (played by Woody the actor) rolls his eyes at the glibness of his loathsome brother-in-law's statement, while Woody the writer and director makes that same sentiment one of his key themes.

Another recurring theme lies in Cliff's afternoon escapes to the cinema. He takes his niece Jenny and when we first meet them, they're coming out after seeing Hitchcock's *Mr. and Mrs.*

Left Dolores (Anjelica Houston) and Judah (Martin Landau) enjoy happier times.

Right "If it bends, it's funny": Alan Alda as Lester, a character said to be partly based on *M*A*S*H* producer and writer Larry Gelbart.

> "Comedy is tragedy plus time."
> Alan Alda as *Lester*

Smith. Woody marvels – just as his young movie-going self always did – at "how wonderful it must be to live like that, with the tuxedos and the evening gowns, whereas this (looking outside at the traffic and daylight) is … awful". Later in the picture, on an illicit break from filming his TV documentary about Lester, he'll take Mia Farrow's Halley to the cinema or they'll eat Indian food, drink champagne and watch a print of *Singin' in the Rain* in his edit suite.

This refrain of escaping into films is one his audience has seen recently in *The Purple Rose of Cairo* and in *Hannah and Her Sisters*, but here it also sets up the film's iconic finale. Judah and Cliff (Landau and Woody) sit at a piano stool at a wedding and debate moral justice in the universe. Judah has, by now, gotten away with murder and he's now squared his evil act with his own conscience – the only thing outside the law that could hold him to any moral code. Having thinly disguised his own story as an idea for a film script, he discusses it with Cliff. "Turning himself in? That's fiction, that's movies. You see too many movies. I'm talking about reality. If you want a happy ending, you should see a Hollywood movie."

Films, and going to the cinema, are an aspect of watching, an act that is this film's dominant metaphor. "What were God's eyes like?" wonders Judah. "Unimaginably penetrating, intense eyes, I assumed. And I wonder if it was just a coincidence that I made my specialty ophthalmology."

One of Judah's patients is Sam Waterston's Ben, a rabbi who is slowly going blind but whose insights are, of course, penetrative and clear. "Without moral structure, there's no basis to know how to live," says Ben. "Look," says Judah, reflecting within the dialogue exactly what the film's structure itself is doing, "we've gone from discussing a small infidelity to the meaning of existence."

There is so much that is of the highest quality in *Crimes and Misdemeanors*. Landau's performance is outstanding (he lost out at the Oscars to Denzel Washington in *Glory*), but so are those of Anjelica Houston as Dolores his mistress, Jerry Orbach as Judah's brother Jack, and Alda's Lester.

In this film, Woody reworks his favourite tricks and techniques, but you hardly notice the repetition. Like Tracy did to Isaac in *Manhattan*, Halley breaks Cliff's heart by going off to London for an unmissable work opportunity. The film will end, as *Annie Hall* did, with a wistful montage of its key scenes spooled over the musings of Professor Louis Levy (played by Martin Bergmann, a professor at New York University). And again, films are both an escape and a clue to the action, with clips from *This Gun for Hire*, *Happy Go Lucky* (1943) and even a long shot of a cinema showing *Buster*, about the Great Train Robber.

Just as Woody used to practise getting away with his magic as a kid, so *Crimes and Misdemeanors* betrays no sleight of hand and pulls off its ambitious intentions with seemingly effortless ease – it might just be the most impressive trick of his entire career.

Left Life imitates art on a bench in Central Park, New York, 1989: Cliff and Halley (Woody and Mia) take a break from shooting their documentary about Lester.

Woody Allen
Film by Film
The 1990s

Working throughout the furore
caused by the scandal of his imploding
private life, Woody Allen continued
to make films that are unpredictable
yet brilliant in their scope and styles,
taking in relationship breakdowns,
fame, musicals, period pastiche
and angry literary comedy – he even
featured in a documentary about a
European tour with his own jazz band.

Left Shadowy figure: the turmoil
of his private life haunted Woody
Allen's movies throughout the
1990s, including as Kleinman in
the expressionistic *Shadows of Fog*.

Alice (1990)

A wealthy Upper East Side housewife, who seemingly has everything, begins to feel uneasy about her life and marriage. She consults a mysterious Doctor Yang in Chinatown, and using his magic herbs she flirts with a love affair, spies on her husband and heads for a new start.

Alice's Christmas Day release in New York signals that it has magical, fairytale qualities. Woody Allen has said that he saw it as a fable but, curiouser and curiouser, insists that there were no intended comparisons to *Alice in Wonderland*. "I could have called her Leslie, and then I would have called the movie *Leslie*," he said.

In that case, I guess, Mia Farrow wearing an Alice band in her hair was simply an afterthought on the part of Jeffrey Kurland's costume department. But like Lewis Carroll's creation, this Alice does go into a wonderland of transitions using Dr Yang's potions and herbs. She can fly, she becomes invisible, she becomes sexually confident, she can commune with the spirit world.

The film is some kind of gift to Mia Farrow. In places, she delivers moments of her finest comic work, particularly as she seduces Joe Mantegna's saxophonist Joe with breathy talk of jazz – "Ooh the soprano, Joe, that'll extend your range." After she has shaken off the herbs' strange spell, she confesses her uncharacteristic flirtation to a friend: "I was talking about reeds and Coltrane. I mean, who's Coltrane?"

Later, Farrow is brilliantly subtle at suggesting increasing intoxication and pleasure when taking hits of an opium pipe at Dr Yang's. This is sweetly enjoyable comedy, big on charm in every sense. It's about a woman who lives high in a fabulous apartment, insulated from the real world, who wears a fur coat as the chauffeur drives her and her children to their private nursery school.

Woody says he based the character on the women he saw whenever he dropped his own kids off at school, and the film's charm is tempered by a slight edge of contempt. Does Woody feel for Alice, or does he secretly think her ridiculous?

When Alice tells her wealthy husband (William Hurt) that she wants to get a job, he witheringly suggests she could work in a clothes shop: "I mean, you do know sweaters." And, of course, he could never believe she might be unfaithful to him.

Alice is rarely laugh-worthy, relying instead on a quaint charm. The film becomes increasingly magical and has to get by on Allen's special effects, which always have a wilfully primitive quality, more like something from 1940s Hollywood than from contemporary blockbusters.

Indeed, for a film about someone wanting to change their life, Woody's enduringly old-fashioned qualities are to the fore here. Chinatown is a land of roasted ducks and louche, red doorways and the character of Dr Yang, as played by veteran Keye Luke in his last role (he died two weeks after the film's release) is straight out of Charlie Chan.

Yet he also features two very successful executive women, an ad boss played by Judy Davis and a TV channel editor played by Cybil Shepherd. Their smart sassiness throws Alice's cosy-jumpered self-pity into stark relief. Alice gets trampled and ignored. Even when she and Joe become invisible together on a lunch tryst, she lets him use this new power to ogle supermodel Elle McPherson in the changing rooms of Ralph Lauren. "Excuse me," complains Elle to the shop assistants, "but there's heavy breathing in there."

Woody and Mia's adopted daughter Dylan – whom Woody adored – features as one of Alice's kids in the film, and you do get a sense, through some of the locations, that new vistas on New York were opening up to the director, places such as the school hallway, the penguin house at the Zoo, the circus and a dinosaur exhibit.

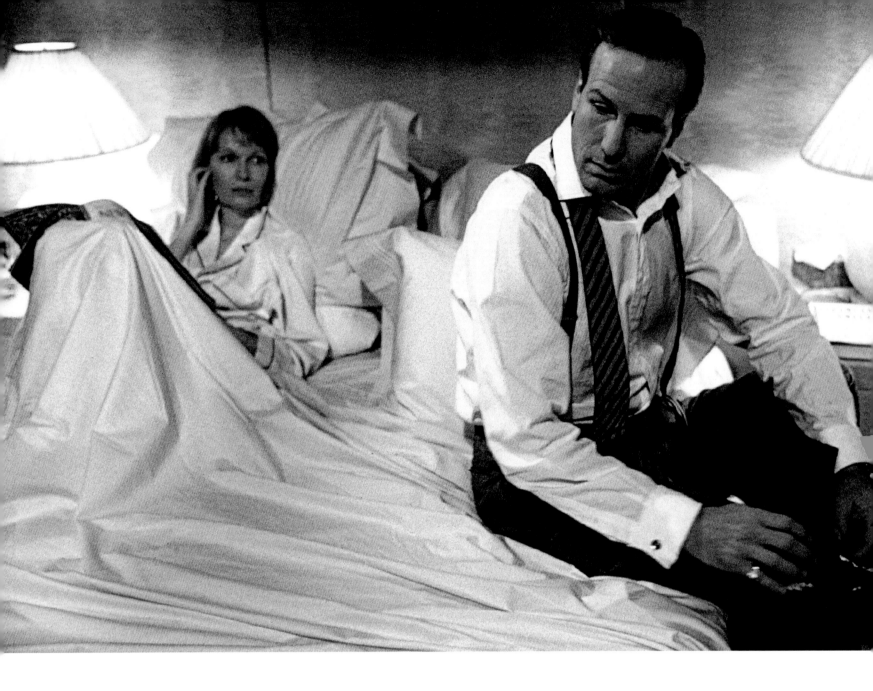

You can't really dislike *Alice* the film. It earned Woody yet another Best Screenplay Oscar nomination. Critics were generally disappointed, though. Roger Ebert rightly said: "It's in the tradition of his more whimsical films, like *A Midsummer Night's Sex Comedy*."

But you can feel torn over Alice the character, who has some infuriatingly passive qualities to go with her yearnings. Is her infatuation with Mother Theresa, for example, a veiled jibe at the saintly Mia herself? Or is it Woody's dig at the desperate need for charity and spirituality in the stratosphere of the Upper East Side rich set – where, of course, he himself lives?

Tinkling away on the soundtrack is Thelonious Monk's version of 'Darn That Dream', and Woody seems intent on dashing hopes here, just as he did to Mia's character at the end of *The Purple Rose of Cairo*. It requires all of Farrow's skills as an actress to smile her way to a kind of happiness.

Shadows and Fog (1992)

Shot in Expressionist black and white, *Shadows and Fog* is set in a 1920s village that might be in Europe. Woody, playing timid clerk Kleinman, is woken in the middle of the night to help catch a serial strangler. Finding himself suddenly accused of the crimes, he bumps into Irmy, a circus performer, who tries to help him.

His final film for Orion Pictures, *Shadows and Fog* was caught up in the company's spectacular financial collapse and became one of the least-promoted and least-seen works in Woody Allen's career. Not even the casting of Madonna, then one of the most famous women in the world, could prevent this becoming his most expensive flop. (It must be said, her appearance as a seductive trapeze artist is briefer than the chorus of any of her hits.)

Shot entirely at Woody's preferred Kaufman Astoria studios in Queens, the film was performed on a specially constructed set, at 2,400 square metres (26,000 square feet) the largest ever built in New York, and the remarkable work of production designer Santo Loquasto. The film is based on a short play, *Death*, which appeared in his collection of writings, *Without Feathers* (1976), and is obviously indebted to the work of Franz Kafka. It's a clear pastiche of *The Trial*.

But, with cinematographer Carlo Di Palma, Woody also created an ode to German Expressionist cinema of the 1920s and 1930s, the films of directors such as FW Murnau and Fritz Lang, whose *M* (starring Peter Lorre as an accused murderer) comes most often to mind. The music of Kurt Weill is used for the score, featuring some rare compositions but also the 'Alabama Song' and the familiar strains of 'Mack the Knife' from *The Threepenny Opera*, co-written with Bertolt Brecht.

With these heavy Germanic influences and Allen's familiar stammering and neurotic hand-wringing act at its centre, this is perhaps his most metaphorical film, alluding to Jewish ghettos and the Holocaust. Kleinman finds himself, at various points, inscribed on a mysterious list, chased by a mob, "sniffed" by an accusatory clairvoyant and called "cringing, slimy vermin" by a workmate promoted over him.

The film's unpopularity perhaps stemmed from its mix of moods. Woody's Kleinman is neither particularly funny nor particularly well acted, and the occasional bit of verbal comedy combines uneasily with suspense, paranoia, looming tragedy and allegorical historical references. Yet, as ever, the text and ideas are fascinating and the images undeniably beautiful.

Mia Farrow is certainly at her most beautiful as Irmy, the sword swallower on the run from her unfaithful boyfriend at the circus (John Malkovich). Bizarrely, she ends up sheltering at a brothel – one of the few places, along with the church and the police station, to be open all night. It's run by Lily Tomlin, the whores include Jodie Foster and Kathy Bates ("Sword swallowing? That's my specialty too!") and John Cusack is a young client.

In a very curious episode, John Cusack offers Farrow's Irmy a vast $700 to sleep with her, an experience to which she eventually agrees and finds strangely empowering. Is this supposed to mirror the experience of Kleinman, who is also being lured into behaviour that might betray his true self?

Amid the sex, Kleinman is constantly harassed for his opinion on the existence of God ("That's the third time tonight somebody's asked me") while the local Doctor, brilliantly played by Donald Pleasence, is keen to capture the murderer so that he might "find out something definitive about the nature of evil".

Eventually, the film finishes up at the circus – another self-contained world of outsiders, freaks, artists and free spirits – with a climax involving the smashing of a mirror (see also *Manhattan Murder Mystery*, just two films later) and magic tricks, another familiar Woody subject. Yet Death gives them all the slip, like some kind of shtetl dybbuk.

It's interesting, too, that the circus illusionist is a Scandinavian, by whom Kleinman is hugely impressed, even considering becoming his apprentice. Perhaps this is a nod to the way Woody sees Bergman. "Everybody loves my illusions," says the magician. "They need them, like they need the air." Is he saying that we need films (and magic and sex) to relieve the awfulness of reality and the inevitable visit from Death?

Maybe. But what does the film as whole mean? It features God, sex and Death (the titles of the three short plays from *Without Feathers*) as well as mob mentality, hysteria and scapegoating. *Newsweek*'s Jack Kroll wrote, "*Shadows and Fog* is Woody Allen's first mystery movie. The mystery: what caused this total breakdown of a unique artist?"

Yet there is a guiding artistry at work in every frame of this career curio. Though the film's only 82 minutes long, there's time for a beautiful interlude reminiscent of the dawn bridge scene in *Manhattan*, in which Woody and Mia ponder the beauty of the black and white night and its "free feeling".

"A clearing in the fog and we can see all the way to the stars – what a perfect moment," she says, wistfully. Kleinman counters: "But it's so fleeting, soon the fog returns and the clouds move. There's so much motion in the world – it's no wonder I'm nauseous."

Florence Colambani called the film a "constrained stylistic exercise". Constrained by what, though? The critic Emanuel Levy wrote: "*Shadows and Fog*, a movie drained of any spark or verve, is not only a failure, it shows a director at a complete loss. The title of the movie turns out to be ironic – it is Allen himself, not the character he plays, who is in the fog."

Exactly who or what lurked in the shadows and fog of Woody's imagination while he was writing this film, we will perhaps never know – but seismic changes in both his working life and personal life were definitely skulking around one of those dark corners.

Right Death looms over Kleinman – a haunted Woody Allen in his Expressionist homage *Shadows and Fog*.

Husbands and Wives (1992)

New York intellectual couple Gabe and Judy Roth are shocked to learn their best friends, Jack and Sally, are splitting up. Their friends' separation begins to reveal deep cracks in their own seemingly solid marriage, with devastating emotional consequences.

Possibly the hardest-hitting Woody Allen film, it was also the toughest to watch on its original release because of the scandal that was then raging so publicly in the background.

"It's over and we both know it," says Mia Farrow's Judy to Woody Allen's Gabe at the film's emotional climax. We *all* knew it.

As well as marking the end of their 12-year relationship, the film was the last in a staggeringly productive and brilliant run of collaborations between Allen and Farrow, embracing 13 films, which began with *A Midsummer Night's Sex Comedy* in 1982.

Allen maintains that he came up with the story for *Husbands and Wives* two years previously, but the scandal that was to drive them apart forever emerged during the last days of the film's shoot. The couple famously lived separately (on opposite sides of Central Park but in view of each other's apartment) and it was when Farrow visited his apartment that she found, on the mantelpiece, erotic Polaroid photographs of her 18-year-old adopted daughter Soon-Yi Previn.

With only a few days of filming left, Mia had to be persuaded back to the set to complete her scenes. Producer Robert Greenhut describes what happened in Robert Weide's *Woody Allen: A Documentary* (2011):

> I remember him answering the phone just before we were about to shoot a sequence, and I could tell something disturbing was happening on the other end. Mia had found out he was having an affair with one of her daughters. Well, it took me three days to convince Mia to come back to work because she felt she simply couldn't bear to see this person any more. But, like a trooper, she came back and finished her job.

Husbands and Wives must, then, stand as a prime example in the difficulties of separating life from art. Woody Allen always maintains that an artist's private life does not influence his work – but how can it not? At the very least, it certainly influences the audience's perception of the work.

Released at the height of the scandal – which dominated front pages for weeks, including a custody battle in which Woody was accused of sexually molesting his and Farrow's daughter Dylan – *Husbands and Wives* is a scathing, sceptical take on love and lasting relationships.

Clearly taking inspiration from Bergman's *Scenes from a Marriage*, Woody's film has a vague documentary structure in which an unseen interviewer (voiced by Woody's costume designer Jeffrey Kurland) questions the characters about their behaviour and emotions a year after the events.

This structure is not adhered to strictly and could be viewed as a lazily employed device. It's technically impossible, and yet this documentary camera's all-seeing eye adds to the maelstrom captured by Carlo Di Palma's skittering handheld photography. The pain in some of the scenes is so severe and intense, you can hardly believe you're watching a Woody Allen film.

Judy's reaction to the news of Jack and Sally's divorce fills the film right from the opening scene. Her nervous frailty recalls Mia

Right A newer model: Gabe (Woody Allen) shakes his head as his friend Jack (Sydney Pollack) runs off with fitness freak Sam (Lysette Anthony) in *Husbands and Wives*.

Right Juliette Lewis plays Rain, a precocious literature student flirting with her tutor, Woody Allen's Gabe.

Farrow trapped in the New York apartment of *Rosemary's Baby*, the actress's breakthrough movie from 20 years previously. If her performance is so delicately knife-edge, though, Judy Davis's performance as Sally is frightening, raw and bleeding – brilliantly so of course. The Australian actress is practically demonic in some of her delivery, particularly in one scene when she arrives at a colleague's house for a date and makes several screaming phone calls to her ex-husband. "What opera are we going to see?" she asks the poor date. "*Don Giovanni*, yes? A Don Juan story? I hate Don Juans. Someone should just cut their fucking dicks off."

Such dialogue was unusually spiky for Woody Allen. As Judy and Gabe Roth (surely a nod to the author Philip Roth), Mia and he have a most unromantic discussion about using a diaphragm before sex. There are references to the "festering wounds of marriage, years of resentment and anger". What happened to, you know, just calling a dead shark a dead shark?

But no, *Husbands and Wives* tears off the flesh and cuts to the carcass bones. Sally's fury at her date's house may be agonizing, but it could also be seen as very blackly comic (well, maybe not for the date guy). Even that cannot be said, though, for the scene when the wonderful Sydney Pollack as Jack has to wrestle his new girlfriend (Lysette Anthony) away from a party because he feels she's embarrassing; that scene is just screamingly horrid.

Woody Allen's Gabe, a novelist and lecturer who then courts his young writing student, is also hard to take. Originally, this part of the preternaturally confident Rain ("my parents named me after Rilke") was played by the English actress Emily Lloyd, star of *Wish You Were Here*. However, Woody replaced her with Juliette Lewis after just a few days. The flirtation and flattery in this relationship is not easy to watch, especially to those viewers uneasy since *Manhattan* about Allen's on-screen penchant for younger women. And there is

Left "It's over and we both know it": the mother of all break-up scenes, Woody and Mia in *Husbands and Wives*, 1992.

> "Art doesn't imitate life,
>   it imitates bad television."
>
>   Juliette Lewis as *Rain*

a most unattractive screen kiss at Rain's 21st birthday party, amid a thunderstorm and a blackout.

And yet, as always with Woody Allen, the richness, skill and intelligence of the work withstands such objections. Indeed, it must be significant that his very next film, *Manhattan Murder Mystery*, has a climax involving the shattering of so many distorting mirrors.

For all its pain and brutal honesty, *Husbands and Wives* contains so much of what typifies Allen's films and what we want to find in them. Just as ownership and belonging might be issues within marriage, these New York apartments are key locations, all cramped and oppressing, the walls closing in as the camera moves along them, sometimes blocked by them, losing characters as they stomp from little room to galley kitchen.

These spaces are also characters, dressed with telling details that reflect their inhabitants' souls. Gabe and Judy's place is lined with books and artefacts. Sally's house is sparse and grey. Rain's parents have a palatial pad with stuffy wallpaper, but overlooking the river. "Welcome to my rent-stabilized den," is the opening line from Sally's soon-to-be beleaguered date.

Everyone drinks white wine – which, I've noticed in Allen's films since *Annie Hall*, they seem to take at room temperature. Conversation is about opera, or analysis, or poetry or Bauhaus furniture. These people are unlikeably opinionated, snobbish and arrogant; when Jack's new girlfriend says they might watch the Grammys on television, he calls it dumb. Later, he confesses to enjoying watching a video with her, "some stupid dopey little thing, the kind of thing Sally would never let me bring in the house – but I laughed like hell. I had a terrific time, and I didn't have to feel guilty about it."

But he does. Allen's characters here are wracked by the guilt of their choices, prisoners of their past decisions as much as they are of their apartments. "So what if she's not Simone de Beauvoir?" Jack feels he has to say to the doubtful (and maybe jealous) Gabe. It's part protest, part confession, all self-justification. Adds Jack: "You're not my rabbi."

Even when the storm subsides, the wreckage is not pretty. Jack and Sally are back together being interviewed on the couch, describing how they recovered their marriage because, well, "it's a buffer against loneliness". What a contrast to those sweet interviews with real-life couples in Rob Reiner's *When Harry Met Sally* (1989), the hit rom-com that paid homage to Woody. And how fascinating that the film's writer, Nora Ephron, appears very briefly as a dinner party guest here.

And then there's Woody himself, of course. His performance as an actor in this film is very strong, one of his best acting performances, although the character is never sympathetic. It's as if he's completely abandoned his early career mission to find a likeable persona for his absurdist thoughts.

His character is mean and self-obsessed. He reacts to the news that Judy has been writing poems by calling it "fooling around with poetry". As she says, "I don't want an objective valuation, I want you to be supportive." Gabe's really a pompous ass.

Later, after declaring how easy it is to seduce students, he writes a novel he's not particularly proud of but which he gives to Rain to read, pathetically seeking her approval. She says it's brilliant, but is "disappointed with its attitudes toward women and relationships". Offended by the criticism, he calls her a "twit" and even swears when she leaves the manuscript in the back of a taxicab, necessitating a bit of a goose chase out to the cab driver's home.

We actually see some of Gabe's novel dramatized while Rain reads it out to herself. This novel within the film is a story comparing two unhappy men (Pepkin and Napp, two names very much from the Woody Allen storybook) and it features the bitterly funny line: "The only time they experienced simultaneous orgasm was when the judge handed them their divorce papers."

But there's also a line in one of Rain's short stories, which Gabe fawningly says he likes – "that bit that says: Art doesn't imitate life, it imitates bad television". Well, sometimes, it's hard to separate them, especially when life is imitating a lurid soap opera too.

Husbands and Wives is a major work of art. But it's also a landmark moment in the life and career of Woody Allen, whose work was never viewed the same way afterwards, half of New York being convinced that he was a pervert and possible paedophile.

For fans, though, what counts is the work, so there's a sadness that this should mark the end of a beautiful cinematic relationship,

one of the finest ever between an artist and his muse. Woody and Mia, director and performer, created a run of magnificent works and characters together: *Zelig*, *The Purple Rose of Cairo*, *Broadway Danny Rose*, *Hannah and Her Sisters*, *Radio Days*, *Crimes and Misdemeanors*, *Alice* and, yes, *Husbands and Wives*. It doesn't get much better than that.

But as Mia's Judy says in this film so sadly to Woody's Gabe when they both realize they have to break up: "All those stories, they're just memories from years gone by, they're isolated moments – they don't tell the whole story."

No, they don't.

Above Woody goes hand-held: the director discusses a shot with cinematographer Carlo Di Palma on *Husbands and Wives*, for which they adopted a new "herky-jerky" style.

Manhattan Murder Mystery (1993)

A light relationship comedy entwines with a murder mystery to create a heady confection of New York, one-liners and intrigue. The director has always maintained that this is one of his most successful pictures.

If you're looking for a sequel to *Annie Hall*, all you have to do is look at *Manhattan Murder Mystery*. Not only does the film reunite Woody Allen with Diane Keaton and writer Marshall Brickman, but it started out life as a subplot in the 1977 original.

In that film, Alvy and Annie were to have been side-tracked by a murder in their apartment building, but this was judged to be one tangent too many and the scene ended up on the scriptwriters' floor. Although Woody told Marshall Brickman he could keep the episode and do what he wanted with it, the story seems to have been locked away in a drawer.

Years later, looking for a lighter story after the intense drama of *Husbands and Wives*, Woody asked Brickman to disinter what he called, merely as a reference title, their old "Manhattan murder mystery" story. With typical Allen alacrity and productivity, work on the new script had already begun before the shooting of *Husbands and Wives*.

It was assumed at the time that Mia Farrow would play the part of Carol Lipton, the wife of Larry, the publisher played by Woody.

Above left We are detectives: Diane Keaton, Ron Rifkin, Woody Allen, Anjelica Houston and Joy Behar plot their trap.

Left Anjelica Houston teaches Woody how to play cards in a scene from *Manhattan Murder Mystery*.

However, Woody and Mia's relationship broke down irretrievably just near the end of the *Husbands and Wives* shoot, and many people expected him to abandon the project. Woody, though, preferred to bury himself in work as a distraction from the media circus of the court case and the bitter custody battle between him and Mia Farrow, and he simply called Diane Keaton to step in, reuniting one of the great comic couples on screen for the first time in over 12 years. Later, Woody spoke to author Eric Lax about this change:

> I didn't have time to rewrite any of it because a thriller like that is very tightly plotted, so you can't alter one thing without it affecting something else further down the line. While Mia had a delightful comic sense, I was always a stronger comic than her. But with Keaton, she was a great comedienne and I would always end up playing the straight guy. I could labour all year and give myself a thousand funny lines, but when the camera hits Keaton, that's what you want to see. She always makes it funnier than I wrote it. Next to Judy Holliday, she is one of the greatest screen comediennes we've had.

Later, he would add the unbeatable remark: "She's such a great maniac."

Critics took the opportunity to see the Liptons as Annie and Alvy grown old together, with the character of Ted (played here by Alan Alda) being best friend Tony Roberts now returned to Manhattan, his career in Los Angeles having dried up. It seems a natural enough interpretation now, but at the time many people preferred not to, finding it hard to forgive Allen for what they were hearing in the press during the lurid trial coverage. The director may have been able to compartmentalize his work from his private life (he was even writing *Bullets Over Broadway* while filming *Manhattan Murder Mystery* and appearing in court); the public was less capable. He was even booed by passers-by while filming one scene on location in Bryant Park.

Viewed from a distance, the film is a gem of light touch comedy blended with a decent little crime mystery, the sort of pulpy fiction you get in TV detective stories or the "airplane reading" of the novel Woody's Larry lends his client, the charismatic author Marsha, played by Anjelica Houston.

But while the tone is playful, the plotting is clever in testing out the constraints and the wear and tear of marriage. The Liptons bicker over ice hockey and the opera ("I can't listen to that much Wagner, I get the urge to invade Poland"), while Paul House, played by Jerry Adler, has clearly had enough of his long relationship with Helen House (Lynn Cohen). Investigating the murder down the corridor provides the Liptons with just the impetus they need to reinvigorate their own marriage. Carol has her fidelity tested by Ted's flirting and mischief, while Larry rises to its challenge and mans up for what is – by Woody's standards – a tense climax.

What viewers will now remember and cherish, though, is the return to the comic playing, location photography and jazz, such as the memorable opening helicopter shot over Manhattan (the first I can recall in Allen's work, although a cliché in so many rom-coms), which is set to a live recording of Bobby Short singing Cole Porter's 'I Happen to Like New York'. There's also a car chase set to Benny Goodman's 'Sing Sing Sing', and the tinkling of Erroll Garner and the deep horn of Colman Hawkins. With Allen and Keaton on fine comedic sparring form, it's sort of what you want from a Woody Allen movie.

The excitement is such that, as the mystery thickens and he realizes his wife's hunch may be right, Larry is forced to remark: "This is the Apple, honey, this is why we don't live in Deluth. Plus, I've no idea where Deluth is."

Having taken inspiration from the husband and wife detective movies of *The Thin Man* series which hooked him in his youth, and referenced classic thrillers with a visit to watch *Double Indemnity*,

Woody borrows his climax completely from Orson Welles's *The Lady from Shanghai*, paying brilliant homage to the hall of mirrors shootout. Just as his characters in *The Purple Rose of Cairo* stepped in and out of the screen, here they step behind an actual movie screen in a dilapidated cinema during a screening of the Welles movie.

It's a virtuoso sequence, shot by cameraman Carlo Di Palma, and one of the most cinematically stylish in all Allen's work. "Never again will I say that life doesn't imitate art," breathes Larry as he unties his kidnapped wife, a salutary moment for the man who always believes fantasy and reality are far removed. "I'll call the police," she says. And, with wonderfully deadpan practicality, he adds: "Yes, and also a glazier."

Woody has called this "a trivial picture, but fun, like a dessert, not a real meal, but a very pleasurable experience", and it's worth noting that it features one of his happiest endings. The Liptons return to their apartment building wiser and fresher and, most importantly, together. And you feel they're going to stay that way – or, at least, that they're not going to murder each other in the near future.

Right "I'm a world-renowned claustrophobic": Woody Allen and Diane Keaton rekindle their comic spark in the lift scene from *Manhattan Murder Mystery*.

Bullets Over Broadway (1994)

In this affectionate 1920s backstage farce, an earnest young playwright discovers he will never be a true artist when a gangster becomes the real author of his hit play – even killing one of the cast to make it work.

Bullets Over Broadway remains Woody Allen's most Oscar-nominated film. That may owe something to this being his first to be distributed by awards guru Harvey Weinstein at Miramax. Or maybe, more simply, it's some of his best-crafted work.

Amazingly, *Bullets* was written during the most turbulent year of Woody's personal life: the bitter court case with former partner and muse Mia Farrow was raging in the background, his name continually splashed across the front pages and in the news bulletins.

The stress must have taken some toll because, unusually, Woody looked for help in writing his next project. "Sometimes, you get lonely in the room," he remarked. He teamed up with Douglas McGrath (husband of Woody's former assistant Jane Martin and a confirmed friend just as half of New York seemed to be siding with Mia), and the two batted around several ideas.

Last on Woody's list of vague outlines was the story where the "gangster turns out to be the playwright". McGrath convinced Woody that this was the right vehicle. The pair would meet at Woody's house, talk around some scenes, take a walk, grab dinner and talk some more. In Robert Weide's lengthy documentary, McGrath recalls that Woody would break off from working and discussing a scene to take hushed calls from lawyers and detectives about the court case in another room.

"I'd hear snippets of somewhat lurid, whispered conversation that were quite bizarre, like 'Can we get a sample?'," says McGrath. "Then he'd come back in and say, 'OK, back to work on our little comic bauble.'"

Bullets may be a bauble but, my, how it glitters.

It is not, perhaps, a great film on its own terms, but it is a brilliant pastiche that adds up to first-class entertainment of the old-fashioned kind. It allows Woody to wallow in his continuously romantic vision of New York, steeped in music from the Great American Songbook (Gershwin, Cole Porter, Jerome Kern) and a world of actresses, gangsters, art deco glamour, martinis and, most importantly, aspiring artists.

For this is one of his films that questions the responsibility of great artists and it contains, within its farcical humour, one of the most discussed lines of his entire oeuvre: "Guilt is petit-bourgeois crap – an artist creates his own moral universe … You gotta do what you gotta do."

Is this a reference to the tawdry allegations going on in the court case? Is Woody really excusing his behaviour in having a relationship with Soon Yi, Farrow's adopted daughter, with an artist's get-out clause? Is it an extension of his own much-quoted response, itself paraphrasing Emily Dickinson, to those who questioned his new love: "The heart wants what it wants"?

The line itself is uttered by a character named Sheldon Flender, a struggling playwright who knocks off a play a year (sound familiar?) but who is happy they never get performed. "I don't write hits," he says. "My plays are art, they're written specifically to go unproduced." The role is played by Rob Reiner, himself hugely successful, so was Woody making some sly comment by giving him such a line?

Reiner's presence resonates in other ways, too. The director of *When Harry Met Sally*, a huge comedy hit with unashamed echoes of *Annie Hall*, he also directed *The Sure Thing*. That was the

Left Jennifer Tilly earned an Oscar nomination for the role of gangster's moll and terrible actress Olive in *Bullets Over Broadway*.

Below Chazz Palminteri as Cheech and John Cusack as playwright David on the set of *Bullets Over Broadway*.

film debut of a teenaged John Cusack, here playing the idealistic playwright David Shayne.

Bullets Over Broadway opens with a discussion between David and his producer Julian (Jack Warner) about the difficulties of raising finance for arty plays. This echoes the financing troubles then facing Woody: Tri-Star, headed by Mike Medavoy, had just pulled out of their three-picture deal citing the unspectacular box office of *Husbands and Wives* and *Manhattan Murder Mystery*, although it is likely they were also cowed by the negative publicity surrounding Allen.

Above "Don't speak!": Dianne Wiest's Helen Sinclair gives John Cusack the *grande dame* treatment.

Right Broadway Woody Allen: the director delves into the costume cupboard on the shoot of *Bullets Over Broadway*, 1994.

Fortunately, a new financier stepped in: Jean Doumanian, one of Woody's oldest friends since the 1960s. Her company Sweetland Films (backed by her billionaire partner, the Swiss-Lebanese banker Jaqui Safra) now offered Woody a larger production budget (and director's fee) of around $20 million, which he lavished on the period details of *Bullets Over Broadway*. Doumanian also allowed Woody – for a while, at least – to continue with full control on the picture. "He's one of those self-sufficient geniuses who do what they want," she told the *New York Times*.

What sets this film apart from mere homage is that it asks a crucial question disguised as a funny plot point: how far would you go for your art? In the film's great twist, Cheech, the gangster played by Chazz Palminteri, is eventually revealed as the brilliant playwright – although, to David Shayne's initial relief, he won't take credit for it. "Where I come from," says Cheech, "we don't squeal."

The subject of authenticity is always key for an author, an artist and an existentialist of sorts like Allen. Indeed, it was something he dealt with as an actor in 1976's *The Front*, covering for a blacklisted writer, and he will return to the theme of a writer passing off someone else's work as his own in *You Will Meet a Tall Dark Stranger* many years later.

But here, Cheech becomes increasingly proud of his work and when he realizes that the squeaky-voiced Olive (Jennifer Tilly) might ruin his work with a lousy performance, he whacks her in one of the great movie killings of all time: "Olive, I think you should know this, you're a terrible actress," he says – and shoots her dead.

Originally, the film was then supposed to continue with Cheech enjoying a big hit with the play and being celebrated around town – only to discover that show business types are far worse than the sharks, double-dealers and crooks he has known, so that he longs to go back to being a gangster. Funny as it might have been, Allen felt that this extra "beat" in the story would add too much to an already packed film, adding another 15 minutes to the running time.

As ever with comedy, an examination of the themes' seriousness just takes away from the laughs and the sheer brio with which it all unfolds, the visual equivalent of those smooth and witty lyricists continually heard on the soundtrack. English

"I'm still a star. I never play frumps or virgins."

Dianne Wiest as *Helen Sinclair*

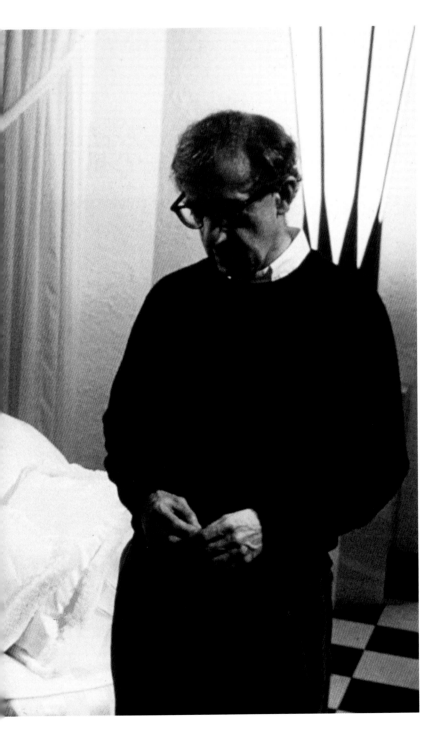

treasure Jim Broadbent is marvellous comic entertainment as Warner Purcell, the compulsive eater with a chicken leg up his sleeve. Jennifer Tilly is terrific as Olive ("Charmed, charmed") and Tracey Ullman gets laughs as Eden Brent with her chihuahua Mr Woofles. When offered a saucer of milk for her dog, she says: "Oh, you needn't bother with that, I breastfeed her … Just kidding!"

But reigning supreme is Dianne Wiest – the only winner out of the film's seven Oscar nominations. She picked up her second award for a supporting role in a Woody film, having won for *Hannah and Her Sisters* fully eight years previously – and in such a different part.

Initially, Wiest could not find the right tone to play theatrical *grande dame* Helen Sinclair, but she lowered her voice until it become increasingly comical. Allen, uncharacteristically, even showed her how to play it, doing his best Norma Desmond impression. "Really? You want it that broad?" she gawped.

But in copying him and adding her own baritone flourishes, she created one of the great comic portrayals of the theatre. "I'm still a star. I never play frumps or virgins." And of course there's her inimitable, yet oft-imitated, catchphrase "Don't speak, don't speak", a line she speaks while squishing her hands into the young, lovestruck playwright's face. Allen says he got the idea from Anna Magnani in *The Rose Tattoo*.

Only Wiest as Sinclair could enter the theatre late for the first rehearsal, saying: "Please forgive me. My pedicurist had a stroke. She fell forward on to the orange stick and plunged it into my toe. It required bandaging."

Later she dramatically raises her martini glass "to an ideal world with no compromise", and you know it's a vain wish. But it's one for which Woody Allen sincerely strains every time he sits down to write – and one he usually gets.

Left Over the top? Woody Allen inspects Jennifer Tilly's wardrobe on the set of *Bullets Over Broadway*.

Don't Drink the Water (1994)

The Hollanders, a noisy Jewish family from New Jersey on holiday in Eastern Europe, find themselves accused of spying and take shelter in the American Embassy.

Filming – or rather, not filming – "the moronic enterprise" that was *Casino Royale* in Swinging London meant his nights were filled with cards and gambling – but that left Woody Allen with days to kill. So, with typical industry, he wrote his first play.

After many drafts and try-outs and having been through several producers, *Don't Drink the Water* opened on Broadway, at the Morosco Theatre in November 1966 and ran for a highly respectable 598 performances. "It was not a great play," Woody has said, "but the stagehands at the Morosco told me they'd never heard laughs like that, wire to wire, the audience just roared and roared. As a laugh machine, it got huge laughs."

It starred Lou Jacobi, who would appear later as the cross-dresser in *Everything You Always Wanted to Know About Sex*, and a young actor called Tony Roberts, who went on to act in Woody's next play, *Play It Again, Sam* and who would become a familiar figure in many of Woody's early films.

Success on the stage led, in 1969, to the inevitable film version. Woody, by then launching his own film career directing *Take the Money and Run*, wanted no involvement in it despite the fact that his own managers Charles Joffe and Jack Rollins were overseeing production. They secured Jackie Gleason as the star, but it was not a hit.

Allen says he never even saw the film until he came to put on his own production for TV – by which time he was actually old enough to play the role of Walter Hollander, the caterer famous for his mashed potato sculptures. Of the Gleason film, Woody says: "It's abysmal, a textbook of how you buy a play and ruin it. I did it a hundred times better."

Above Woody Allen directs Michael J Fox in *Don't Drink the Water*, shot in the Ukrainian Embassy, New York, 1994.

Left "We're not spies, we're from New Jersey": Woody Allen and Julie Kavner as Walter and Marion Hollander.

I'm not so sure. As Woody admits, the play does have plenty of jokes and it should "be an evening of laughs even if the PTA are doing it". *Don't Drink the Water* is, indeed, often performed by amateur dramatic societies and students – several wooden productions of it can be seen in home videos posted on the Internet. But Woody's own production, shot in two weeks in the Ukrainian Embassy in New York, doesn't feel much more professional than many of those.

Although Julie Kavner is good as Marion Hollander, she doesn't have many jokes and comes across as a nag, and Mayim Bialik as the daughter has an even thinner role. Meanwhile, Woody's acting as Walter feels lazy and behind the beats of the comedy.

Dom DeLuise steals the show easily as the priest-turned-magician and while Michael J Fox exerts his ever-boyish charms as

the Ambassador's hapless son in charge of getting the Hollanders home, the 1994 version feels hopelessly dated, even while it owns up to being a period piece.

The gags are stale, the casual xenophobia is unpleasantly out of touch (there are jokes about harems, bad foreign food and Woody dressed in a burka) and the pace is so sluggish it can't be enlivened by Woody's desperate-looking insistence on jerky camera moves by his regular movie cinematographer Carlo Di Palma.

Perhaps there was the urge to capture the performance as if it were "live" theatre, and it's understandable that Woody was tempted by the thought of committing to tape a definitive reading of his old play for future generations. I think, though, that this proved a lot harder than he thought it would, and it needed more care – or at least, you know, some rehearsals.

The film aired on US television just before Christmas 1994 for ABC's *Sunday Night Movie* slot. It wasn't shown in a European cinema until a Woody Allen career retrospective at the 2004 San Sebastian Film Festival. I was there and I can tell you nobody laughed. Perhaps the joke was supposed, over time, to have flipped to be squarely on the American family, but this audience of loyal Woody fans didn't get it, and the film looked very ugly blown up on the big screen.

I wondered what they must have put in the water at the Morosco back in 1966, and where I could get some.

"O cursed fate, some thoughts
are better left unthunk."
The Greek Chorus

Mighty Aphrodite (1995)

When sportswriter Lenny Weinrib traces the mother of his adopted son, he is shocked to discover she's a helium-voiced prostitute. He tries to improve her life, which leads to trouble for his own marriage.

With Woody Allen working as assiduously and productively as ever throughout the upheavals in his personal life, can we discern in his work anything new that might reflect outside influences?

Most obvious is the theme of adoption, which has played a large role in his personal life, leading to happiness as well as heartbreak. There have been landmark court rulings allowing unmarried couples to adopt (he and Mia Farrow never married) as well as shattering decisions that restricted his access to his children.

Woody insists that the film does not reflect his own experiences, and will admit only that the storyline was inspired by watching Mia with her many adopted children – one of whom is, of course, now his own wife. The question of genes, nurture and hereditary traits do crop up here, and are handled by someone who has dealt with such issues at close quarters. He made this film during what was undoubtedly a period of stress and heartache for him, centred around his own adopted children, and it's fascinating that he should be able to make art from such material, turning it into a light comedy when it was anything but that in life.

As for Woody the persona, I think he does look older, maybe a little tired (what am I, his mother?), but that's about the most you can say of the man we see on the screen. The baggier look actually suits the part of Lenny Weinrib very well and I wish we could have seen more of this character and the world of sportswriting:

Lenny is a kind of Danny Rose figure, and I could see Woody playing out a very fine story set in boxing gyms, race tracks and football training sessions.

Mighty Aphrodite merely skims these worlds, mainly because Mira Sorvino walks away with the film as Linda Ash. It's a part that won her an Oscar, and it is indeed a bravura comic performance. Later, talking to critic and filmmaker Stig Björkman, Woody suggested it deserved comparison with Marilyn Monroe.

Her Linda is far more than the rather cartoonish character Woody probably wrote on the page (although the screenplay did earn him another Oscar nomination, his 12th in the category for Best Original Screenplay) and she invests genuine emotion in the character. She skilfully balances a wounded sadness – as shown in her speech confessing to giving up her child for adoption – with a peppy, comically breezy attitude to her professions of hooker and porn actress: "You didn't want a blow job, so the least I could get you was a tie."

The device of the dancing and narrating Greek chorus also lends *Mighty Aphrodite* more depth than the average comedy, ushering in themes of destiny and luck as well as providing some laughs through their mix of high-minded grandiloquence and New Yorky colloquialisms: "O cursed fate, some thoughts are better left unthunk. Please, Lenny, don't be a schmuck."

It's not much more than a comic gimmick. Take out all the chorus scenes (many of them filmed in Sicily's Taormina), and the main narrative is unaffected, although we'd miss a couple of nicely harmonized song and dance routines (choreographed by Graciela Daniele) as well as some gags. F Murray Abraham's chorus leader

Left Woody Allen tries to keep Mira Sorvino calm at the race track in *Mighty Aphrodite*.

breaks conventions by chatting with Woody's Lenny at key moments back in New York: "Remember Achilles," he warns, as Lenny attempts to takes on Linda's pimp. To which Lenny's retort is classic Woody: "He only had an Achilles heel, I gotta whole Achilles body."

The chorus does occasionally chime with some of Woody's more probing comic work on God and Fate. In a celebrated moment, it appeals, "O Zeus, most potent of Gods, we cry out to thee." In reply comes an answer phone message: "Hi, this is Zeus, I'm not home right now, but leave a message and I'll get back to you as soon as I can." It's on a par with the "if he would just cough" line from *Love and Death*.

So, yes, *Mighty Aphrodite* recycles familiar Woody material and obsessions. When Lenny and Amanda (Helena Bonham Carter) toy with names for their new son, he suggests Groucho, Harpo, Django, Thelonious and Sugar Ray – remember, this is a man whose kids are called Satchel, Manzie and Bechet.

But mainly *Mighty Aphrodite* is a brightly executed movie, as richly enjoyable and diverting as any of Woody's fable-like New York stories and crowned with a top-notch comic turn from Mira Sorvino.

Other actresses, including Cameron Diaz, did read for the role and Mira got the part only after a second stab at it. Woody was at London's Dorchester Hotel on a promotional tour for *Bullets Over Broadway* – back then, a rare occurrence – and Sorvino arrived dressed in character, with full hair and make-up. "She was dressed so tarty, I'm surprised they let her up," he recalled.

Right Woody Allen's Lenny is shocked to discover the mother of his adopted child is a prostitute – Linda Ash, played by Mira Sorvino.

"You didn't want a blow job, so the least I could get you was a tie."

Mira Sorvino as *Linda Ash*

Below Woody Allen as Joe with
Natasha Lyonne as his daughter DJ
on the Grand Canal, Venice 1996.

Everyone Says I Love You (1996)

Musical numbers from the Great American Songbook punctuate the story of a year in the life of a wealthy New York family, taking in love, death, politics, an escaped convict and a Groucho Marx party.

Woody would wait until 2014 before helping to turn *Bullets Over Broadway* into his first bona fide stage musical. But you can feel the joy of a man toying with one of his favourite genres all the way through *Everyone Says I Love You*, perhaps the most purely enjoyable, romantic film in his entire oeuvre.

The first thing a viewer will notice is that these people can't sing. Despite being big Hollywood stars, they were not cast for their singing voices and indeed weren't even told they were doing a musical until shooting had started. Woody wanted to pay tribute to the great musicals that had transported him from Brooklyn to Manhattan in his youth, to the white-telephone world of Fred Astaire and Ginger Rogers, but he took the route of amateur rather than auteur.

Thus the technique here owes more to the "sung through" musicals of Dennis Potter, such as *Pennies from Heaven*, and of Jacques Demy, such as *The Umbrellas of Cherbourg* and *The Young Girls of Rochefort*. (Woody had even worked with Demy's cinematographer, Ghislain Cloquet, on *Love and Death*.) Woody has likened the vocal style to "shower singing" and the idea was to break the fourth wall of musical convention and have characters sing their feelings, the better to get across the poetry contained in the lyrics in some of the finest American songs – to act it, rather than sing it.

Back in the 1990s, they just didn't make musicals any more, so perhaps big things were expected of Woody. Perhaps there were hopes that he could recapture the giddy whirl of MGM-style numbers. These would be disappointed. Indeed, many audiences were baffled – including Miramax executives. Distributor Bob Weinstein apparently walked out of the first test screening yelling at Allen, "I hate it". Yet it seems to me the most perfect and delightful way of doing a modern musical, of giving normal people the motivation to burst into song.

The film is narrated by Natasha Lyonne, playing a character called Djuna "DJ" Berlin, who tells the story of how she came to be part of a loose, loveable, loaded family. She's immediately aware of the construct, too: "We're not the usual type of family you find in a musical comedy," she says.

Djuna's father, played by Woody, is Joe Berlin, a novelist who now lives in Paris (Woody's dream come true). He is divorced amicably from her mother Steffi (Goldie Hawn), who's now married to Bob (Alan Alda) and they all live in a sumptuous Upper East Side apartment and seem to live life like it's still the 1930s. (Some critics notice a direct nod to one of Woody's writing heroes, George S Kaufman, and his play *You Can't Take It with You*, which also become an Oscar-winning movie.)

One story strand here is a reworking of the plot device from *Another Woman*, this time to comic effect as DJ eavesdrops on the therapy sessions of Von, a beautiful woman (Julia Roberts) who is the client of her friend's mother. Later, on vacation with her father in Venice, they bump into Von, and DJ uses that information to help him woo her.

It's complicated. Yet Allen weaves all his plots and characters in very sweetly and unfussily. Everyone here is really after one thing – love, the first delirious tingles of which surely give anyone reason to sing. The film's title, taken from a song in the Marx Brothers' *Horse Feathers*, says it all.

Woody's long-running debt to Groucho Marx is made concrete in the film's finale in Paris, when Woody and Goldie Hawn dress up for a Christmas Eve party in full Groucho glasses and face – slightly better versions of the same masks Woody had put on Virgil Starkwell's parents in *Take the Money and Run*.

Woody does a passable Groucho impression and Goldie spars with him terrifically, to the point where you wish they had performed with each other before. As a duo, they have the sort of easy and loving comic chemistry that he and Keaton used to create. Their dance by the Seine, using wires to lift Goldie up, has a lovely simplicity as well as a romantic impossibility.

The film's choreography is devised by Graciela Daniele, who had also created the Greek chorus steps in *Mighty Aphrodite*. Witty and inventive throughout, it makes use of hospital corridors, Harry Winston's jewellery store, the Yves Saint Laurent shop window and even a funeral home.

The actors use their own voices, including Woody himself, who delivers a couple of verses of the film's refrain 'I'm Through With Love'. (He was later modest about his talents, saying that he was able only to "croak out half a song".) Only one actor did no singing at all: Drew Barrymore, who soon convinced Allen that her voice was too terrible even for this enterprise. He agreed, saying: "She sings so badly, deaf people refuse to watch her lips move." Drew was eventually dubbed by Olivia Hayman.

Audiences at the time did make the rather dull accusation that watching Woody woo the far younger Roberts was a bit creepy. However, it is clear that this is a doomed romance, another exploration of dream fulfilment as he lies his way into her affections, hilariously pretending to know about Tintoretto or the best way to get to Bora Bora, "or at least, uh, one of the Boras".

Frothy and charming as it is, this isn't entirely without substance. Roberts's Von is a classic Allen character, desperate for reality to match her idealized views yet disappointed when it does (mainly because that reality is in itself a product of someone's lies). "I have seen my dream come true, so my fantasy doesn't torture me any more," she declares. "That's so neurotic," he tells her.

And, as so often, the spectre of Death appears, this time sending a message from beyond in the form of Grandpa. At his funeral, he gets

Right Sing, sing, sing: Woody directs Edward Norton and Drew Barrymore, New York, 1996.

out of the coffin as a ghostly figure and performs, with other ghosts, a version of 'Enjoy Yourself (It's Later Than You Think)'.

Some critics hated the film. Jonathan Rosenbaum declared it "grisly to behold". Kenneth Turan declared in the *LA Times*: "Much of the film's story is half-hearted, its jokes hit or miss, and what starts out feeling genial ends up unavoidably thin." But Janet Maslin wrote in the *New York Times*: "It's a world of serene privilege and surreal possibility, a delightful and witty compendium of the film maker's favourite things." And Roger Ebert put it down as one of his favourite Woody Allen films: "Here is a film that had me with a goofy grin plastered on my face for most of its length … It would take a heart of stone to resist this movie."

Its charms seem numerous and irresistible to me. Quite apart from hearing the beauty of these classic lyrics put across/read with heartfelt emotion, it looks great. Working with Carlo Di Palma here, Woody creates as gorgeous, rarefied and romanticized a New York as he did in the black and white of *Manhattan*. (Later, he did briefly discuss, with his co-author Marshall Brickman, the possibility of making that film into a musical.) And I just love the Halloween sequence, when all the kids in the building perform elaborately costumed pieces for their trick or treat rewards: the 'Chiquita Banana' dance (the debut of future Broadway star Christy Michelle Romano)

is adorable, and Woody captures it beautifully, as well as everyone's reactions to it.

It's fascinating that this picture, coming so soon after the bitter break-up of his family with Mia Farrow, is probably his most harmonious portrait of family life, the various members all getting on beautifully with each other.

Meanwhile, however, Woody's "film" family was under pressure. Financial concerns at Sweetland Films were growing, and costs were being cut. His long collaboration with Robert Greenhut as producer was now over and Woody still needed a hit. His next film would tear everything apart.

Above They're not through with love – in his third film with Woody, Alan Alda dances with the gorgeous Goldie Hawn.

Right "Tintoretto is my hero": Woody Allen somehow shares Julia Roberts's deepest passions in *Everyone Says I Love You*.

> "[Drew Barrymore] sings so badly, deaf people are afraid to watch her lips move."
>
> Woody Allen

Deconstructing Harry (1997)

A bitter but ingenious comedy in which a famous, foul-mouthed novelist travels to his old university to accept an award while friends, relatives, ex-lovers and fictional characters attack him from all angles.

"It's about a nasty, shallow, superficial, sexually obsessed writer, so of course everyone's going to think it's about me," said Woody Allen on the release of *Deconstructing Harry*. He was right.

His image and "brand" were still recovering from the split with Mia Farrow and the subsequent court case, and this film seemed to be Woody screaming back, an angry stab of self-justification. One thing it definitely wasn't doing was saying sorry.

That's exactly what makes this one of Woody Allen's most fascinating films to examine, if not one of the most pleasant to watch.

The intensely unlikeable Harry Block can be seen as a portrait of the writer in crisis. An alternative perspective is available: the film is bookended with star Annie Ross singing 'Twisted', a 1952 song with the refrain "My analyst told me that I was right out of my head …", so perhaps Harry Block is simply the untameable id, the naughty dark side given free rein. You can say things in fiction that you sure can't say in life.

What shocks many viewers is that Woody Allen had for so long created a warmly likeable persona through which to convey his thoughts and on whom he could hang all life's absurdities. But here as Harry, it's as if he's saying goodbye to all that, blowing it apart, perhaps to start anew.

Hearing Woody Allen swearing (twice using the C-word to describe different women) and talking about blow jobs is like catching your parents having sex. But once the floodgates are open, how he lets the profanities flow, as if Harry's got Tourette's. Maybe he has.

Certainly the idea of controlling oneself better in art than in life is a recurring theme, one that Woody's been toying with since *Annie Hall* (when, incidentally, he also went into a nervous panic just before an awards ceremony). But no matter how badly behaved this Harry is, what seems to have really offended anyone in his vicinity is his art.

"You take everyone's suffering and turn it into literary gold," screams scorned lover Judy Davis at him, brandishing a gun. Later, his sister and her husband scold him for the unsympathetic portrayal of Jews in his work, accusing him of being a self-hating Jew. "Hey, I may hate myself, but not because I'm Jewish," Harry counters. His ex-wife (played by Kirstie Alley) does nothing other than yell at him in the street – rather like Woody himself, playing Ike in *Manhattan*, yelling at Meryl Streep in response to the tell-all novel she has written.

Harry's characters, as in many of Woody's comic stories and writings, have names straight out of the shtetl: Goldberg, Epstein, Fischbein, Pinchik, Mendelbaum. But from the five or so dramatizations of the tales that we see (Allen was using up some of those discarded ideas he keeps on scraps of paper in that famous desk drawer), Harry's writing doesn't seem particularly vicious or revelatory.

This disconnect is one of the film's tonal weaknesses, but it's also the source of some very decent jokes: the *Star Wars*-themed bar mitzvah; the descent into Hell ("fourth floor: book critics and insurance salesmen"); the actor (played by Robin Williams) who goes out-of-focus, prompting his wife (Julie Kavner) to ask, "Did you eat shellfish?"

As he did in *The Purple Rose of Cairo*, Woody lets his fictional characters run around. When Harry's creation Ken, a husband who cheats with his wife's sister, does meet Harry, there's a neat clash. "You created me and you don't even recognize me," says Ken. "I'm you, thinly disguised of course, with a bit more maturity and a different name." (Ken is played by Richard Benjamin, who also appeared in *Goodbye, Columbus*, which inevitably sparks associations with the writer Philip Roth, whose novella was the source for that film.)

Above When Harry met Billy:
Woody's Harry Block with
Billy Crystal and Elisabeth Shue.

Left Better the Devil you know:
Woody poses on the "Hell"
set of *Deconstructing Harry*.

Echoing what the aliens tell Sandy Bates in *Stardust Memories*, we might forgive Harry were he to tell funnier jokes. As it is, he's got a few good lines, but they're all rather bleak. As his sister tells him: "Your life is nihilism, cynicism, sarcasm and orgasm." To which Harry replies: "Hey, in France I could run on that slogan and win."

Maybe the film itself would have succeeded better commercially had Woody not played Harry. He did try to enlist Elliot Gould, Dennis Hopper, Robert De Niro, Dustin Hoffman and Albert Brooks. All were unavailable. It was only as the shoot neared that Woody reluctantly agreed to play Harry. And his acting is not good here. It's lazy and tired, with about three default poses: the hands waving out front as if pushing away an attack, or hanging palms up at the sides or clasped to the top of his head.

Ultimately most people in his life hate Harry. The kidnapping of his own son (this shortly after Allen himself went through custody battles) has finally prevented Harry from being honoured at the ceremony – he is arrested and slung in jail – so he must imagine one for himself. Of course, Harry's characters all forgive him and, in a rather brilliant scene, gather to applaud him; the music playing is a version of 'I Could Write a Book'. Harry tells them: "You've given me some of the happiest moments of my life."

While Woody biographer Eric Lax has said, perversely, that "it's actually a very sweet movie", critic Florence Colombani calls this finale "a breathtaking moment, when it seems that Allen is saying farewell to the cinema, or at least to his previous films".

Expect neither Woody nor Harry were finished, far from it.

Back in his real life, Harry is unblocked and inspired and we think once more of Ike's voice over at the start of *Manhattan* as he begins typing out a story. "I like it! A character who is too neurotic to function in life but can only function in art."

Back in his real life, Woody attended the Venice Film Festival, which opened with *Deconstructing Harry* and where he accepted their Golden Lion for lifetime achievement. Later he was nominated yet again for an Oscar for Best Screenplay. And he married Soon-Yi.

Wild Man Blues (1997)

Documentary maker Barbara Kopple follows Woody and Soon-Yi Previn on a three-week tour of Europe's finest hotels as Woody plays clarinet in a series of concerts with his New Orleans Jazz Band.

While Woody Allen was often on television and in the public eye during his early career, the 1980s found him conducting ever fewer publicity engagements.

When the scandal over his affair with Soon-Yi hit the headlines in 1992, however, he found himself in the glare of almost daily tabloid exposure as well as having to give evidence in a public court. It cannot be denied that the scandal had an effect on Woody's hitherto loyal audience and on the perception of the image he had so carefully created of himself on screen. By 1996, his box office clout, if not the quality of his films, was suffering a notable dip.

He was now being bankrolled by his friend Jean Doumanian's Sweetland Films and distributed by Miramax Films – and experiencing, for the first time since his film career began, the stirrings of commercial imperative from producers and sponsors.

Woody's old friend and band mate Eddy Davis now made a suggestion: why not tour Europe with the New Orleans Jazz Band that normally played on Monday nights in Michael's Pub, New York? Allen agreed. Doumanian believed that there was currency in the sight of Woody being feted by his loyal European audience, and she had the idea of making a film out of the event, persuading Woody to let the cameras into his private life for the first time ever.

Thus the chief attraction of *Wild Man Blues* (named after a Jelly Roll Morton track) is for Woody Allen fans to see their idol as up close and as personal as he might allow. Of course, they have to watch him puff and nod his way through plenty of New Orleans jazz, but since this is one of his enduring life passions, it seems to offer a decent way in to his soul.

Despite his protestations of modesty, Allen and his band are more than competent, if definitely unspectacular. But Kopple is an Oscar-winning documentary maker, and offers us a careful balance that includes rare, if unspectacular, insights into Woody, his life, his travel peccadilloes and, of course, his newish lover.

Kopple's work is subtly revealing and not always particularly flattering to Woody. True to form, he does come across as a genuine neurotic and "world-renowned claustrophobic". He moans and kvetches about shower drains, omelettes, dogs – and getting his laundry back in one piece (in Milan, he's concerned it'll come back "breaded"). Soon-Yi remains patient and accommodating yet gently and subtly supportive, while his sister Letty does all the fussing, coercing and arranging.

Woody's entourage travel by private jet (separate from the rest of the band) and stay in the finest suites of the grandest hotels in Madrid, Vienna, Venice, Milan, Geneva, Turin, Paris and London. Woody reveals he has to have a separate bathroom all to himself "for my unctions and vanishing creams and the lotions that give me this look". Did I spot a bottle of Old Spice aftershave in his wash bag?

We see him on a treadmill in trainers and unattractive brown socks. We watch him and Soon-Yi take a dip in their private suite swimming pool. In Venice, he makes a fuss about the little waves from a water taxi and later, on a supposedly romantic gondola ride with Soon-Yi, he complains his "knuckles are white, my heartbeat raised". Frankly, one is surprised she doesn't push him into the canal.

Later, at the next in a series of after-show functions in Italy, he introduces her to some guests, jokingly, as "the notorious Soon-Yi Previn". Through all the meet-and-greets with various mayors and

the wives of sponsors, Woody is, at least, more civil than his character Sandy Bates in *Stardust Memories*, which this film cleverly invokes (as much as it does Fellini, even using Nino Rota's music for the Italian section). Woody is never less than polite and only complains gently about the general ridiculousness of the paparazzi and of the crowds waiting patiently outside his hotel for an appearance. "Stick around, I'll be coming out for a glimpse later," he teases.

It's hard to tell if Woody is happy at any point. Even when he's blowing hot up on the stage, you can't be sure. His regular set ends, he explains in a rare moment of speech, as many New Orleans parades did, with a rendition of 'No Place Like Home'. "When I'm in New York, I miss Europe," he says to Soon-Yi in a private moment. "And when I'm in Europe, I miss New York. I just don't want to be wherever I am at any given moment. That's my chronic dissatisfaction, anhedonia."

That, of course, was the title he wanted to call *Annie Hall*, and we're reminded of that film again when, in London, he gets sick before his gig and takes to his bed at the Dorchester Hotel. "These people can hate me in my own language," he wails.

These are keen and valuable insights, though one suspects Woody is often aware of Kopple's camera, no matter how unobtrusive she is. It's interesting that here he is using the documentary format to redress any perceived imbalances in his public image, given that at many times in his career already he's played with the documentary form himself, partly as a way to create that very image. *Take the Money and Run, Zelig, Husbands and Wives* all used documentary

elements, and in *Crimes and Misdemeanors* Woody even played a documentary maker himself. Anyone who has also seen those films will inevitably be wondering if documentaries are to be trusted.

This one climaxes, on his return to New York, with lunch at his parents' apartment, which plays out like a scene from a Woody Allen film. His parents have a collection of his Oscars on their shelves and Woody dumps all the trinkets, baubles and mementoes from his European trip on his Dad, who seems only to be interested in the quality of the engraving. "Why did they call you Gracie?" he asks his son, pointing to one Italian plaque. "That's *Grazie*, Dad, it means 'thanks'."

This scene also includes his mother Nettie complaining how her son never stuck at anything, how he always stayed in his room as a boy ("What were you doing in there?"), how he'd have been better off as a pharmacist ("Maybe you'd do more business as a druggist than as an actor") and how he should have married a nice Jewish girl. Soon-Yi sits by, patient as ever.

Weirdly, it's a scene we've sort of witnessed before, in *Radio Days*, in *Crimes and Misdemeanors* and in *Annie Hall*. "This was truly the lunch from hell," says Woody to nobody in particular, as if mentally noting it down for future use, again.

Celebrity (1998)

In this gleaming monochrome tribute to Fellini's *La Dolce Vita*,
a celebrity journalist grows disenchanted chasing the fame and beauty
of his subjects while the wife he leaves becomes famous and finds love.

Generally remembered as one of Woody Allen's worst films, it's actually rich with memorable moments, bitter laughs and staggering beauty.

Boosted by the growing clout of having fame-hungry Harvey Weinstein and Miramax as part of the producing team, *Celebrity* is probably Woody's starriest and best-looking cast: Charlize Theron, Melanie Griffith, Winona Ryder, JK Simmons (selling bleeding Jesus statues), Isaac Mizrahi, Joe Mantegna, Bebe Neuwirth, Hank Azaria, Famke Janssen, Gretchen Mol, and Debra Messing

It's like flicking through a particularly glossy black and white issue of *Vanity Fair* magazine (you can even spot *VF*'s famed photographer Annie Leibovitz in a crowd of paparazzi). Every gorgeous frame drips with glamour, glistening in the magnificent lensing of Bergman's cinematographer Sven Nykvist, who brilliantly contrasts the light and dark to emphasize the inky blackness beyond the pop and flash of celebrity.

The film is worth seeing for the photography and camerawork alone.

If nothing else, this film demonstrates the lasting pulling power of

Woody Allen. The man gets who he wants: the hottest, newest stars, the biggest names – he clicks his fingers and they still come running. And generally, nobody comes out of it badly. No actors were harmed in the making of this film.

Except maybe Kenneth Branagh.

What sunk the film on release – and it really did sink – was the general reception of Kenneth Branagh playing Lee Simon, the celebrity profile writer who gets sucked into (literally) the vortex of the world he's supposed to be impartially covering. Branagh, playing the "Woody surrogate" role, delivers what everyone regarded as a Woody impression, replete with the stammers and tsch-sounds that are the hallmarks of Allen's acting. Yet Woody actually writes these linguistic tics and imprecisions into the text, so they're on the page and, frankly, Branagh is just being faithful to the text when he hits them all.

Viewing the film now, with years of distance, you simply see the character of Lee Simon for what he is – a bit of a square with ideas way beyond himself. Branagh's performance seems far less distracting, particularly now that the actor is also known as a director and no longer has to live up to the tag of being "the new Laurence Olivier". He's actually very good in the earlier parts of the film and succumbs to Woody parody only in the later, bigger speeches – and even in these he has a crumpled, crushed vulnerability that ultimately earns our sympathy.

I think the problem is almost unsayable, so let me try. Branagh doing Woody Allen – or, at least, the Woody Allen persona famous from so many self-penned film roles – is tantamount to an actor "Jewing up". It's possible that in the casting process Woody the director identified some kind of connection with the Belfast-born

Above left Charlize Theron dazzles on the catwalk, playing a supermodel in *Celebrity*.

Left Melanie Griffith plays a movie star being interviewed by Kenneth Branagh's Lee.

thesp. The trouble is, you couldn't really get more non-Jewish than
Ken Branagh, and here he is adopting the nasal, neurotic, yiddish-
inflected rhythms of New York. For many viewers, I suspect that this
is uncomfortable.

Celebrity also suffered, ironically, from the glare of celebrity itself.
It was the first film to star Leonardo DiCaprio since he had become
a global phenomenon in *Titanic*, and he is on the screen for only 10
minutes – a huge disappointment to the star's legion of new fans, who
felt Leo had been slighted.

But what a bravura 10 minutes it is. Leo is incandescent,
tearing up the screen and a hotel room. He plays Brandon Darrow,
a spoilt Hollywood actor complete with his entourage – one of
whom is played by Sam Rockwell with shocking hair, and another
of whom is a young Adrian Grenier, who went on to be the star of
the TV show *Entourage*. Branagh's Lee tries in vain to sell Brandon
a screenplay while keeping up with the gang as they booze, snort
drugs and cavort with women in a hotel room after a boxing match
in Atlantic City. Lee cannot enjoy himself for one minute without

trying to peddle the screenplay, even in bed during a foursome.

Charlize Theron is also problematic, despite being superb in
her scenes as a supermodel. I think Woody diehards may have been
offended that her character is said to suffer from the condition of
being "polymorphously perverse". That's how Alvy Singer described
Annie Hall so memorably. You can't just reuse that expression, and it
was starting to feel that Woody was running out of new things to say.

The Fellini parallels are many, including an airborne opening
in which the inhabitants of a city are all looking upwards. In *La
Dolce Vita* a Jesus statue is being flown over Rome; here, a plane
is skywriting the word *HELP* high above Manhattan. It's a great
opening sequence by a director who's pretty good at such things by
now. Woody might not have figured out endings, but he sure knows
how to open a picture.

Along the way, Allen takes swipes at plastic surgery, health, fashion,
psychotherapy, journalism, self-help – and television. The Felliniesque
carnival reaches its apogee backstage at a TV studio where neo-Nazis
share bagels in the green room with a rabbi, members of the South
Carolina Klan, a mafia boss and a teenage obese acrobat.

There's also a private screening for media types, who fawn over
a famous film critic. "He used to hate every movie," explains Joe
Mantegna's character. "Then he married a young big-bosomed
woman and now he loves every movie."

Another scene that offended many viewers, still recovering from the sexual allegations laid at Woody's door several years earlier, was one in which Judy Davis goes to meet a now-famous prostitute for help with her sexual confidence. The pair practise fellatio on a couple of bananas. I can't say it's a particularly edifying sight, though as the scene plays on, it does actually become quite funny thanks to Bebe Neuwirth's utterly brilliant performance.

Of course, Allen has mocked many of these subjects before. Probably nothing can top his trashing of popular culture than the withering speech he gave Max von Sydow in *Hannah and Her Sisters*. Yet *Celebrity* still displays the prescience of a great artist. This was made years before reality shows, selfies and the narcissism of Facebook and Twitter, and it bristles with a sense of doom about where such idolatry is headed.

Even when Lee does think he's found true, romantic love and connection with Winona Ryder's bohemian actress, this is flung back in his face. Fame, and the pursuit of fame, are toxic and you will get hurt, says this film.

Nevertheless, celebrity cameos also include Donald Trump, basketball player Anthony Mason and magician David Blaine. The film is using fame, youth and beauty as magic tricks, revealing nothing but darkness. *Celebrity* tries to hold on to the ephemeral, beginning and ending on the shot of that cry for *HELP* written in the sky, but fading to black even before the word is complete.

Fame fades, love fades, youth turns to age. "Ask not for whom the toilet flushes," quips Branagh's Lee at one point as he realizes his life is passing quickly. All this is true. And yet, whisper it, *Celebrity* the film will be one that endures.

Right Kenneth Branagh rolls the dice as Leonardo DiCaprio and Adrian Grenier look on in *Celebrity*.

Sweet and Lowdown (1999)

The 1930s jazz guitarist Emmet Ray and his affair with a mute
girl provide the subject for a beautiful "biography" about an artist,
his music, his drinking, his fears, failures and dreams.

Of the 10 films Woody Allen directed in the 1990s, he featured in only half of them. If he'd spent the 1970s establishing his screen persona and the 1980s deepening his range as a director, the next decade was spent toying with both those sides of his art.

His 1990s films are about hiding preconceptions, frustrating our expectations of him, even shattering them. It's as if he sometimes wished to disappear, wipe away an image he himself had constructed, on screen and off.

Sweet and Lowdown was to be the final film in a decade of behind-the-scenes turmoil – court cases, dwindling audiences, changes in financiers and distributors, a "notorious" new love. Those years were now drawing to a close: Woody was married to Soon-Yi, settled and happy again, even if there were many people unable to regard him or his work in quite the same light.

I do think the work shows his awareness of this shift in attitude. Following *Bullets Over Broadway* and *Deconstructing Harry*, this was another film dealing with the behaviour of an artist and how that behaviour affects those around him. The morality of an artistic universe seems to fascinate the Woody Allen of this era: after the censures and fissures caused by his actions in his own private life, he signs off the decade with a film about the world's second best jazz guitarist.

And yet, this was a project that was one of his longest-gestating ideas. He had originally pitched it to United Artists right after *Take the Money and Run* as a script entitled *The Jazz Baby*, and it was not what the studio were expecting from their new comedy hit machine. Even though his new contract gave him remarkable freedom to do what he wanted, Woody didn't want to force through a project his backers weren't enthusiastic about, so he simply went away and wrote *Bananas* instead.

Nearly 30 years later, he finally was able to let *The Jazz Baby* grow up, changing the title to that of a George Gershwin tune he'd actually used on the *Manhattan* soundtrack (but, curiously, would not reuse in this new film). Woody returns to the mockumentary format he had employed in *Husbands and Wives*, *Zelig* and *Take the Money and Run*, enlisting a number of jazz aficionados – including himself – as "talking heads", or maybe that should be "nodding" heads.

Between them, they relate the stories they'd heard of Emmet Ray, creating a gentle parody of the way so much jazz mythology has sprung up. The eminent sleevenote writer and jazz author Nat Hentoff is one such contributor, as well as *Bullets Over Broadway* co-writer Douglas McGrath. Other experts are simply made up, such as Daniel Okrent's character AJ Pickman, the author of *Swing Guitars: American Perspective Series*.

The picture they paint is of Emmet Ray (Sean Penn), the self-confessed "best guitarist in the world – apart from this gypsy in France …". Emmet is haunted by the eminence of Django Reinhardt (a real-life jazz legend whose music Woody will use extensively again in *Midnight in Paris*) and the film makes continuous comic currency out of Emmet's "pathological phobia" of Django. I wonder if there isn't a self-referential element here, of Woody and his inability – in his own eyes – to ever match Ingmar Bergman or Fellini? Probably only in so much as it's common for many artists to be paralyzed by what greatness has come before them. I'm not sure

Right Sean Penn shows
Woody his air jazz guitar on
the set of *Sweet and Lowdown*.

Right Right Samantha Morton's performance as deaf-mute Hattie earned her an Oscar nomination.

Below Sean Penn's Emmet Ray aims for the stars to brighten up his set.

Woody himself ever has been, except maybe in his vain attempts at perfection in making *September*.

Unusually for a Woody Allen artist, Emmet Ray, despite his hang-ups about Django, is not in crisis. Unlike his other creations Harry Block, David Shayne, Gil Pender or Isaac Davis, Emmet simply flows with beautiful music and enjoys considerable acclaim and success, as much as is possible in Depression-hit Chicago.

Emmet is undone by his own flaws – drinking, petty thieving, bad accounting, womanizing and self-loathing, all of which is quite brilliantly played by Sean Penn. He received an Oscar nomination for the role and spent months learning the fingering to numbers such as the film's key refrain 'I'll See You in My Dreams'. Not that he played the actual recordings – that was left to West Coast virtuoso Howard Alden, whose sublime repertoire of plucks and slides does Django, and Emmet, proud.

But the glory of Penn's performance is not just in the physicality of the playing or the walk or the voice (all excellent for sure), but in the way he achieves a look of spiritual grace and serenity while in the act of playing.

Twice in this beautifully constructed work, Emmet will shatter his own dreams – once farcically, then tragically, which neatly flips round Karl Marx's famous dictum about how history repeats itself. In the first instance, Emmet's grand idea to enter the stage sitting in a specially built crescent moon becomes a painful comic sequence in which he falls off it and then burns it. Later, he will smash his own guitar in frustration at his own mistakes in love and his inability to reach the heavenly firmament he hears in Django's music.

All the while, Emmet declares, "I gotta be free, I'm an artist." It's his excuse to not let himself fall in love with Samantha Morton's mute Hattie, whose own moon face is one of the most extraordinary things in all Woody Allen's work. Originally told to study Harpo Marx by Allen, she captures that essence but creates something more like one of the silent screen girls who accompanied Chaplin or Keaton. Her silence means that, rather than being a physical partner in the choreography of the comedy, she becomes a foil to Emmet's egotistical garrulousness.

Hattie, the comic silent screen heroine, will be contrasted with the voracious screen goddess embodied by Uma Thurman playing socialite Blanche, sashaying and glowering like Marlene Dietrich. It puts Emmet in the classic Woody Allen on-screen dilemma/fantasy of being torn between two very different but beautiful women.

Emmet's quest for pure artistry ultimately undoes him and he disappears into myth, leaving only a couple of RCA Victor recordings behind. His fate is to become a footnote, an attendant lord rather than Prince Hamlet, to quote one of Woody's key poems (TS Eliot's Prufrock crops up in *Love and Death*, *Celebrity* and *Midnight in Paris*).

Sweet and Lowdown is often overlooked by people making lists of the great Woody works. But it is an absolutely gorgeous piece, handsomely designed – as all of his nine period films are – by Santo Loquasto, who gives it the hue of nostalgia. It was shot by China's Zhao Fei, most famous for *Raise the Red Lantern* and a man who didn't speak a word of English. He was now bathing America in chinoiserie (such as the red lanterns in the jazz clubs and a wonderful Chinese outfit for Thurman's Blanche) and leaving a warm, sensual glow.

The film can be enjoyed for its many obvious delights, but it can also be seen as Woody Allen once more working through his enduring struggle to square his artistic life and his worship of great artists with the prosaic duties of a human being trying to keep together a consummately professional career and a workable personal life.

Woody Allen Film by Film

The 2000s

Despite box office wobbles,
Woody Allen has no trouble attracting
the freshest, most outstanding acting
talent to tell his unique filmed stories.
He embarks on a surprising European
odyssey that will re-invigorate
his creativity and delight a new
generation of fans.

Left Woody Allen pictured at his
production company office in New
York City, 12 December 2001.

Small Time Crooks (2000)

Ray Winkler attempts to rob a bank by tunnelling in from the shop next door, where his wife Frenchy has set up a business baking cookies as a front. While the robbery fails haplessly, the cookies make them a fortune – but a life of sudden wealth drives the couple apart.

Having reached an entirely new generation and audience with his excellent voice work as a neurotic insect in the animated hit *Antz* (1998), Woody Allen kicked off the new century by sealing an unlikely new deal with the cartoon's producers DreamWorks.

The three-picture contract was strictly for comedies but still allowed Allen his customary creative freedom. He responded to the new circumstances by writing three films at the same time, all based on ideas that had been lying in his famous drawer for some while. "I thought I ought to start making some of these ideas because I'm getting older and who knows what could happen to me? I don't want to have them lying around in my drawer as unrealized, unattempted great comic ideas that I never got into."

Small Time Crooks is, thus, his purest comedy in ages, free of any of the philosophical concerns or tragic elements that had so deepened his work over the previous 25 years. Yet it is far from a return to the joke-filled zaniness of the "early, funny" films and indeed marks a period in which he would rely on old-fashioned charm to comfort older audiences – on whom, presumably, the new generation of gross-out comedies and super-hero franchises were lost.

Perhaps it is most similar to *Broadway Danny Rose*, with Allen again playing a working-class character, though it doesn't have half that film's polish or wit. *Small Time Crooks* has a nice idea – critics have seen parallels in a 1942 comedy *Larceny Inc.* and the 1958 Italian caper *Big Deal on Madonna Street* (*Il Soliti Ignoti*), starring Marcello Mastroianni – but it does seem off the pace and behind the beat.

For the first time, the 64-year-old Woody is beginning to look tired in the comic lead, particularly with the physical comedy. Nor

They took a bite out of crime.

WOODY ALLEN
TONY DARROW
HUGH GRANT
GEORGE GRIZZARD
JON LOVITZ
ELAINE MAY
MICHAEL RAPAPORT
ELAINE STRITCH
TRACEY ULLMAN

does he give himself many funny lines. Woody the writer may have created Ray Winkler, but I'm not sure that Woody the actor fully got the character, and the film might have benefited from another actor playing the lead – or, at least, an actor without such a strong screen comedy persona.

Instead, Tracey Ullman, Hugh Grant and Elaine May are the film's chief attractions. For all Frenchy's bluster, Ullman brings a real softness to the part, especially in the middle section when she gets a whiff of elegance and sophistication and a hint of what she thinks will be a better class of life.

Her pride at learning all the "A" words in the dictionary is deliciously played: "I was agog, and I can asseverate the pianist deserves accolades." We also feel for her when her cookie empire crumbles, and it's to her credit we feel for her emotionally and not in the least financially.

Grant, meanwhile, is excellent as the caddish art dealer who sees Frenchy as an opportunity. He does the part very well and wrings comedy out of the lines while still maintaining his own characteristic delivery.

Special mention must go to the legendary Elaine May, finally making an appearance for Woody Allen, having been asked by the director to appear in his very first film, *Take the Money and Run*. (In that film, he also played a hapless robber, Virgil Starkwell.)

The part of Frenchy's daft sister is not exactly flattering, but May plays it beautifully and she has a definite chemistry with Allen's Ray in the later part of the film, when her character develops more confidence: "The man said I reminded him of his wife, who's dead. I assume he meant when she was alive …"

This was to be Woody's last film with Sweetland Films and producer Jean Doumanian. The two longtime friends became involved in a costly lawsuit, with Allen suing for fraud. Could this explain the plot twist in which Frenchy is defrauded by accountants and bankrupted?

Whatever the elements from real life that went into the fiction of *Small Time Crooks*, it isn't a film out of the top drawer. It has a certain visual grace (thanks to Chinese cinematographer Zhao Fei) but a comic ambition that it can't always match. The themes of class and the illusion of getting rich quick are ideas explored only cursorily, characters are left dangling and there's a lack of warmth. Ultimately, this is an unusually inconsequential film, and it feels as baggy as some of Ray's jackets look.

The Curse of the Jade Scorpion (2001)

New York insurance investigator CW Briggs is hypnotized
by a stage magician and used to commit a series of high society
jewel robberies – crimes that he is then sent to solve.

At the mid-point of his three-picture deal with DreamWorks,
Woody Allen went through a bitter court battle with his old friend
and recent producer Jean Doumanian and her partner Jacqui Safra.
Nothing, though, could put Woody off his yearly routine – his sister
Letty Aaronson simply stepped up as producer.

Maybe it was just a steep budgetary learning curve, or maybe
DreamWorks were intent on buying their way to securing a hit with
their comedy hero, but *The Curse of the Jade Scorpion* came in as the most
expensive Woody Allen film ever made, with a budget of $26 million.

Not content with being a record-breaker at the top end, the film
also broke new ground at the bottom of the scale: "I feel that maybe –
and there are many candidates for this – but it may be the worst film
I've made," said Woody after it flopped miserably.

Is he right? Woody's key criticism was that he cast himself in the
lead (he did ask Tom Hanks and Jack Nicholson first). He had begun
to look a bit creaky in certain roles in the 1990s, and now, at 65, he was
certainly looking too old and too small to be a leading man, especially in
a role that riffed on Hollywood icons such as Humphrey Bogart, Cary
Grant, Fred MacMurray, Alan Ladd or even Edward G Robinson.

Of course, Woody had already compared himself unfavourably to
Bogie to great comic effect in *Play It Again, Sam*, but this was a different
blend, an attempt to mix screwball comedy and film noir. I'm sure
Woody understands the two genres intimately and intelligently, but he
can't seem to get the balance right here. A film with himself as the star
will always tempt the audience to look for laughs – and if the laughs aren't
there, well, it's not much of mystery or suspense thriller in its own right.

Set in 1940 – a title card tells us this with rare precision – the film
indulges both its production designer and cinematographer. Santo

Loquasto's sets are fabulous, and cinematographer Zhao Fei, who
spoke no English, seems to have an intuitive feel for the atmosphere.
(It's a mystery, however, that of all Woody's films, this homage to film
noir is shot in colour, sumptuous as those hues may be.)

Woody's dialogue has the right feel too, trading insults with
Helen Hunt's Miss Fitzgerald in the office ("Germs can't live in your
bloodstream, it's too cold"). He also creates an unlikely sexual heat
with Charlize Theron's Laura Kensington (a bombshell concoction
part Lauren Bacall, part Veronica Lake) in the bedroom. It's just a pity
his acting can't pull off such lines as "What you need is a roll in the
hay" or "How about I slap you around a little bit?" Diane Keaton may
have bought it in *Play It Again, Sam*, 30 years earlier, but nobody does
now. "Don't call me toots," says Hunt, practically sneering.

Woody's music choices are still very much up to scratch, though.
The marvellous Duke Ellington tune 'Sophisticated Lady' is well
suited to a femme fatale's sashay, and the dixieland swing of Wilbur
de Paris's 'In a Persian Market' is the perfect accompaniment to the
magician's exotic trigger words "Constantinople" and "Madagascar".

Maybe Woody was too close to the source material, too respectful of
it, to spoof its conventions. Comedy audiences of the new millennium
had been through the *Naked Gun* silliness of Jim Abrahams and the
Zucker brothers and they were used to the zany sketch films of Will
Ferrell and Ben Stiller; Woody's latest simply didn't have its timing
right, on screen or off it. For the first time, he looks out of sync.

The Curse of the Jade Scorpion opened in the late summer of 2001,
its head resolutely buried in the sands of time. Only a couple of weeks
later, global events would converge on New York City and shake its
certainties and confidence to the ground.

Left Woody still gets the ladies: office girl Elizabeth Berkley agrees to an unlikely date with insurance investigator CW Briggs.

Below Charlize Theron radiates "screen heat" in her second role for Woody Allen.

Sounds from a Town I Love (2001)

A response to the shock of 9/11, this short film was commissioned as part of a fundraising Concert for New York City held just six weeks after the attacks on the Twin Towers.

Although little more than three minutes in length, *Sounds from a Town I Love* is Woody Allen's wake-up call.

It features a host of New Yorkers on the streets, all on their cell phones – I'm not sure anyone had even used such a modern device on screen in a Woody feature film – and we overhear single snatches of their conversations.

As such, it's a collection of one-liners about the city, Woody going back to the sort of writing that began it all for him. For instance, an old Jewish lady says: "It was a themed Bar Mitzvah: *Deep Throat*."

Elsewhere, a smart woman is stressing about her white poodle named Binky who has "escaped from alcohol rehab". A tubby man crosses the street, saying: "I love this town – it's the only place you can be paranoid and right so often." A young woman walks past unflustered as she says: "So that's $4 million, and it's a one bedroom?"

There are quick turns from Woody alumni such as Hazelle Goodman from *Deconstructing Harry* and Bebe Neuwirth from *Celebrity*. His *Bullets Over Broadway* co-writer Douglas McGrath loiters on one corner, blithely chatting away: "We were at Balthazar last night and on the next table were Brad Pitt, Julia Roberts, Tony Blair, Tiger Woods, the President and Osama Bin Laden – I'm telling you, it's the in place to be right now."

And suddenly, there's Tony Roberts, Woody's old sparring partner, sitting on a park bench, telling someone on the other end: "You can't just pick up your business and move out of New York. No, you can't. You're the head of the Port Authority."

These little quips cumulate to encapsulate city life in all its modern absurdity, showing up New Yorkers' resilient strengths and comic flaws. An old man is describing his mugging on the way back from the opera: "They took my gas mask, my flashlight, all my Cipro …" Even the neuroses of dating in the city make a return, as a young woman breathes excitedly to her interlocutor: "We're so wrong for each other, but that's not the only attraction …"

My personal favourite is the man gossiping: "He did Don King's hair, he did Donald Trump's hair too – then they caught him and put him back in Bellevue." Classic New York, classic Woody.

Sounds from a Town I Love also showed on the bill with a short by Martin Scorsese, only the second time these two iconic yet totally different New York filmmakers had shared billing.

If that was a surprise, Woody then made a personal appearance – his first ever – at the 2002 Oscars ceremony. He introduced a tribute montage to New York, compiled by his friend Nora Ephron, with a short bit of on-stage stand-up, his first such routine for nearly 30 years. Hollywood received his entry with a standing ovation. "Thank you," he stammers, shooting a nervous look off-stage. "That makes up for the strip search."

He was clearly determined to show his enduring love for New York and to appeal for filmmakers to keep coming to the city. But he was also keen to show he was vital and funny as ever and still making films.

In the speech, he even told the assembled Hollywood grandees that he was about to start shooting his new picture: "It's a romantic movie, about a foot fetishist, this guy who falls in love with a Harvard professor and she's absolutely beautiful and she's brilliant and, tsch, she's written this paper on existential philosophy and, uh, he becomes sexually aroused by her foot notes."

If only he had made that one …

Right After years of no-shows, Woody makes a surprise appearance at the 74th Academy Awards, hosted at the Kodak Theater, Los Angeles.

Hollywood Ending (2002)

In this light comedy, Woody Allen plays Val Waxman, an Oscar-winning film director fallen on hard times. When his ex-wife suddenly hires him for a studio picture, he is struck by blindness but carries on as if nothing were hampering his artistic vision.

Although it opened the Cannes Film Festival, the film was Woody Allen's first not to receive a cinema opening in the UK. It went – the insult is too much to bear – straight to DVD.

Let's be honest. It's not a great film. It bears a likeable resemblance to good Woody Allen movies, but it lacks pace and laughs and Woody himself isn't very good in it. He looks old and tired and the sight of him fondling a busty starlet such as Tiffani Thiessen is unpleasant.

Still, you'll always find someone who'll praise a Woody Allen film or insist that it is, to use that dreaded critical term, "a return to form". Oddly, this is one that Woody himself thinks was pretty good, as he told Eric Lax in 2005:

> The biggest personal shock to me of all the movies I've done is that *Hollywood Ending* is not thought of as a first-rate, extraordinary comedy. I was stunned that it met with any resistance at all. I thought it was a very, very funny idea and I executed it absolutely fine. I don't think many people would, but I would put it toward the top of my comedies.

Many critics, including myself, reluctantly and with heavy heart, disagreed. For the *Washington Post*, Stephen Hunter wrote: "It is minor Woody Allen from that saddest of all possible worlds: the one where there may be no more major Woody Allen left. It feels old, tired and given-up-on, maybe three drafts shy of minimal production level."

Perhaps it didn't help that Woody fired his cameraman Haskell Wexler after two weeks. "I didn't get along with him, he was so fanatic and never stopped bothering me to make shots," Woody later explained. In one self-referential gag in the finished film, the character Val demands a foreign cinematographer because "they bring a unique texture". In real life, Wexler was replaced by Wedigo von Schultzendorff.

Curiously, at 112 minutes, this is one of Woody's longest films and one where a deal of tightening might have helped. It's interesting to note this was the first film Woody made without his regular editor Susan "Sandy" Morse, who had pieced together all his films since *Manhattan*. Her absence may explain why there are just too many scenes which ramble without gags – and in today's cinema, that is commercially unviable. It's not as if the leaden scenes are thickening the plot or ratcheting up tension, either. Driftwood moments such as this are most unusual in his films.

It's a pity because his chemistry with Téa Leoni (playing his studio exec ex-wife) is very good. Some of their repartee fizzes, although there are lengthy gaps between any giggles.

Sure the idea about a blind filmmaker is strong, but it makes this essentially a one-joke movie, albeit a decent joke. However, it takes at least 45 minutes even for that central joke to be made. And, given the possibilities for jokes about the lack of artistic vision in Hollywood movies, Woody doesn't really run very far with it, too often resorting to easy slapstick, such as bumping into the furniture.

Of course there are some sharp observations about the film business, relationships ("You were cheating on me not just behind my back but under my nose, that's twice a day"), life in LA ("You hated travelling by car, I hated travelling by mud slide"), some decent one-liners ("I would kill for this job, only the people I want to kill are the

people offering me the job"), as well as one expertly well-timed and
hilarious pratfall gag of which Buster Keaton would have been proud.

But I got a sinking feeling watching *Hollywood Ending*, the last
of his three-picture deal with DreamWorks and the final one in the
run following *Small Time Crooks* and *The Curse of the Jade Scorpion*.
He was panting, crawling exhausted over the finish line and the
cast (George Hamilton, Tiffani Thiessen, Debra Messing) had a
distinctly "TV star" feel, as if even his legendary pulling power was
deserting him.

Worse, Allen really did seem disconnected here, as if he were
filming in a vacuum and had failed to take a look around at the rest
of the world. It seemed too that he was badly in need of a refresher
in the art of comedy.

Elvis Mitchell wrote in the *New York Times*: "Once the energy
from the jokes dies down, we're left with a project so stale you feel
like opening a window to let some air in."

Anything Else (2003)

Comedy writer Jerry Falk spends days chatting with his new mentor
Dave Dobell, who gives him advice on his neurotic actress girlfriend,
his slimy manager and how to survive the forthcoming urban apocalypse.

I'm going to start by being honest: I think *Anything Else* is the worst
film Woody Allen ever made.

It shouldn't be, because it's got all the usual ingredients. Yet there's a
sense here – one that has been coming over the last couple of pictures –
of ghostly retread, of a filmmaker going through the motions.

It's as if the film were directed by the Annie Hall who detaches
herself to watch from the end of the bed as she and Alvy make love.
"Now that's what I call removed," says Alvy.

Desperate for a hit from their investment, DreamWorks may well
have encouraged Woody to go back to the rom-com template that
had made him so groundbreaking, to retool his take on it for a new
generation who, maybe without even knowing it, were still getting
Annie Hall hand-me-downs at the multiplexes.

Cast in the lead role of comedian Jerry Falk (is anybody under the
age of 30 still called Jerry?) was Jason Biggs. A limited but amiable actor,
he had a large following through the successful but crass sex comedy
franchise *American Pie*, so this should have been a smart commercial
move. The film also echoes the style of *Annie Hall* as Biggs frequently
addresses the audience directly, and it opens with a joke.

That joke is told by David Dobell, a strange and unlikeable older
man played by Woody Allen himself, who has set himself up as Jerry's
mentor. The gag is about a boxer getting badly beaten in the ring.
His mother turns to a priest at ringside and asks him to pray for her
son. "I'll pray for him," says the priest. "But if he could punch, it
would help …"

As Dobell says: "There's more insight in that one joke into what
I call the Giant So What than in entire books of philosophy." And we
think, for a delicious moment, that we might be back on classic Allen

ground, discussing the absurdity of life and relationships through the
prism of humour and philosophy.

Yet it never works out like that. Even as we flash back to Christina
Ricci's Amanda lolling around in her knickers and vest, it evokes
Annie Hall yet never achieves the pace and dexterity – or the sexiness
– of its illustrious predecessor. Some of the writing is droll as ever:
"I couldn't decide between giving you Sartre or O'Neill – whose
nihilistic pessimism would make you happiest?" But even with Woody
delivering his own material, it feels limp and never finds a heart. We
simply don't care about any of these people.

"The Pentagon should use her hormones for chemical warfare,"
says Dobell of Amanda. It's a great line, but most of the time he's
so uninspiring you wonder why Jerry is spending any time in his
company. Woody may be many things, but I've a feeling mentor is
not one of his strong suits – and it shows in this performance. What's
more, like any decent comedian, he's not great at giving someone else
better – or, in this case, any – gags.

To keep the *Annie Hall* parallels going, there's even a cocaine skit.
In *Annie Hall*, Alvy skewers the entire coke culture with a sneeze, a joke
that's over in a second but has lasted decades. In *Anything Else*, the coke-
taking palaver goes on for three minutes and has no punchline at all.

There are scenes with people talking out of shot in a bathroom, there's
pill popping, observational long shots from across the street, analysts, trips
to the art house cinema, Central Park, Billie Holiday on the soundtrack,
the paranoia of anti-Semitism, even the split screens – it's all there again,
just like in 1977, but it just doesn't feel authentic or fresh this time.

So, for me, *Anything Else* is the worst effort because it makes the
least effort, and not even Lady Day can save it.

Above Nice ride: Woody Allen and
Jason Biggs play comic mentor
and disciple in *Anything Else*.

Right Woody doffs his cap during
the shoot of tragicomedy *Melinda
and Melinda*, New York.

Below A Day at the Races:
Will Ferrell, Radha Mitchell
and Steve Carell at the track.

Melinda and Melinda (2005)

The story of a desperate woman arriving at a dinner party splits into two divergent but contemporaneous plots: one a comedy, the other a tragedy. The genres and storylines intertwine to create a maze of neurotic New Yorkers who can't work out if they're happy or sad.

Mirroring the round table storytelling structure of *Broadway Danny Rose*, *Melinda and Melinda* has an ingenious device defining its frazzled toing and froing.

Four intellectuals are having dinner at a restaurant and the argument turns to whether life is intrinsically comic or tragic. It's one of the long-running Woody questions, although in *Annie Hall*, he famously stated through Alvy that life was divided into the "horrible and the miserable".

However, our diners here want to debate: which one of these literary bedfellows can better encapsulate the human condition?

One character, whose trade is writing comedies (played by Woody regular Wallace Shawn), suggests that "human aspirations are so ludicrous and irrational that, in the end, all you can do is laugh". As an experiment, it is suggested, they take a simple starting point for a story – an unstable, near-suicidal woman arrives uninvited to a dinner party – and tell it both ways.

Allen had mixed the two previously in *Crimes and Misdemeanors*, but here he is being more playful and experimental and giving one (or is it two?) of his best-ever female roles to Australian actress Radha Mitchell, playing both Melindas.

The role was originally intended for Winona Ryder, but off-screen issues (the actor had been caught and tried for shoplifting) meant that the picture could not get insurance, or "bonding", with her as star. Woody must have been having a mischievous moment because he also wanted to cast Robert Downey Jr, another actor who was also at a much-publicized crisis in his personal life and undergoing some rehab. Again, the insurance men would not have it.

But it's still a pretty cool cast, with indie style icon Chloë Sevigny and black British actor Chiwitel Ejiofor (Allen's first major black character), as well as star comedian Will Ferrell, shortly after *Anchorman* made him a Hollywood giant, turning in a very likeable performance as the Woody surrogate, Hobie. Ferrell's Hobie is a struggling actor whose big idea for every role is to play it with a limp.

It's a remarkably youthful picture, as if Woody had decided to show the cast of popular sitcoms such as *Friends* and *Seinfeld* how the master could still capture the zeitgeist of New York relationships, just as he had first nailed them back in the 1970s.

To a certain extent, Woody does this successfully, helped by that strong and good-looking cast. (Ferrell's comic stablemate Steve Carell even shows up, well before his career had reached stardom.)

The actresses in particular were honoured to become part of the Woody Allen lineage.

Chloë Sevigny recalls she had been contacted and met with him a few times about appearing in his pictures. "Meeting is not really the right word. It's very brief. He shakes your hand, says it's nice to meet you and you go away. After you've done this a couple of times, you start to think it'll never happen, so you forget about it.

"Then the phone rang one day and this voice said: 'Hello, this is Woody Allen, would you like a part in my next movie?' I mean, you just say Yes. You don't check your schedule, nothing, you don't ask questions, you just blurt out Yes. And the next time he sees you is first day of shooting, on set, in costume. As processes go, it's pretty unique."

Her co-star Amanda Peet was equally in awe of working with a hero. "When I feel depressed or worse, I put on *Hannah and Her*

Sisters and it soothes my brain," she says. Curiously, the summer prior to filming, Peet heard she'd got the part while she was shooting the comedy *Something's Gotta Give*, where she found herself playing opposite Diane Keaton, "which was nerve-wracking enough".

"I made a complete jackass of myself and found myself blurting out lines from *Annie Hall* and *Manhattan*. It must have been super annoying, but Diane was so lovely and patient about it and she was thrilled for me when I told her I'd got a part in Woody's next movie. But all she had as advice was a warning: 'Don't quote him back to him, and turn up on time'."

For Radha Mitchell, the task was even more daunting. "If you think of all the great women who've acted in his films before you, well you'd just freeze on set. I had to block it out, but I confess that in the build-up I held my own personal Woody Allen festival in my flat. I watched maybe 12 or 15 films back to back. I have no idea if it was helpful or not, but my God did he make some amazing movies."

After being cast, the next time she had contact with him was on the first day of shooting, on set. He asked her to start with a long monologue. "It's so crazy. Not for him, I'm sure, but for an actress … I kept thinking I was going to get fired because all he'd say was Action and Cut. That was it. Then he'd go home early for a bath and say: 'Thanks that was great, see you tomorrow.'

"Then I realized we were all in the same situation. I mean the others didn't even have a copy of the script yet, didn't even know what their parts were, so I knew and it hit me, what making a Woody Allen movie is all about: anxiety, anticipation, uncertainty."

For her script, Radha differentiated her two Melindas, one in pink for the comic version, the other in yellow for the tragic Melinda. "I didn't even really know which was which, so in my head I decided that it's basically the same Melinda, one with faith in life, the other who's lost faith."

She also based each Melinda on a different Woody Allen woman – Judy Davis for the tragic, yellow Melinda and Mia Farrow in *The*

Right Amanda Peet runs lines
with her aspiring, limping actor
husband, Will Ferrell.

Left "I look like the wreck of the
Hesperus": Australian Rahda
Mitchell mines Melinda's self-esteem.

Purple Rose of Cairo for the comic, pink one. "It was a life-raft at the
start but eventually, you know, you just learn to trust the text. Doing
Woody is like doing Shakespeare, with this beautiful language nobody
really speaks in real life, but it gives you this mode to switch into, a
magic realm of reality that's slightly enhanced."

Melinda and Melinda premiered at the San Sebastian Film Festival
in northern Spain in September 2004 but was not released in the US
or UK until March 2005. Commercially, it wasn't hugely successful,
despite the new box office draw of Ferrell. Critically the reception was
lukewarm, with many critics merely reminded of earlier, better Allen
films addressing similar themes.

Under the headline "How Woody Became a Hack", Wesley
Morris wrote in the *Boston Globe*: "Allen has grown tired of complex
characters. He appears to be making movies because that's what he's
always done, but the love and the ideas and the zip are essentially gone."
Florence Colombani, who wrote about Allen for the series *Masters of
Cinema*, describes *Melinda and Melinda* as the last of a series of "lazy,
misanthropic" films and sees in the title character a recurrence of
Charlotte Rampling's Dorrie from *Stardust Memories*.

I think such a view is unfair. *Melinda and Melinda* attempts a very
skilful balancing act. It is often funny, thanks to Ferrell's deliciously
long-limbed performance, bringing a newer, taller perspective to
classic Woody-style clowning. Sevigny and Ejiofor are very attractive
and Mitchell herself is impressive, twice over, although the roles failed
to give her the career boost one might have expected.

Shot by Vilmos Zsigmond, the film plays out in a beautiful,
New York, early-summer light that's very seductive and suitably

playful. And while there are some familiar jazz standards to enjoy,
the tragic angle, as it often does, ushers in some striking classical
pieces, such as the strings of Bartók. As critic Roger Ebert pointed
out: "If Woody had never made a previous film and if each new one
was his Sundance debut, it would get a much better reception."

It seems to me that *Melinda and Melinda* signals a recovering
of poise and a re-oiling of the creative process, as the two sides of
Woody Allen battle for supremacy to achieve an uneasy balance.
The stories contained therein – both about betrayal, infidelity and
the fickleness of the heart – are neither his funniest nor his most
impactful in terms of sadness and drama, but it is one of the
works that best plays out the creative process, both of writing
and film making.

You get a sense of characters as creations that can be altered,
played with, dropped into situations at their creator's whim. But
if this particular creator is a God, he isn't a cruel one – he cares for
these characters and, for all their vanities and foibles, he likes them,
even loves them and feels pity for them.

The philosophy here is: these creations don't need the mercy
of an implacable, cruel God, they're quite capable of screwing things
up for themselves.

Significantly, this was to prove a turning point. Having shot
every – or most of every – film in Manhattan since 1977, *Melinda and
Melinda* was to become the last of his films shot there until 2009's
Whatever Works. And after toying here with the fine, blurred line
between comedy and tragedy, it's surely interesting that for his next
film Woody Allen will come down firmly on one side of the net.

Match Point (2005)

Still one of Woody Allen's more divisive films, it is also his most erotic and thrilling picture. *Match Point* cemented Scarlett Johansson's star status in a murder mystery that is in many senses atypical of Allen's work: set in London, with few jokes, rising tension and Caruso on the soundtrack rather than the usual jazz.

Shot in London during the drab summer of 2004, *Match Point* ushered in an itinerant era in Woody Allen's work, one that would lead to three more pictures shot in London, as well as one each in Spain, Rome, Paris and the south of France.

Prior to *Match Point*, Allen had rarely left New York to make his films since the Los Angeles episode of *Annie Hall* or the Venice and Paris scenes in *Everyone Says I Love You*. However, after a period of declining commercial success for his films set in New York, Allen was forced to look further afield for financing. The situation was, frankly, precarious. Critical acclaim and box office returns for works such as *Melinda and Melinda* and *Anything Else* were thinning and audiences and critics, even ardent fans, sensed a certain creative impasse had been reached. There was a feeling that Allen's best days were behind him as he reached his 70s.

Having originally written *Match Point* as a murder mystery that took place among the wealthy Hamptons "set", Allen and his team found it hard to raise money. At the same time, production and tax breaks had picked up in the UK, with government-backed bodies such as the UK Film Council and Film London making it a favourable and fertile ground for visiting filmmakers.

When it was announced that Allen would be shooting in London, huge excitement was injected into the London scene, particularly as the BBC had boarded as co-producers. Practically every actor in town wanted to be a part of it and film fans speculated (and expected) that he would, of course, be making a *Manhattan* or an *Annie Hall* for London, the sort of smartly sophisticated comic love letter to the city they had long craved.

In truth, that was never Woody's desire; he simply wasn't making those kinds of pictures any more – and hadn't for ages. The culturally transposed script *Match Point* wasn't ever going to result in that kind of film. This dark story, referencing Dostoevsky, was one of Woody's most sombre and philosophical since *Crimes and Misdemeanors*. It deals with fate and luck, looking at how life and morality turn on matters of chance, such as that of a dead net cord in a tennis match, where the ball hits the top of the net and could fall either side.

The opening quotation is key:

The man who said, "I'd rather be lucky than good" saw deeply into life. People are afraid to face how great a part of life is dependent on luck. There are moments in a match when the ball hits the top of the net, and for a split second, it can either go forward or fall back. With a little luck, it goes forward, and you win. Or maybe it doesn't, and you lose.

It is spoken, in voice-over, by Chris, a tennis professional (Jonathan Rhys Meyers), who marries into a wealthy family but has a passionate affair with Nola Rice, an aspiring American actress (Scarlett Johansson). When Nola gets pregnant, Chris murders her to keep her quiet – an

Right Scarlett Johansson plays Nola Rice in the midst of her ill-fated love match with Jonathan Rhys Meyers, playing tennis pro Chris.

"The man who said, 'I'd rather be lucky than good' saw deeply into life."

Jonathan Rhys Meyers as *Chris Wilton*

innocent elderly neighbour is also killed – and he gets away with it, continuing his sham marriage for the sake of easy wealth.

British actress Emily Mortimer was chosen to play Chloe, the prim, sweet-natured British girl who gets engaged to the tennis pro even while he cheats. She won the role partly thanks to an earlier appearance in *Lovely and Amazing*, directed by Nicole Holofcener, a filmmaker often dubbed "the Female Woody Allen". She recalls her thrill at getting cast but also her shock that she wasn't playing a typical Woody Allen part:

> I had never dreamed of appearing in a Woody Allen film. I thought of him as strictly New York and it wasn't going to be for an English actress. However, when I got my first part in an American indie movie, I thought I'd do it a bit "Woody Allen", a bit neurotic. It turns out that Woody saw it and it ended up being my only audition. He called me in, I met him, he shook my hand, looked me up and down, and said goodbye. Next time I saw him was on set. The problem was that I was playing a character untypical to his work. It wasn't a comedy, I wasn't an uptight New Yorker in a hat and cool flares and it was all a bit of shock.

What was her interaction with the director?

> Woody hardly says anything on set. You bring your interpretation of the character with you and he just does a couple of takes and suddenly it's three o'clock, he's shouting, "Cut" and everyone goes home for tea. How marvellous. It's very civilized, I suppose, but underneath you are convinced you've been rubbish, that he's hating your performance. It's rather clever, though, if it's a strategy at all, because it makes you determined to know all your lines so much more for the next day, to really work on your next scene overnight and be totally sure of what your character wants.

Match Point had its world premiere at the Cannes Film Festival in May 2005, shown out of competition because Allen insists he will not countenance his films "competing" against others.

Recalls Emily: "All I can remember is standing at the top of those red steps, Woody's arm around me, Scarlett on the other side, the photographers shouting up at us and him grinning like a moron and muttering his words of warning: 'Remember, none of this is real, it can all end tomorrow.'"

Match Point was warmly received at Cannes and became Allen's biggest box office hit in the United States and around the world. It thus marked the resurgence of his career, taking more than $100 million, outstripping *Hannah and Her Sisters* and *Annie Hall*.

The least receptive to it were British critics, who lamented what they felt was a tourist's eye view of London and stilted dialogue. On its later release in the UK, Philip French in the *Observer* wrote: "I have enjoyed almost all of Woody Allen's films. It therefore gives me no pleasure to say that I found *Match Point*, the first picture he has made in this country, extremely disappointing … The basic problem from the outset is that Allen, so much at home with the mores, pretensions and idioms of his native New York, is an ugly duckling out of water in England."

Allen had used so many sparkling London locations in the film that trade body Film London produced a pamphlet Movie Map guide to its various chic landmarks, including boutiques such as Paul & Joe in Notting Hill, restaurants such as Locanda Locatelli, the Royal Opera House, Queen's Tennis Club, and 30 St Mary's Axe, the distinctive skyscraper better known as the Gherkin.

Physical landmarks aside, *Match Point* is notable for being the sexiest Woody Allen movie. Kate Winslet was initially cast as Nola, but she needed to spend time with her young family and Allen was told that he already had enough British actors in the cast to fulfil any production deals. This freed him to cast the hottest actress in American cinema and, always one to fall for a muse, to discover for himself Scarlett Johansson's on-screen electricity. This led to him making scenes that, for Allen, are practically erotic, involving blindfolds, massage oils and an unforgettable wet tumble in the rain and long grass.

Scoop (2006)

Following a tip from beyond the grave, an American student journalist in London teams up with ageing stage magician Splendini to solve a murder mystery.

Considering his hard time with the press over the years – particularly after the headlines recording the controversy of his break-up with Mia Farrow and his new relationship with her adopted daughter Soon-Yi during the early 1990s – it is surprising that journalists and newspapers haven't featured more regularly in the work of Woody Allen.

Reporters have been briefly but witheringly satirized in *Stardust Memories* and *Annie Hall*, Lee in *Celebrity* has a freelance job as a profile writer, Diane Keaton's Mary in *Manhattan* reviews art, Lenny Weinribb in *Mighty Aphrodite* is a sports writer – and that's about it. And yet given Woody's nostalgic streak, and the fact that he got his early comic breaks filing jokes for columnists, newspaper settings would seem to offer ripe material for him.

That had been the case for some of the great films of the past, including films noirs. Yet the closest Allen himself came to such a setting was playing CW Briggs the insurance investigator in *The Curse of the Jade Scorpion*, the film where he tried to mix screwball with film noir. Now, in *Scoop* Scarlett Johansson's Sondra Plansky refers to Rosalind Russell (star of Howard Hawks's *His Girl Friday*) as her inspiration, while Woody as the Great Splendini has a throwaway gag about the greatest of all journalism films, *All the President's Men*, in which he identifies himself as the "little one" – part of a long-running series of in-jokes referring to the number of times he's tried to cast Dustin Hoffman in his films.

Scoop is the first Woody Allen film to be set around journalists – part of it was even filmed in the old offices of my own former newspaper, the *Observer* in London's Farringdon – although neither Woody nor Scarlett seems to have much idea what the craft entails.

The story mechanism begins when a deceased reporter Joe Strombel (Ian McShane) gets his last great scoop on the ferryboat piloted by the Grim Reaper. Through a magic trick during a Great Splendini show, he materializes to keen cub reporter Sondra and tips her off as to the identity of London's biggest serial killer since Jack the Ripper.

It's the starting point for a caper that should have been the London equivalent of *Manhattan Murder Mystery*, with Woody and Scarlett riffing sweetly while they investigate posing as father and daughter, thankfully removing the on-screen relationship of any creepy sexual element.

Of his four London films, *Scoop* feels like the biggest opportunity missed. Woody has done little research into the great tradition of Fleet Street, even if one early scene features some hacks drinking in a pub and telling stories about Joe, faintly echoing those storytelling comedians in the deli in *Broadway Danny Rose*. Sadly, the device is quickly dropped.

But with Woody actually appearing, this might have been a chance to play up the cultural differences with a fish-out-of-water comedy. There are frustratingly tantalizing hints throughout, as Splendini makes jokes about Jews while mixing among posh English folk in country estates ("I was born into the Hebrew persuasion but I converted to narcissism"). He also admires the gardening: "Who did the hedges? I must get their number because back home my topiary moose is starting to look shabby around the antlers."

I wish there had been lots more of this. He could have made one of those excellent, alienated outsider films made by directors exiled in London, such as Antonioni's *Blow-Up* or Joseph Losey's *The Servant*.

Instead we get weak gags about a fox hunt, the Tower and a particularly bad one about Trollope being a woman he once dated. There are also references to Indian restaurants, driving on the left and the image of Woody at the wheel of a Smart car, a funny shot that only reminded me of the far funnier one of him petrified in a car with Christopher Walken's Duane in *Annie Hall*.

"I was born in the Hebrew persuasion but I converted to narcissism."

Woody Allen as *the Great Splendini*

Below Spot the difference: Woody Allen as the Great Splendini in *Scoop*.

Scoop does have more breezy charms than its reputation as "his worst film ever" suggests. But this, his second film to be financed by BBC Films, was deemed so weak that it never received a cinema release in the UK – the second such ignominy to befall Woody after *Hollywood Ending*. Instead, the film premiered belatedly and without much fanfare on BBC television.

It's a pity, because Woody and Scarlett make a decent comic team, sparring with banter as he calls her "precious child" and "blessed offspring" and she snarls at him to "stop telling people I sprang from your loins."

It's clear she has good comic instincts and that Allen is besotted with her skills. However, their decision to keep Sondra unglamorous, even frumpy, in cardigans, round glasses and teeth braces seems slightly perverse, particularly when she's being wooed by the handsome and wealthy Hugh Jackman. We are treated to a brief hint of Scarlett's sexuality, which the director harnessed so joltingly in *Match Point*: in one scene, she wears a sporty red swimsuit while pretending to drown, but it's a rare shot of excitement in a film that badly needed more.

Interestingly, scenes of characters playing poker crop up here and in Woody's next two London films (*Cassandra's Dream* and *You Will Meet a Tall Dark Stranger*); I can't think of any other scenes in the rest of his entire filmography. It could be that Woody can't shake the memory of the bad time he had in London filming *Casino Royale* in the mid-1960s, when he had nothing to do but play cards all night with a series of visiting film stars.

What can we glean from this latest on-screen appearance by Woody Allen? He has retreated into mentor roles, yet doesn't appear adept at handing on advice or accrued wisdom. Indeed, you get the sense he rather wishes he could still play the love interest and get the girl, still play Cary Grant's Walter Burns to Scarlett's Hildy Johnson. Even the magic of film can't achieve that – and I think this director knows that not even the great Woody Allen can fool time itself.

Right Have I Got News for You: Woody Allen and Scarlett Johansson scan the British press, London 2006.

Cassandra's Dream (2007)

Two cockney brothers, Ian and Terry, ask their rich Uncle Howard
to clear their mounting debts. In repayment, he demands they
murder one of his business partners, leading to tragic repercussions.

For his third London film in a row, Woody Allen returned to the
foreboding and dread that characterized *Match Point*. This time,
however, there would be no Americans and no sightseeing tour.
Cassandra's Dream was as pure a tragedy as he had ever written, with
not a single joke on view.

Unfortunately, that doesn't mean people didn't laugh. *Cassandra's
Dream* attracted some of the worst critical reactions of Woody's career,
including a one-star review in the *Guardian*: "This feels like it was
knocked together by complete amateurs … and should probably be
deleted from the records."

Even veteran Woody admirer Philip French in the *Observer* wrote:
"*Cassandra's Dream* is a succession of ill-staged scenes… characters
look awkwardly at each other as they exchange ill-written dialogue full
of clunking exposition … A fine British cast is badly directed, woeful
line-readings are retained."

Yet when I saw the film premiere at the Venice Film Festival in
September 2007, it filled me with a real sense of dread. I felt my throat
tighten. Partly because I could also feel critics' pens being sharpened,
but also because this was a film so unlike Woody Allen, so laden with
doom and dark, scudding clouds, that I even wondered if the old
director was feeling all right?

Reader, he was fine. Mischievous as ever, in fact, when I met him,
Soon-Yi and his cast afterwards. He was delighted with his discovery
of Hayley Atwell (playing neurotic and dangerous actress Angela),
whose debut film this was and who has now gone on to be a big star in
Hollywood; Colin Farrell was surrounded by family and friends – "the
Dublin mafia" is how Woody introduced them to me.

I use personal anecdotes here because I felt alone at the time. I

was unsettled and disturbed by *Cassandra's Dream*, more than by
any Woody Allen film before, and felt that this was a strange, eerie
addition to his oeuvre. I also knew that the London audiences and
critics would be as disappointed by it as they had been by *Match Point*
and *Scoop* (which even went undistributed in UK cinemas). I felt
embarrassed by their ingratitude.

With these later Woody works, you have to let them percolate.
They're not *Annie Hall*, or *Bananas*, or *Crimes and Misdemeanors*,
but they are the work of an artist still trying new things as he nears
80 years old and consequently are harder to place in our constantly
evolving mental parlour game of rating our favourite (and least
favourite) Woody Allen films.

The grand themes of *Cassandra's Dream* may be ones he's visited
before – guilt, morality, murder, luck – but never quite so seriously,
or without the leavening of any humour. In *Match Point* the tennis
ball had hung tantalizingly on the net cord; in *Cassandra's Dream*,
as Farrell's Terry says, "we cross the line". But don't Shakespeare's
tragedies share similar structures and point out similarly destructive
flaws in human behaviour?

This film could certainly do with tightening up and a more
judicious pruning might weed out some repetitious dialogue, but
the sense of ineluctable fate is still ripe and dramatic. Despite their
completely different accents, Ewan McGregor, Farrell and Sally
Hawkins all deliver strong performances.

Given that Allen admits his vision of New York is a romanticized
one gleaned from the films of his youth, it is hardly surprising that
some of this film feels as if it's stolen from the kitchen sink dramas
of the 1960s, or at least from Mike Leigh. In fact, the roles of the

Above Woody prepares himself for the *Cassandra's Dream* press conference at the 2007 Toronto International Film Festival.

brothers' parents are played so broadly by Clare Higgins and John Benfield, it made me wonder if Woody had even spent time watching the grim BBC soap opera *EastEnders*.

Production designer Maria Djurkovic goes to town with garish floral wallpapers in the working-class flats and houses, contrasting it with the sleek airlessness of the modern hotel rooms where Uncle Howard (Tom Wilkinson) stays, or the smart Belgravia apartment of the murder victim Martin Burns (Phil Davis).

The mechanics of tragedy are carefully woven into the story. The film began life as a play written by Woody for a New York theatre a few years earlier, where perhaps its unities of place and plot would have been more obvious. "The order of things, it's out-of-kilter, I got to straighten it out," says the guilt-wracked Terry.

Crimes and Misdemeanors had, at an early stage, the working title of *Brothers*, and that particular family dynamic is explored even more closely here. Also under the lens is the notion of class and ambition, themes Allen clearly feels to be both inherent and essential in British stories.

Critics may have battered *Cassandra's Dream* (the name of the brothers' sailboat in the film), but perhaps it has now weathered the storm. The *New Yorker*'s Richard Brody was the first to try to right the ship, placing the film on his list of the decade's finest: "Few ageing directors so cogently and relentlessly depict the grimly destructive machinery of life."

Nor do they keep experimenting. The music is an original score by feted American composer Philip Glass, the first time Woody has worked with one since *Everything You Always Wanted to Know About Sex*. I found the dissonant strings and crescendos wholly effective. "It's still easier for me to use recordings," said Woody of his collaboration with Glass, "but then you don't get to work with a genius."

Vicky Cristina Barcelona (2008)

Woody's late-career European tour continues with a bright and breezy love postcard to Barcelona, free love and youthful misadventure with one of his most attractive casts in one of his sunniest films.

Although he had consistently expressed his approval of grey British skies and gentle temperatures, insisting they were very pleasant for shooting, Allen must have secretly been pining for the sunshine.

Having secured funding from Spanish sources such as Mediapro and the Catalan government, he set about filming in Barcelona with touristic relish. However, in a brief spoof diary he wrote for the *New York Times* during the shooting, Woody recalls: "Arrived in Barcelona. Accommodation's first class. Hotel has been promised half star next year, provided they install running water."

The story goes that when offered the chance to shoot in Spain, Woody actually had no script ready. He reached inside his trusty ideas drawer and found a love triangle story he'd written years before, to be set in San Francisco. In that spoof diary he notes: "Received offer to write and direct film in Barcelona. Must be cautious. Spain is sunny, and I freckle. Have no idea for Barcelona – unless story of two Hackensack Jews who start an embalming firm could be switched."

The character of Vicky (Rebecca Hall, doing a perfect though female version of the Woody Allen voice) is supposed to be in the city studying for a masters thesis on Catalan identity, although it is clear that neither she, nor Woody, has much clue about such matters. Still, it is just the sort of thing a young, wealthy American student would go and study for a summer. Any excuse.

Vicky's friend Cristina (Scarlett Johansson) is much looser, much freer, ruled by her heart and instincts. Going by the film's title, it's almost as if these two polar opposites together sum up the character of the city, which Woody and his Spanish cinematographer Javier Aguirresarobe (who would return for *Blue Jasmine*) capture with alluring sensuality and dappled romanticism.

And if it's all a bit "Gaudi and guitars", I think that's probably the idea. As Woody himself recalled:

I've been to Barcelona several times in my life, but I didn't have any vast knowledge of it. When I got over there, the art director took me to all these places. You get help from people. So everybody on the crew cooperates and tells you: "Oh, they would never talk like that," or "They would never eat in this restaurant if they're 25 or 30 years old, no, they'd go to this one." So gradually as you do it, you get to look like you know Barcelona, like with London, when in fact, you're faking.

Interestingly, Javier Bardem's artist offers to whisk Vicky and Cristina away on his private jet, and takes them to the beautiful town of Oviedo, in the north of Spain, where they spend a very entangled weekend. One tourist hot spot not included in the film is a statue of Woody Allen, erected there in 2003 – much to his mystification:

Why a statue of me? It's one of the great mysteries of Western civilization. I never did anything there, I never saved anybody's life and when they told me they were putting a statue of me there, I thought it was a joke. But it's a good

Right Penelope Cruz in her Oscar-winning role of temperamental artist and photographer Maria Elena.

"…you get to look like you know Barcelona…when in fact, you're faking."

Woody Allen

statue, it looks good, but it's completely undeserved. People
keep stealing the glasses from it, which is crazy because
they're welded to the statue. Guys come with blowtorches
at night and they take off the glasses – I've even been there
when I've had half my glasses missing.

Penelope Cruz arrives halfway through the movie – and, frankly,
steals it. Her performance as Maria Elena, the mentally unstable ex-wife
of Bardem's artist, earned her an Oscar for Best Supporting Actress.

Allen has said that Cruz heard he was embarking on a project
in Spain and contacted him, while she remembers it differently.
Already famous for her work with Spanish director Pedro
Almodovar in films such as *Volver*, she says that Woody cast her
immediately. Comparing the two directors, she says:

> Woody and Pedro write the best women parts. I don't know
> why, but maybe they have an appreciation of how neurotic
> we are sometimes. I'm lucky they think I'm the right actress
> for this – although I don't think I'm particularly neurotic
> myself, of course. But they seem to know us and love us, and
> the actresses they work with repay that because you feel safe
> with them, and they allow you to behave in the character.

Cruz recalls how she became the go-between for the two directors:

> They both admire each other and they would send messages
> back and forth through me – I was always the messenger –
> you tell him this and tell him that. It was mainly things like
> "Send them good wishes for the first day of the shoot", or
> when we opened in Cannes, Pedro texted me to tell Woody
> good luck, that kind of thing.

Was Almodovar envious that his longtime muse had gone to
another director?

> Oh no, Pedro is never jealous. But I know what you mean,
> but actually I was so pleased to see them get on so well, it was

Right Spanish practices: Woody
directs a love triangle of Javier
Bardem, Penelope Cruz and
Scarlett Johansson.

like when new family meet each other, you know?

Though Cruz enjoyed working with Allen, she did have some disappointment:

> Well, yes, I was really hoping he'd be in this movie. I wanted to act with Woody – that was always my dream and it still is. Even when I read the script I thought he might somewhere appear. Maybe one day that can happen and I can act with him in a movie. But if he didn't appear, we all wanted him to read the narrator part, the voice-over. I think we all assumed he would be reading it. It just sounded so much like him, you know. But, no, he didn't, but we only found this out at the premiere. I don't know why he didn't do it.

In fact, actor and well-known voice artist, the late Christopher Evan Welch provided the authorial voice in the film. Had Allen himself done the narration, I think it would have established some authorial control over these characters and given some ironic, knowing detachment to their behaviour, like an older head looking down on the fecklessness of youth.

Woody's familiar voice would have directed the tone of the piece towards the humorous side because, although it was generally taken to be a comedy, Allen himself never envisaged it that way. "I thought I was writing a straight love story," he said later. "It's gotten many more laughs than I anticipated."

Indeed, the film was nominated for a Golden Globe in the Best Comedy or Musical category, and *Vicky Cristina Barcelona* became one of Allen's most successful commercial hits and received mostly positive reviews from his supporters, earning comparisons to the French filmmaker Éric Rohmer.

Notable, too, is the soundtrack, which departs from Woody's signature jazz to feature a variety of Spanish guitar sounds, from indie to flamenco. The theme tune 'Barcelona', for example, is by the little-known local band Giulia y los Tellarini, but also featured are the international artists Paco de Lucia (on the beautiful track 'Entre Dos Aguas') and Juan Serrano. Says Allen:

> I knew I wanted Spanish music for *Vicky Cristina Barcelona*, but I didn't know much Spanish music. I nosed around and picked up a few stray items here and there, and by compiling the tunes of a few known players and composers with the tunes of relative unknowns, found myself with one of the most lovely scores in all of my films. It's an eclectic mix, to be sure, but mostly Spanish and reflecting the feeling of Spain – or certainly Barcelona as I've portrayed it.

Above Woody wears his signature sun hat to shoot a scene at Gaudí's Sagrada Familia.

Below Woody discusses a scene with
Penelope Cruz and Javier Bardem,
who later married in real life.

"Woody [and Pedro
Almodovar] write the
best women parts ... "

Penelope Cruz

Whatever Works (2009)

Grumpy old professor and veteran New Yorker Boris Yelnikoff gets a new lease of life when Melodie, a pretty young runaway from the South, turns up on his doorstep, eventually followed by her parents.

In the middle of a run of seven films made outside Manhattan, Woody Allen returned to his home territory for *Whatever Works*. An impending writers' strike meant he couldn't create new material, so to maintain his remarkable record of making one film a year Woody simply dusted off an old script he'd written in the 1970s. Then it had been intended as a play for the comic actor Zero Mostel, with whom he had appeared in the 1976 film *The Front*.

Allen cast Larry David, co-creator of the hit sitcom *Seinfeld* and then creator and star of his own show, *Curb Your Enthusiasm* – both TV programmes that owed large debts to the comic (and Jewish) sensibilities of 1970s Woody Allen.

Fans were understandably excited by the prospect of two comedy legends combining. David had, in fact, appeared in *Radio Days* (he's unrecognizable and practically invisible as the communist neighbour) and in "Oedipus Wrecks", Allen's contribution to *New York Stories*, he'd played the belligerent producer of the magic show during which Woody's mother vanishes.

Although David himself was concerned his acting range couldn't handle playing a feature-length character like Boris, Allen's casting instincts – led as ever by Juliet Taylor – were correct. David's Boris is one of the grouchiest creations in all Woody's work, second only to the bilious Harry Block, and a seemingly natural extension of the irascible "Larry" character from David's *Curb Your Enthusiasm*. Fans would wonder why Woody couldn't have played Boris himself, though.

There was also much to anticipate in seeing if absence had made the director's cinematic heart grow fonder for New York. Interestingly, the film was positioned as something for the hip indie crowd, as if a new voice was about to break downtown. It was made the opening-night film of the relatively new Tribeca Film Festival, on 22 April 2009.

Well, *Whatever Works* is OK. Or, as Larry might say in *Curb Your Enthusiasm*, "preety good, preety good". But honestly, not great. Woody still has an experimental streak: Boris directly addresses the audience through the camera, while other characters in the film can't see us and think Boris has gone crazy talking to himself. "They pay good money for tickets so some moron in Hollywood can buy a bigger pool" is his attitude and he assaults us with invective from the get-go, enumerating a not particularly sharp assassination of modern culture. "We're a failed species," he harangues. "They've had to install automatic toilets in public restrooms because people can't be trusted to flush a toilet. You have to take what little pleasure you can find in this chamber of horrors. I hate fruits and vegetables."

The trouble with Boris is that, as played by Larry David in his boxer shorts and dressing gown, there's nothing sympathetic about him at all. He calls everyone, including the impermeable Melodie (Evan Rachel Wood), "brainless inchworm", or "bedraggled microbe". Nor is he believable as a Professor of quantum mechanics, for which "he was almost nominated for a Nobel Prize".

And I think audiences of a new millennium were generally fed up of seeing a young girl throw herself at the feet of a much older man – even if there is the concession in this script that Boris initially resists her overtures. "What can I possibly offer you beside hypochondriasis, reclusive rages, morbid fixations and misanthropy?" he asks Melodie. She marries him anyway.

Apart from a few updated references to Darfur and President Obama, there is little here to suggest Woody has moved with the

Below Grumpy Old Men? Woody
Allen and Larry David work it
out on *Whatever Works*.

Right Woody directs Evan Rachel Wood and British actor Henry Cavill at a market in New York.

Below right Southern runaway Melodie falls for Boris despite the age gap and "the hypochondria and misanthropy".

Below Evan Rachel Wood and Patricia Clarkson at a waxwork museum – Donald Trump and Abraham Lincoln look on.

new century as a filmmaker or comedian. Melodie and her mother (Patricia Clarkson, summoned to appear again, after *Vicky Cristina Barcelona*) visit the wax museum in a scene containing jokes about Billy Graham and Ronald Reagan (just ask a parent). And I'm fairly sure the jokes about Southern rednecks are past their sell-by date too.

Even working with the brilliant cameraman Harris Savides (known for cool collaborations with David Fincher and Gus Van Sant) didn't bring much new to Woody's New York vision, which actually feels more touristy than usual. After all that European wandering, I was looking forward to Woody getting his Jewish humour back – but while the city has changed, Boris is still eating at Yona Schimmel's Knish shop. (I took my fiancée there shortly before I proposed and, oy, the indigestion with the nerves, not good …)

Look, this doesn't mean *Whatever Works* is lousy. Yes, it was far from a hit at the box office, but there are still some fine Woody moments. When Melodie's mother Marietta asks for a place fun to go in New York, Boris suggests: "How about the Holocaust Museum?" When a suitor turns up for Melodie, he politely compliments Boris: "She explained to me your theory about life being meaningless, sir." Replies Boris: "Well, don't let it spoil your evening …" And when one of his friends takes a shine to Marietta, Boris puzzles: "For me, I lose all erotic inclination if a woman is a member of the National Rifle Association."

Sadly, these moments are rare. And even if the familiar Allen themes about "luck playing a bigger part in your existence than you'll ever know" are hammered home, they don't feel as authentic as they once did. *Whatever Works* was a piece of philosophy that had helped Woody in the past to make the best of things despite the terrors of reality. Was it really still working for him?

You Will Meet a Tall Dark Stranger (2010)

A mother, Helena, and daughter, Sally, experience upheaval
in their marriages. As all parties seek affection elsewhere, they
discover the human heart is untrustworthy and true love an illusion.

Woody Allen was back in London for the fourth time, and locals could have been forgiven for thinking he might finally make an incontestable success of capturing the city's spirit on film the way he'd so often immortalized New York.

Lukewarm appreciation for his UK output had not dimmed the director's international reputation – financing came mainly from Spain's Mediapro – and he attracted one of his starriest ensembles to *You Will Meet a Tall Dark Stranger*, a roundelay of broken hearts and silly dreams.

Antonio Banderas, Naomi Watts (as Sally), Josh Brolin, Freida Pinto and Anthony Hopkins give their all, ably supported by British comedy talents including Lucy Punch, Gemma Jones (as Helena) and Pauline Collins. The result, however, is thematically shaky and tonally unsure of itself, content to languish in that register of bittersweet contemplation typical of several of these later films.

To his credit, Allen does at least capture a certain London milieu from which most British filmmakers have repeatedly recoiled – namely a world of art galleries, writers, booksellers, publishers and upper-middle-class wealth, which also takes in the opera and Mayfair boutiques. It's a pity that, after four attempts, he still can't find some British music to accompany his images the way he did so easily in Paris, Barcelona and Rome. The film is, I believe, one of the great, surprise failures of this late period.

But, as the omniscient narrator (Zak Orth, who had appeared in *Vicky Cristina Barcelona*) tells us at the start, this is a "tale of sound and fury signifying nothing". If the sound of Benny Goodman is an ill fit for London, the fury surfaces only once: in the film's best, most Allenish scene, things boil up between the failed writer Roy (Brolin), the

heartbroken Sally and her fatefully deluded mother Helena, the characters criss-crossing in and out of the room drinking whisky and seeking painkillers. The emphasis, then, must fall on the nothing.

All the familiar and favourite Allen themes present themselves, including a prostitute on the make, a stalled writer, an older man falling for a younger woman, faith as misplaced spiritual mumbo jumbo ("it's cheaper than the psychiatrist at least"), fear of mortality, fear of failure and, above all, infidelity and the impossibility of lasting love.

Alas, the ideas and the characters fail to gel satisfactorily and the film lacks charm and agility. Only a couple of lines get laughs: when Hopkins's bimbo blonde girlfriend complains the play he took her to "wasn't even scary", he patiently replies, "I think Ibsen meant the ghosts to be symbolic …").

Actually, there's something ghostly about watching this film – it feels like a Woody Allen film but it's too thin and transparent. We're going through the motions along with the filmmaker and sometimes I think we're supposed to provide our own punchline.

It's a great pity, because Naomi Watts turns in a very decent performance as Sally, the frustrated wife of Josh Brolin's failing novelist, keen to start her own family and art gallery and whose patience is quickly running out. Watts's scenes are the most complex and nuanced in the picture and, like Téa Leoni in *Hollywood Ending*, she might have joined the ranks of classic Woody women had she only been in a better film.

In the end, these characters can't find answers in love, art or the afterlife. The title jokes on the old fortune teller's hokum designed to feed the illusions of poor suckers, but of course it also refers to

Above Crystal gazing: Naomi Watts looks for answers, with Gemma Jones and Roger Ashton-Griffiths.

Allen's old chum, Death, from which Anthony Hopkins's Alfie in particular is in piteous flight.

If the overall theme is of time running out, opportunities slipping away, here you feel it more for the director himself and this particular film, rather than any for the characters in it. As AO Scott wrote in the *New York Times*: "There are hints of farce, droplets of melodrama, a few dangling loose ends and an overall mood of sloppy, tolerant cynicism. Mr Allen has both mastered his craft and grown indifferent to it."

And yet Woody's films always have something to say and at least try to fathom human existence far more than your typical event cinema. For those who don't flock to the superhero summer blockbusters, his films are still annual cinematic events and for that we remain grateful. To quote *Macbeth* again, tomorrow and tomorrow and tomorrow … there's always another Woody Allen film coming along to surprise you.

Midnight in Paris (2010)

An American writer in Paris wanders into a 1920s time warp and hangs out with Hemingway, Picasso, Dali and Fitzgerald – only to find that falling in love with the past is no answer to love's problems now.

It takes something to match the opening sequence of *Manhattan*, but Woody Allen comes close in *Midnight in Paris* – and as homages to one's own work go, it's certainly up there with the best.

Static shots of Paris unfold for nearly four minutes to the mellifluous strains of 'Si Tu Vois Ma Mère' by Sidney Bechet. (It just had to be Bechet, the New Orleans saxophonist and clarinettist who relocated to Paris in the 1950s and after whom Allen named the first daughter he adopted with Soon-Yi.)

Shot by Darius Khondji, the Persian-born, Paris-based cinematographer, these are literally tableaux vivants, locked-off shots but with cars and people moving unaware across the screen. The images combine tourist views with more mundane street corners, mixing day with night and sunshine with rain and back to sun again.

It is a beguiling beginning, a fitting start to a film that is about both nostalgia and the present. Unusually for Allen, the familiar credits then begin as people talk underneath and we are plunged right into a conversation between Owen Wilson's Gil and his impatient but pretty fiancée Inez, played by Rachel McAdams. They are on holiday in Paris with her wealthy, conservative parents.

Gil, a Hollywood screenwriter, is struggling to finish his first novel and hopes Paris will inspire him; he's swept up in romantic notions of living there in a garret and wandering its streets in the rain. Inez accuses him of "being in love with a fantasy".

Were it not clear enough that Wilson, as Gil, has stepped into the "Woody" role here, we hear him ask: "What if I'd stayed here in Paris all those years ago and not got caught up in churning out all those movie scripts?" These are sentiments Woody himself has entertained many times since falling in love with Paris filming

What's New Pussycat? back in 1964. Gil's wanderings will take him – and us – back even further than that.

But before he travels through time, Gil and Inez take a trip to Versailles in the company of her ex-boyfriend, the insufferable intellectual Paul, smugly played by Michael Sheen. When Gil explains his novel's protagonist works in a "nostalgia shop", it gives Paul the chance to dismiss the entire theme as a "denial of the painful present".

This, says Paul, is "golden age thinking – the erroneous notion that a different time period is better than the one one's living in. It's a flaw in the romantic imagination of those people who find it difficult to cope with the present."

These are, of course, very familiar Woody Allen themes, already explored in *The Purple Rose of Cairo* and *Radio Days*, and yet he takes a very playful tack in this film. It is a vintage Peugeot that transports Gil back to the bohemian 1920s.

Wilson's performance is admirable in these sequences, playing it better than Woody himself ever could and cleverly delaying the realization of the magic that's happening to him. Indeed, the very fact that he gets lost, at midnight, on the Rue Saint-Étienne-du-Mont when he can't find his way back to the hotel (Le Bristol, since you were wondering), is because he doesn't possess anything so modern as an iPhone or a device for using Google Maps. Such old-fashioned notions and plot points still obtain in Woody Allen films; the last time he referred to anything remotely technological was in *Sleeper*. Sometimes, it's as if his films themselves are denials of the present.

Gil meets Scott Fitzgerald and Zelda ("I'm stunned, stupefied, anaesthetized, lobotomized," she drawls) and hears Cole Porter

playing 'Let's Do It' at the piano. Then they all go to watch Josephine Baker dance – Wilson's bemused face and dazed eyes are wonderfully funny here. The venue is Bricktop's (Chez Bricktop), the nightclub where Bechet played and which was run by the famous jazz world character Ada Bricktop Smith, who had actually appeared in *Zelig* as one of the "talking heads".

When he's back in the real world, we feel for Gil as he tries to explain his amazing night to Inez and she utterly rejects him, even when he takes her to the same spot the next night. She runs off before the chimes strike midnight and then, sure enough, the vintage car passes again. This time, Hemingway is inside, hilariously yet movingly played by Corey Stoll. Discussing another of Allen's favourite subjects, Hemingway laughs in the face of Death: "You will never be a great writer if you fear Death. The artist's job is not to succumb to despair but to find an antidote for the emptiness of existence." Brilliantly, he then asks: "Do you box?"

Of course, the Woody connections continue. Hemingway's grand daughter Mariel played Tracy in *Manhattan*, but back on

this screen, Hemingway introduces Gil to Gertrude Stein (after remembering to say "Hello Alice" to the woman, Alice B Toklas, who answers the door). Stein is entertaining Picasso and his beautiful muse Adriana (Marion Cotillard) in a scene that builds up to one of Wilson's best-delivered lines: "So, how long have you been dating Picasso? God, did I just say that?"

Midnight in Paris also comes with its very own "Marshall McLuhan moment": Gil is able to use the story he's learned at Stein's house to put down Paul when, on the next day in the present, they all visit a gallery and find themselves in front of Picasso's portrait of Adriana (actually, *La Baigneuse*).

Gil becomes increasingly comfy with his midnight flits to the 1920s, although also obsessed with the beautiful Adriana. Jokes flow about Salvador Dali, Man Ray and Luis Buñuel ("You think that makes sense? I'm travelling through time, from the twenty-first century? Well, you guys are surrealists …") and when Gil explains his problem, "a man in love with a woman from another era", it immediately echoes Cecilia in *The Purple Rose of Cairo* and her line "He's fictional but you can't have everything."

There's a wealth of references to everyone from *Nightwood* author Djuna Barnes – "That was Djuna Barnes? No wonder she wanted to lead" – to TS Eliot – "Prufrock's like my mantra," says the stunned Gil, "though where I come from, people measure out their lives in coke spoons." (I like this line, but I can't help wondering if coke spoons aren't themselves a little old-fashioned for modern-day California.) The film then goes further back to La Belle Époque – Adriana's favourite era – to meet Toulouse-Lautrec, Degas and Gaugin at the Moulin Rouge. This Gil will eventually have to leave Adriana there, just as Cecilia is left by her Gil; the fact the two characters' names are the same cannot be mere coincidence.

Meanwhile, in the present, Gil has a connection with a pretty girl (Léa Seydoux) who sells vintage records in the Paris flea market, specializing in Cole Porter. Uncommonly for a Woody character, he is rewarded with a happy ending, maybe because he realizes his folly over the course of a film. "I'm having an insight, it's a minor one, but I'm having it," he says – and he acts accordingly, becoming master of his own destiny, both as a man and as artist. Woody is on the side of this particular creation and imbues him with a resolve he himself never had.

Perhaps I should confess to being a Francophile myself, someone who has roamed the streets and bars of Paris and chased the shadows of existentialists and American authors, jazz legends and Oscar Wilde, Émile Zola and countless painters. So for me, *Midnight in Paris* is a terrifically enjoyable film – and I was delighted to see I wasn't alone. It became Woody Allen's biggest ever hit, bringing in more than $100 million at the global box office, trading on the star power of Owen Wilson and, no doubt, the romance of Paris. There was also considerable publicity in the casting of Carla Bruni Sarkozy, then France's First Lady, as a tour guide at the Rodin museum. It was a coup that caused quite a fuss of expectation as the film opened

"I'm having an insight – it's a minor one, but I'm having it."

Luke Wilson as *Gil Pender*

the 2010 Cannes Film Festival, though perhaps wisely, she didn't appear on the red carpet.

The casting may have reflected the financing difficulties of his late career (this time, finances came from Spanish outfit Mediapro, through Gravier Productions, which Woody owns with his sister Letty), but the finished picture is as good as anything he might have made in the 1980s or 1990s; the plentiful Django-style guitar riffs often brought *Sweet and Lowdown* wafting back to my mind.

It earned Woody another Oscar, his third, for Original Screenplay and it was also nominated for Best Picture that year, something that was once commonplace for Woody Allen films but which hadn't actually happened since *Hannah and Her Sisters*. It was also nominated for Best Production Design, which was particularly well deserved and a huge endorsement for his choice of new collaborators, Anne Seibel and Héléne Dubreuil, who had taken over following the retirement of his longtime designer Santo Loquasto.

There's always someone somewhere hailing the latest Woody Allen film as a "return to form", probably because they've forgotten, in the intervening months, just how unique his style and writing is amid the mass of mainstream product. But *Midnight in Paris* is a cut above – this is funny, beautiful, playful, romantic and smart, but it is never off-puttingly clever or arcane, wearing its erudition lightly and, who knows, maybe introducing a new generation to Gertrude Stein or Picasso or Hemingway or Sidney Bechet. How many films can you say that about these days?

It may ultimately reject nostalgia as no way to live, but it certainly makes an attractive case for respecting the past before you get on with the disappointments of the present. And, this being a Woody Allen fantasy, it suggests you might even end up with a pretty young French girl for your troubles.

Left The red carpet treatment: Adrien Brody, Léa Seydoux, Owen Wilson, Woody Allen, Rachel McAdams and Michael Sheen at the Cannes premiere of *Midnight in Paris*.

To Rome with Love (2012)

Four entirely separate comic stories are woven around each other in a fresco film featuring tourists, opera, a prostitute, newly-weds, sudden celebrity, wandering architects and a neurotic actress.

Woody Allen has said it was the traffic and chaos of Rome that inspired the portmanteau style of *To Rome with Love*. "Everyone out on the streets, sitting on steps or in cafés, the constant motion … all the romance and emotion – it needed a number of stories."

However, he was also keenly aware of the Italian tradition of omnibus films, though their various stories were usually helmed by several directors, rather than one. They had been a feature of the country's output in the 1950s and '60s, and were a genre to which he'd already nodded in his own such film, *Everything You Always Wanted to Know About Sex*, which featured an episode vaguely parodying Antonioni and Woody himself speaking Italian. He'd also contributed to a similar exercise alongside two Italian Americans, Martin Scorsese and Francis Ford Coppola, when making the triptych *New York Stories*.

Woody originally titled the picture *The Bop Decameron*, suggesting in advance something both jazzy and connected to Boccaccio's medieval collection of tales, which had been filmed by Pasolini in 1971. Then he altered its name to the jokey *Nero Fiddled*. Finally he arrived at the more romantic final title – doubtless because the other choices were not great anyway, nor reflective of the content, and because *Midnight in Paris* proved such a hit partly by trading on that city's evocative name in the title.

The film opens with a traffic cop addressing the camera. "In this city, all is a story," he says, although this narrative framing device is quickly dropped, only to return with a different character in the film's final shot. Perhaps such carelessness is indicative of this later-period Woody Allen, but it also allows a certain looseness and freedom as the director intertwines his four stories.

In *Hannah and Her Sisters*, *Crimes and Misdemeanors*, even in *Melinda and Melinda* and *You Will Meet a Tall Dark Stranger*, he had at least found something to connect his disparate narrative threads. Here, Rome itself is the common character and it looks alluring, warm and magnificent throughout, shot by Darius Khondji, who'd done such a fine job for Paris.

One early shot describes a beautiful circle around a spectacular Piazza as if drawing a ring of enchantment around the soon-to-be-lost newly-wed from the provinces, Milly (the pretty Alessandra Mastronardi). Her story becomes a sort of sex comedy, involving her having an adventure with a famous actor and a petty thief. Her husband, meanwhile, is mistaken for a client by a sexy prostitute (a voluptuous Penelope Cruz), who then has to stand in for Milly when uptight relatives burst in. The uncles and aunts have booked a tour of the Vatican for their nephew and his new bride. "I know it well," says the prostitute.

The newly-weds' story is told entirely in Italian. ("I always wanted to be a foreign film maker," Allen told the *Daily Telegraph*. "But I'm from Brooklyn, so I couldn't be. But all of a sudden, I've become one to such a degree that I'm even writing subtitles. I'm thrilled with that.") As is the second Italian story, involving the comedian Roberto Benigni as office worker Leopoldo Pisanello, who wakes up one morning to find he is suddenly famous and in demand by the voracious paparazzi as well as on TV news shows. He's asked how he likes his toast, what shaving foam he prefers and if he wears boxers or briefs.

This satire on fame of course chimes with Woody's hero Fellini and his Roman films such as *La Dolce Vita*. It's something Allen has touched on several times before, in *Stardust Memories* and *Celebrity*,

although here it's more of a fable and taken to the limits of absurdity. Benigni plays it very nicely, in the broad Italian style.

The remaining two stories concern American tourists and are probably the stronger for it. The first features Woody Allen's own return to the screen for the first time since *Scoop*, six years previously. He plays Jerry, a retired Dad visiting his daughter (Alison Pill), who has just become engaged to a handsome, idealistic Roman lawyer. "I could never be a communist like him," stammers Woody. "I couldn't share a bathroom."

Woody's performance is one of his funniest for ages, helped by sparking off one of his favourite actresses, the brilliant live wire Judy Davis, who plays his psychiatrist wife, Phyllis. "Don't psychoanalyze me," he warns her. "Many have tried, all have failed."

Jerry is a retired opera producer who is piqued back into action when he overhears his daughter's intended father-in-law Giancarlo (Fabio Amiliato) singing in the shower. Convinced he has discovered a new star, he puts on an entire production of *Pagliacci* – with Giancarlo singing on stage in a mobile shower, complete with soap and loofah.

It's a funny idea, a perfect example of something Woody would have written down on one of his yellow pieces of paper and stuffed in his drawer: a man who can sing beautifully only when he's in the shower. Like a latter-day Danny Rose, Jerry has big plans and sees the hesitant Giancarlo singing in his shower in Vienna, Paris and New York: "He'll be the most popular opera singer in the world." Adds the ever-sceptical Phyllis: "Certainly the cleanest."

And then there's the final thread, which bears some resemblance to *Midnight in Paris*: Alec Baldwin is an American tourist wandering the streets of the now-trendy old quarter Trastevere, where he lived 30 years ago. Now an architect, he bumps into a young version of himself, a student, played by Jesse Eisenberg, a bright and intelligent young actor who, perhaps more than any other, appears born to play Woody Allen roles.

Magically, Baldwin assumes some kind of invisibility (much like Bogart in *Play It Again, Sam*, or indeed the ghostly character he himself played in *Alice*) and gives advice and warnings to the younger man as he embarks on an ill-considered flirtation with his girlfriend's visiting friend, a highly strung, highly pretentious actress played by Ellen Page.

This segment has wistfulness and wisdom, suffused with a youthful recklessness that is frowned on by the older, sceptical man. "With age comes wisdom," supposes a chastened Eisenberg when it all goes awry. "With age comes exhaustion," counters Baldwin.

To Rome with Love is a bit baggy and perhaps longer than it need be, although that hardly makes it any the less enjoyable. It is skilful, perceptive and often very funny as well as stunningly beautiful throughout. It's no profound masterpiece, but it does have a playfulness that contrasts youthful idealism with a sense of encroaching mortality, of time catching up. It's much better than many critics would have had us believe at the time of release, one of Woody's diverting delights, and watching it is a visual pleasure.

Woody Allen: A Documentary (2012)

Documentary maker Robert Weide gained unprecedented access to the
life, home and film set of Woody Allen, discussing his work and processes
with the man himself and a star cast of admirers and collaborators.

Although this is a film *about* Woody Allen rather than one *by* him, it would not have been possible without his full cooperation. It shows so much of him at work and at thought, as well as so many of the people key to that career, that you can't understand the man without it.

The film's energy is exhilarating for a documentary, helped by the fact that director Bob Weide is clearly a lifelong fan. He is also a fine filmmaker and comedian in his own right, having won awards for his work on the long-running series *Curb Your Enthusiasm*, on which he collaborated with occasional Allen player Larry David.

Weide's two-part television documentary – which was shortened for theatrical release and shown at the Cannes Film Festival in 2012 – is particularly precious for the little coups involving Woody's most private aspects. One such is the moment he allows Bob and his camera – and therefore us – into his writing room. We see the bed on which Woody lies to think and scribble, as well as the hallowed Olympia typewriter bought for $40 when he was 16 years old and on which he has tapped out every play, article, script and one-liner ever since. As Philip French wrote in the *Observer* when reviewing this film: "Has any instrument since Shakespeare's quill been the conduit of more pleasure to mankind?"

Allen himself appears comfortable in Weide's company. This is very different to Barbara Kopple's *Wild Man Blues*, which maintained a distance and merely observed Woody on his European tour. Weide's camera is more trusted, sitting in the car as Woody takes us on a tour of his old neighbourhood – a moment so special we actually feel, for a fleeting moment, like Annie Hall herself.

Woody shows us his old house and recalls sitting on the stoop. We nip around the corner to where he went to the cinema – the place is now a mall of some sort. He even treats us to a sinister anecdote about a nanny who, he alleges, tried to smother him in the crib. His only comment is to shrug: "Had she succeeded, the world would have been short of a number of great one-liners …"

The film is excellent on the early years, on the creation of the talent and persona, tracing Woody's progress from joke writer for newspaper columns to summers in the mountain resort of Tamiment, writing for Sid Caesar, and his early days as a shy, struggling stand-up encouraged only by the management duo of Charles Joffe and Jack Rollins.

These clips and notable TV appearances with, say, chat show host Dick Cavett, show how carefully Allen was building his career and "brand" so that his comedy could reach the largest possible audience – even if that meant boxing a kangaroo for laughs. (I think the kangaroo won.)

Rather like this book, Weide then takes a chronological journey through Woody's films, using clips and interviews and critics. Everyone's present, including Diane Keaton and an extremely eloquent Mariel Hemingway. Understandably, only Mia Farrow is missing, and the documentary doesn't shy from that scandal and its fallout.

Just as groundbreaking is the footage from the set of *You Will Meet a Tall Dark Stranger*, the first time Allen had allowed filming of one of his sets since *Sleeper*. (We see footage of that film early on, showing him laughing uncontrollably at the comic magic of Diane Keaton.)

Both Naomi Watts and Josh Brolin are filmed trying to work out their scenes, and Woody is shown doing his very hands-off yet very precise directing. Both Brolin and Watts are clearly working hard but remarkably unsure of themselves for such top-of-their-game actors. "It's the worst week of my life," says Brolin.

Weide's film gets into Woody's edit suite and even travels to Cannes for the film's premiere and shows Woody right at the centre of the circus – "a surreal, preposterous thing". He's still getting laughs, though: "My relationship with Death remains the same – I'm, uh, strongly against it."

It is a superb film biography, fascinating and thorough, as well as very funny in its own right and full of Woody in his various moods and modes. Interestingly, one still feels he's playing some kind of continuous game.

Perhaps more typical than anything are the film's closing sentiments, when Woody is asked to reflect on his remarkable career. "When I look back on my life I've been very lucky. I've lived out all these childhood dreams. There was nothing in my life that I aspired toward, that hasn't come through for me. But despite all these lucky breaks, why do I still feel that I got screwed somehow?" And he laughs.

"But despite all those lucky breaks, why do I still feel that I got screwed somehow?"

Woody Allen

Above Still looking at life with raised eyebrows: Woody Allen himself goes under the lens in Robert Weide's detailed documentary.

Blue Jasmine (2013)

Jasmine is a fallen New York socialite clinging to the past yet looking for a fresh start while staying with her impoverished sister in San Francisco.

Woody Allen's films rarely respond to world events. It has both helped and hindered him, rendering his films timeless yet sometimes also leaving him looking out of touch.

Blue Jasmine appears to be about the banking crisis that pulled the world into recession in 2008. The film is centred on a wealthy Manhattan socialite (Cate Blanchett) fleeing the ruins of her husband's business empire.

Although the director himself would not confirm that events were based on real life, commentators were quick to compare the film's collapsed investment scheme to that of convicted New York fraudster Bernie Madoff and his notorious Ponzi scheme. That said, it's clear Woody, like most people, didn't really understand the ins and outs of the financial labyrinth.

It's why he puts us squarely in the brittle mind of Jasmine, who understands the implications even less than we do, a woman who floated blissfully while the money flowed but was left floundering as it washed down the plug hole.

The film might even suggest that we are all in Jasmine's position, offering here a metaphor for the world to chew on. Personally, I think Woody's topicality here only goes so far – he could just as well be referring to the Great Depression of 1929 as the 2008 financial crisis. Although Jasmine is a less likeable character, her delusions of grandeur are not that far from poor Cecilia's illusions in *The Purple Rose of Cairo*.

She is a pitiably self-obsessed figure and, when we first meet her, she's telling her story to a complete stranger on a plane – a lovely slow-burn visual gag, which I'm sure Woody borrowed from one of his favourite comedies, *Airplane!*. Jasmine's fragility teeters on the tightrope of comedy: she's laughable, but when you realize she's suffering a sustained mental breakdown, it becomes more troubling and our attitude towards her will wobble throughout the film.

As played by the Oscar-winning Blanchett, she's a latter-day Blanche DuBois, the deluded character from one of Woody's favourite plays, *A Streetcar Named Desire*. He has quoted from Tennessee Williams's Blanche several times before, including in *Whatever Works*, when Patricia Clarkson arrives in New York from the South. Woody even played a comic version of Blanche in a famous scene from *Sleeper*, immediately finding himself bested by Diane Keaton's impression of Brando as Stanley.

There are other parallels: the obvious existence of streetcars in San Francisco and the fact that Jasmine is staying with her sister Ginger (Sally Hawkins) just as Blanche stays with her sister Stella.

Blanchett is magnificent in the role and stormed to victory at the Oscars, taking the film to yet more levels of commercial success for Allen so late in his career. In interviews – and she gave many on that Oscar

Right Fendi-ing for herself: Cate Blanchett plays Jasmine, a socialite who can't adjust to impoverished new circumstances.

Overleaf Red Jasmine: Cate Blanchett saw parallels with *A Streetcar Named Desire*, as Jasmine goes to live with her sister but clings to the glamour of her past.

"You never know if he's down on you or if he's just not happy with his writing."

Cate Blanchett on director Woody Allen

trail – Blanchett talked about the swiftness of Woody's casting (two brief phone calls, the last ending with "OK, I'll see you in San Francisco"), being left to her own decisions on wardrobe, her fear of being fired, her eventual pleasure following Woody's enigmatic directing.

"You never know if he's down on you or if he's just not happy with his own writing. I could ask him a question and get the briefest response, which probably meant it was a stupid question. Sometimes, though, he would really indulge me and we'd get some lengthy discussion. I was even a bit confused because I'd heard he only ever does two takes, but there were some scenes where we did eight or nine takes. That made me a bit paranoid. But the great thing is that he never allows you to get precious, because there's just no time for it. It's like he's already on to the next thing, thinking about his next movie, probably, or at least where he's going for dinner."

Blue Jasmine is highly unusual in Woody Allen's oeuvre, which is in itself remarkable. How often over the previous 20 years has he been criticized for repeating himself and yet how often, too, has he surprised doubters and loyalists alike by coming up with something totally new?

Blue Jasmine has all the frustrating elements that Woody's detractors enjoy pointing out – expository dialogue, an insistence on old-fashioned jazz to the exclusion of all other modern music, an approach to plotting stuck in the middle of last century. Why, for instance, does Peter Sarsgaard's Dwight not simply Google Jasmine and find out about her past?

And yet, *Blue Jasmine* is also about a retreat into fantasy, about a woman so closeted by her own wealth that she has no need to get involved with reality. It's also about how so blinkered an existence can harm others: we see the pain she causes Ginger, her own sister, so sweetly played by Sally Hawkins, whose reactions and behaviour act as a measure of Jasmine's blind arrogance and self-absorption. In one of the film's several flashback sequences, she visits Jasmine's Manhattan residence, and I love her nervous little curtsy on entering.

Increasingly the norm for these later films is the absence of Woody himself on screen. Yet his presence is, of course, still everywhere. What effect has this had? I think it has allowed him to experiment with tone increasingly deftly. He has often dealt in the margins – between comedy and drama, fantasy and reality, past and present – and found there the true tensions of creativity.

And *Blue Jasmine*, aided by the brilliance of Blanchett, strikes an extraordinary balance. If in his previous tragicomic masterpieces such as *Hannah and Her Sisters* and *Crimes and Misdemeanors*, there was tragedy when Woody was off screen and comedy when he was on it, in *Blue Jasmine* both co-exist in the same frame. Woody even casts two stand-up comedians – Andrew Dice Clay and Louis CK – to play sad figures.

Jasmine herself is a figure both comic and tragic. For example, her intimate knowledge of where the vodka bottle sits on the shelf is quite funny, yet it is so often her first response to any stress that it becomes tragic to watch. Similarly, the dentist Dr Flicker (Michael Stuhlbarg) lunges at Jasmine in a scene that is funny and, at the same time, deeply awful. Even Jasmine's luggage is funny – and yet it isn't, especially if you're her sister and it's clogging up your tiny apartment.

A denizen of the Upper East Side, Woody must have known quite a few Jasmines during the crash – such women are not far removed from his creation in *Alice* – and the character writing here is among his keenest ever.

Peter Bradshaw's five-star review in the *Guardian* describes the film thus: "The mix is just right: a bittersweet cocktail exactly measured. It is delivered with such ease and storytelling skill in the disposition of scenes and management of tone, and the elements of melodrama and soap are carefully controlled to give the right champagne fizz. Without ever playing anything overtly for laughs, Allen gets a tingle of exquisitely sad comedy to run right through his picture from first to last."

Right Blanchett poses with her Oscar at the 2014 Academy Awards. "Audiences want to see films with women at the centre," she said.

Magic in the Moonlight (2014)

Stanley Crawford, a British stage magician and rationalist, travels to the French Riviera to debunk a pretty American clairvoyant who has a wealthy family under her spell.

Magic has been as constant as jazz in the work of Woody Allen, something lingering from childhood days spent practising card tricks and sleights of hand in his Brooklyn bedroom.

By his own admission, his films have been a life-long act of prestidigitation, sometimes throwing us off the scent of his personal philosophical despair and depression, sometimes cloaking over his private life. Of course, there is much more than this to explain magic's recurrence in his work, and Woody has spent many films pondering the tussle between magic and reality and those who would happily believe in one over the other.

Magic in the Moonlight, about a sceptical magician unmasking a mystic, thus revisits well-trodden Allen territory. But it does so very beautifully, bathed in the golden light of the Côte d'Azur, captured by Darius Khondji's cinematography and with gorgeous costumes, locations and props – all part of the magician's apparatus designed to distract from the fact that this is a trick we've seen many times already.

This, his twelfth period piece, allows Allen to retreat even further into his bubble of nostalgia, returning here to a Gatsbyish heyday. You do wonder why it couldn't have been set in contemporary times – there are plenty of wealthy people around now as there were then, and just as many spiritual charlatans and TV magicians; perhaps it's all just an excuse for Woody to get out his old jazz records.

To be honest, *Magic in the Moonlight* scrapes by on the charms of Woody's new leading lady Emma Stone, an actress who has all the hallmarks of a fine Woody heroine: beauty, brains, wit, style. As Sophie Baker, she looks fabulous in a variety of splendid costumes (designed by Sonia Grande) and you can understand why the gullible American family are so in her thrall, particularly Brice, their gormless puppy of an heir (nicely played by Hamish Linklater).

Colin Firth has the task of debunking Sophie, but his Stanley rarely rises above an insistent whine. Dapper as he may look in his tweeds and woollens, his character can't seem to balance the screwball comedy with the scepticism. There are elements of *A Midsummer Night's Sex Comedy* and *The Curse of the Jade Scorpion*, as well as *Scoop* (three of Woody's weaker films, unfortunately) in a film that looks romantic but which lacks romance.

"I believe that the dull reality of life is all there is but you are proof that there's more, more mystery, more magic," says Stanley to Sophie, which at least strikes a hopeful note that life is not quite as "nasty, brutish and short" as Woody and Stanley would have us at first believe.

In one of the film's most memorable scenes, Stanley and Sophie shelter from a storm in the Nice Observatory, designed by Gustave Eiffel – surely reminding us of Ike and Mary soaked in Central Park's Planetarium in *Manhattan*. And although this new film misses a certain electrical charge, it does have complicated philosophies buried within its civilized trappings, as all Woody Allen works do. While Stanley undergoes a sudden, scarcely believable conversion, Sophie is still a fraud, albeit a really attractive one.

Thankfully, what Woody called "the ugly curtain of reality" in *The Curse of the Jade Scorpion* falls before we can really ponder the implications of a kiss between Stanley and Sophie. It's an ending which merely provides further evidence that for all Woody's

philosophy, the key to happiness isn't much more complicated than a young girl's pretty face.

The film was received (and marketed) as a light summer comedy, but its release was surrounded by new scandal. His estranged daughter Dylan again raised accusations of historical abuse and Mia Farrow claimed that their son Ronan was actually fathered by Frank Sinatra. Besieged, Woody even felt obliged to defend himself with an open letter to the *New York Times*.

Despite such scuttlebutt, the film slipped out without much harm done. Or rather, the lukewarm box office and tepid reviews were very much the film's fault.

Jason Bailey, fresh from writing his lively *Ultimate Woody Allen Film Companion*, would later ask Woody about using films as an escape from life. It's a question often asked of this director.

"Since I was a little child, I escaped by … sitting in the movies all day long. And then when I got older, I escaped into the world of unreality by making movies. So I've spent the last, I don't know, almost 50 years … escaping into movies., But on the other side, when I get up in the morning, I go and I work with beautiful women and charming men, and funny comedians and dramatic artists, and I'm presented with costumes and great music to choose from, and sets, and I travel a certain amount of places every year. So my whole year … for my whole life, I've been living in a bubble, you know. And I like it. I'm like Blanche DuBois that way. I prefer the magic to reality and have since I was five years old. And hopefully, I can continue to make films and constantly escape into them."

So now we know.

Irrational Man (2015)

A dissolute philosophy professor arrives at an East Coast college and embarks on affairs with both a faculty wife and a pretty student before deciding his key to happiness lies in committing a perfect but dreadful crime.

Following his European odyssey, Woody returned to America and his occasional milieu of college professors (Michael Murphy's Yale Pollack in *Manhattan*, his own Gabe Roth in *Husbands and Wives*). However, for the first time since the early 1970s, his American story takes place entirely away from New York City.

Irrational Man is set in the fictional Braylin College and was shot over the summer of 2014 in Newport, Rhode Island, at the campus of Salve Regina University and at various spots around Newport, Providence. The setting gives the film a breezy brightness with scenes of students sitting on lawns and riding bicycles, youths dappled with sunny optimism.

Into this bucolic, intellectual setting staggers Joaquin Phoenix's Abe Lucas like a black cloud, swigging whisky from his hip flask, his paunch visible through his sweaty T-shirt. Despite his drinking, Lucas is still the cause of much excitement, a philosopher with a maverick mind and reputation. "He'll be like Viagra to the department," giggles one faculty employee.

But Abe is at rock bottom – his own "Zabriskie Point", as he calls it in his opening voice over, referring perhaps to both the desert of his emotional life and to the Antonioni campus film from 1970 (given the lack of cell phones, iPads, rucksacks and the like among the students at Braylin, this Woody Allenized campus looks more like something from last century, at least).

Abe is unable to find any joy in life, despairing of his achievements and writings. He can't even have sex with Rita Richards, the unhappily married science professor played by Parker Posey, who is nevertheless romantically drawn to Abe's maelstrom and seduces him with pot and whisky. "I wish you would run away to Spain with me," she tells him.

Also caught up in Abe's self-torment is student Jill Pollard, played by Emma Stone, in her second consecutive Woody film. Her performance here

is, I think, streets ahead of her pretty turn in *Magic in the Moonlight* – and Woody agrees. In Cannes before the premiere of *Irrational Man*, he told me:

> I first saw Emma in a movie while I was on my treadmill and I thought she was very pretty but also very funny in that movie [*Easy A*], so I called her in to our office to have a chat and hoped I could find a way to work with her one day.
>
> And she was wonderful in *Magic in the Moonlight*, but when I was thinking of who could play Jill while I was writing *Irrational Man*, well I could only think of her. I mean, I needed a student who was young and pretty and smart, so Emma was perfect, but I had never seen her do anything dramatic before and I didn't know how tremendous her range was. And she surpassed all my expectations. I knew she could be funny, but I didn't know what a deep and wonderful professional actress she was – really, better than I could ever have hoped.

Stone's Jill is the daughter of music professors and a gifted pianist. To the distress of her boyfriend Roy (Jamie Blackley), she becomes infatuated with her teacher Abe. It is initially a platonic relationship, but Jill soon realizes that she is "fascinated to be around someone so complex as Abe" and that he has "tapped into her romantic fantasies".

Abe and Jill overhear a conversation in a diner – a woman is devastated that a judge has been influenced by her ex-husband's lawyer and is about to take away custody of her children – and Abe is suddenly rejuvenated, physically and intellectually, by thoughts of murder.

Irrational Man is one of Woody's most talkative pictures. Both lead characters have detailed voice-overs reflecting on their actions but, within the story, much of the film is also taken up with discussions between Phoenix and Stone. At first they stroll along talking about

"I'm simply a product of the philosophers I've read."

Woody Allen

Right Joaquin Phoenix plays Abe Lucas, a famous philosophy professor teaching a summer course at Braylin.

philosophy; later, it's morality, responsibility, randomness, chance and existential choice. Kant, Kierkegaard, Simone de Beauvoir and Heidegger are just some of the names peppering the conversation. Meanwhile Abe gifts Jill a volume of poetry by Edna Saint Vincent Millay, like Michael Caine in *Hannah and Her Sisters* expressing his love via e e cummings.

Woody conjures up a rarefied university setting, but here there are no jokes about anyone looking into the soul of the student sitting next to them. It's definitely one of his "serious" pictures, though one somehow suffused with lightness, romance and amateur sleuthing, a film that blends the dread of *Match Point* with the legerdemain of *Manhattan Murder Mystery* and a touch of *Scoop*. Mention of Dostoevsky relates to the former (both films feature a copy of *Crime and Punishment*) while Stone, of all Woody's muses, channels a bit of the old Diane Keaton magic.

Meanwhile, the use of bouncy jazz pianist Ramsey Lewis on the score ushers in some of the most propulsive music Woody's ever borrowed, at least since Benny Goodman's 'Sing Sing Sing' (used for the car chase in *Manhattan Murder Mystery*).

Woody explained the use of grooves such as 'The In-Crowd' and 'Wade in the Water': "It's got a relentless, pulsating beat that works very well for the visual material whether people are driving to it or walking to it or behaving badly to it. There's a hot tone and rhythm to it, so it suggests the tempestuousness in every character's soul."

Using the widescreen camerawork of Darius Khondji for the fifth time and reunited with longtime set designer Santo Loquasto, Woody finds in *Irrational Man* a marvellous poise. His direction is effortless and his screenwriting spry and playful (watch out for the flashlight), able to

blend suspense with philosophical intelligence and bitter irony so you hardly notice the skill or the layers of meaning.

What light does *Irrational Man* shed on Woody in his 80th year? The title is taken from a William Barrett book, a popular volume in the 1960s which introduced many Americans to existentialism. To those detractors who say Woody, since the 1992 scandal, has been trying to excuse his behaviours through the subliminal messaging of his films, *Irrational Man* will provide more fodder. It is another story in which a middle-aged man has an affair with a much younger woman, although it has to be said Stone's Jill is in full control of her own decisions. "He's an original thinker who shouldn't be judged by middle-class rules," says Jill in Abe's defence. "He's radical, but he's not nuts," she adds.

Irrational Man may not come to rank as one of his most popular movies – as Phoenix's Abe mutters: "A book about Heidegger and fascism, just what the world needs…" – but both stars are excellent. (Stone, in particular, delivers the best performance of her young career.) Morevoer, the film's deceptive depths swirl on elegantly in the mind long after.

There are also some brilliantly executed set pieces of tension, action and violence, which still show a unique, master director in full control of all his film-making faculties and always capable of surprise.

Immediate reviews from Cannes were warm yet unspectacular, the general consensus being that this was not first-grade Woody Allen. But it's a film that needs time (something which nobody really has in Cannes) to percolate because, yet again, Woody has hit a different note in his continuing exploration of the human condition, a different combination of his previous tones. He can still wrongfoot even his ardent fans.

At the film's Cannes premiere, he looked well, fit, strong and quick-witted, and his film bursts with youth and inquiry, still posing questions, still digging for answers. Woody may be approaching 80, but he could certainly still teach all those students a thing or two.

Left Starring alongside Joaquin Phoenix in *Irrational Man*, Emma Stone takes her second consecutive role in a Woody Allen movie as student Jill Pollard, who becomes fixated with her professor's teachings.

The Last Word

Unlike his films, which always seem to know how to sign off with a poignant flourish just at the right moment, there's no telling when Woody Allen's extraordinary run of film making might end.

As I write, audiences around the world will be enjoying *Irrational Man* in cinemas while Woody himself will already be editing his next film which, we know, stars the A-list talents of Bruce Willis, Jesse Eisenberg and Kristen Stewart.

He will no doubt already be writing the film after that and also – the surprises never cease – creating his first comedy series for the web-based retailers and producers Amazon. He is as busy as ever and will barely have time to celebrate his 80th birthday on 1 December 2015.

Woody himself may not care for old age. When I asked him how he felt about it at Cannes in 2010, he said: "I find it a lousy deal. There is no advantage to getting older. You don't get smarter, you don't get wiser, you don't get more mellow, you don't get more kindly – nothing happens. But your back hurts more, you get more indigestion, your eyesight isn't as good and you need a hearing aid. It's a bad business getting older and I would advise you not to do it if you can avoid it."

I doubt, too, he'll spend the day looking back on any of his old films. But what a landmark occasion that 80th anniversary offers fans and historians to reflect on an outstanding contribution to how we view cinema, comedy, philosophy and even jazz.

Of the 50 or so films Woody Allen has made, very few of them could be considered controversial, unless you count *Stardust Memories* and *Deconstructing Harry*, which are only controversial within the body of the rest of his work. Funny, moving, beautiful, prescient, diverting, piercing, uplifting, wise, whimsical and perceptive - all of those and more would be relevant descriptions. Yet it is becoming clear that Woody Allen will also be remembered as one of cinema's most controversial figures, mainly because of one big decision and one big,

horribly persistent, yet unproven rumour in his private life that have coloured many people's view of his art.

Woody's all-encompassing presence in his films and on our screens, year after year, means we can trace his imprint from chat shows and stand-up comedy routines to zany clown and romantic lover, through to chameleon, showbiz hustler, bitter writer, small-time crook to ageing magician. There's a time-lapse photo to be done that might chart Woody through these ages – but to be honest, I don't think the face behind the glasses and under the hair will have altered very much. Our perception of him is what alters.

But is Woody Allen any different as a film maker in the 25 films before he began his relationship with Soon-Yi to the artist who has made another 28 films since? More than any other film star, he has invited us to be a constant audience to his on-going stand-up routine, using his life, lovers, observations and fears as inexhaustible material as well as defence mechanism. As he gets nearer the "thinning out" fate of that skeleton in the classroom in *Manhattan*, we feel we know him and we might even feel he knows us by now, like Tom Baxter in *The Purple Rose of Cairo* who spots Cecilia in the stalls for the fifth time that week.

We can occasionally produce Woody, just like Alvy did with Marshall McLuhan in the cinema queue, to answer questions and bat witticisms at press conferences and in interviews. We can quote him but we cannot really know him.

I don't think his parents did rent out his room when he was kidnapped; he probably never shot a moose; he certainly never woke up 200 years in the future; he didn't try to assassinate Napoleon; his mother never appeared above the Chrysler Building; his brother doesn't think he's a chicken or, if he does, he's not laying any eggs.

"Life is full of misery, loneliness and suffering and it's all over much too soon," he said. But has that really been an accurate reflection of his own life? All we can really say is that Woody Allen's films have shown us characters that look a lot like him, even when dressed as a sperm. Some of the women playing female characters in his films have also been his real-life lovers, although most of them haven't.

But he has adopted children; he has had a relationship with a much younger woman; he has imagined going back to 1920s Paris; he has lain on a therapist's couch; he did listen to the radio and he did take refuge in movie houses.

To paraphrase Sonja and Boris: if this isn't the best of all possible worlds, then it's certainly the most confusing. His films have reflected universal truths – some of which I'm sure Woody Allen himself believes, some of which he simply believes will get a laugh. His adult life has been a constant well of creativity and productivity that has summed up man's position in a chaotic universe. And he has achieved this by creating a fictive universe to reflect it, one that's just as confusing and absurd as the real one, only shorter and without any washing up.

Above "New York was his town and it always would be." Woody Allen in the town he idolized, on Bleecker Street, shooting *Alice* (1990)

And so we come back to it. "You're always trying to get things to come out perfect in art because it's real difficult in life," said Alvy. But it's the art that remains: the jokes, the ideas, the escape. It offers a glimpse into Woody's real life, into his thoughts and worries. The rest is mystery. After all, what is that our business?

The only truth is what the cameras recorded. And on screen and on paper, Woody Allen has certainly made a life of making art, something which, we also know, is real difficult to do. It may not have come out perfect every time, but he has always been there, every year, sculpting his world, our world, into the shape of those small but perfectly formed moments of movie magic.

Index

Bibliography

Four Films of Woody Allen: Annie Hall, Interiors, Manhattan, Stardust Memories. Faber and Faber, 2003.

Bailey, Jason. *The Ultimate Woody Allen Film Companion.* Voyageur Press, 2014.

Bendazzi, G. *The Films of Woody Allen.* Ravette, 1987

Biskind, Peter. *Easy Riders, Raging Bulls.* Simon & Schuster, 1999.

Bjorkman, Stig, ed. *Woody Allen on Woody Allen.* Rev. ed. Faber and Faber, 2004.

Colombani, Florence *Masters of Cinema: Woody Allen.* Cahiers du Cinema, 2010.

Farrow, Mia. *What Falls Away: A Memoir.* Doubleday, 1997.

Girgus, Sam B. *The Films of Woody Allen.* 2d ed. Cambridge Film Classics, 2002.

Hirsch, Foster. *Love, Sex, Death and The Meaning of Life – The Films of Woody Allen.*

Lax, Eric. *Conversations with Woody Allen.* Aurum Press Ltd, 2008.

Meade, Marion. *The Unruly Life of Woody Allen, A Biography.* Weidenfeld & Nicolson, 2000.

www.EveryWoodyAllenMovie.com
www.WoodyAllenWednesday.com

Photography Credits

The publishers would like to thank the following sources for their kind permission to reproduce the pictures in this book.

Above "Nothing like warm cockles": a frozen Woody Allen pictured by legendary Magnum photographer Ernst Haas, on location in Hungary shooting *Love and Death*. Behind him, a dummy soldier flies through the air during a test for a scene.

I am grateful to all of the many people who have interviewed Woody Allen before me and written so elegantly and passionately about his work.

I have used the quotes and insights of critics and biographers who were reviewing Woody's films and meeting him long before I came along, and I am merely adding to that body of opinion and appreciation.

I'd like to thank Matthew Lowing, my editor at Carlton Books, for his enthusiasm and guidance and Caroline Turner at Hyperactive Publicity for her generous assistance.

6. Steve Schapiro/Corbis, 13. Arthur Schatz/The LIFE Picture Collection/Getty Images, 14-15. John Minihan/Evening Standard/Getty Images, 17. Brian Hamill/Getty Images, 18-19. Sunset Boulevard/Corbis, 20. Arthur Schatz/The LIFE Premium Collection/Getty Images, 23. Nancy R. Schiff/Getty Images, 24. Brian Hamill/Getty Images, 26-27. ITV/Rex, 29. Ebet Roberts/Redferns/Getty Images, 31. Brian Hamill/Getty Images, 32. Mirrorpix, 33. Robert Rosamilio/NY Daily News Archive via Getty Images, 35. Marc Hauser Photography Ltd/Getty Images, 36. Ted Thai/The LIFE Picture Collection/Getty Images, 37. Arthur Schatz/The LIFE Premium Collection/Getty Images, 39. Munawar Hosain/Fotos International/Getty Images, 40-41. CBS via Getty Images, 43. Keystone/Getty Images, 44-45. Hulton Archive/Getty Images, 47. Snap/Rex (left), Courtesy Everett Collection/Rex (right), 49. Sunset Boulevard/Corbis, 51. & 52. Courtesy Everett Collection/Rex, 53. Sunset Boulevard/Corbis, 54-55. & 57. Steve Schapiro/Corbis, 58. Moviestore Collection/Rex, 60. Sunset Boulevard/Corbis, 61. Courtesy Everett Collection/Rex, 63. Paramount/Getty Images, 64. & 65. AF archive/Alamy, 67. Sipa Press/Rex (top), Steve Schapiro/Corbis (bottom), 68. & 69 Steve Schapiro/Corbis, 71. Marka/Alamy, 72. Archives du 7e Art/Rollins-Joffe Productions/Photo12, 73. Snap/Rex, 74. Sunset Boulevard/Corbis, 75. Archives du 7e Art/Rollins-Joffe Productions/Photo12, 77. Ernst Haas/Getty Images (top & bottom), 78. Archives du 7e Art/Rollins-Joffe Productions/Photo12, 79. Courtesy Everett Collection/Rex, 81. Brian Hamill/Getty Images (top), Moviestore/Rex (bottom), 82-83. & 85. Brian Hamill/Getty Images, 87. & 88. Snap/Rex, 90. Brian Hamill/Getty Images, 91. Sunset Boulevard/Corbis, 92-93. Snap/Rex, 94-95. Keystone-France/Gamma-Keystone via Getty Images, 97. Brian Hamill/Getty Images, 98. Moviestore Collection/Rex, 101. Courtesy Everett Collection/Rex (top), WarnerBrothers/Getty Images (bottom), 102-103. Orion/Getty Images, 104. Brian Hamill/Getty Images, 106. Snap/Rex, 106-107. & 108-109. Moviestore Collection/Rex, 109. Orion Pictures Corp/Everett/Rex, 111. Orion/Rollins-Joffe/The Kobal Collection, 112-113. Moviestore Collection/Rex, 113. Orion/Rollins-Joffe/The Kobal Collection, 114-115. Brian Hamill/Getty Images, 116. Courtesy Everett Collection/Rex (top), Orion Pictures Corporation/Photo12 (bottom), 118-119. United Archives GmbH/Alamy, 120. Archives du 7e Art/Orion Pictures Corporation/Photo12, 123. Orion/Everett/Rex, 124. Brian Hamill/Getty Images, 126. Orion/Rollins-Joffe/The Kobal Collection/Hamill, Brian, 127. Snap/Rex, 129. Snap/Rex, 130. Archives du 7e Art/Orion Pictures Corporation/Photo12, 131-132. Brian Hamill/Getty Images, 135. Snap/Rex, 137. Brian Hamill/Getty Images (top), Snap/Rex (bottom), 140. Moviestore Collection Ltd/Alamy, 142. Archives du 7e Art/Orion Pictures Corporation/Photo12, 143. AF archive/Alamy, 144-145. United Archives GmbH/Alamy, 146-147. Orion Pictures Corp/Everett/Rex, 149. AF archive/Alamy, 151. Orion Pictures Corp/Everett/Rex, 153. Brian Hamill/Getty Images (top), Rex (bottom), 154-155. Snap Stills/Rex, 157. Brian Hamill/Getty Images, 158. TriStar/Getty Images (top), Tri-Star/Rollins-Joffe/The Kobal Collection (bottom), 161. Snap/Rex, 163. Moviestore Collection/Rex (top), Magnolia/Sweetland/The Kobal Collection/Hamill, Brian (bottom), Archives du 7e Art/Miramax Films/Photo12, 165. Brian Hamill/Getty Images, 166-167. Snap/Rex, 168. & 169. Buena Vista/The Kobal Collection, 170. Brian Hamill/Getty Images, 172-173. Snap/Rex, 174. United Archives GmbH/Alamy, 176-177. Lawrence Schwartzwald/Sygma/Corbis, 178. Mondadori Portfolio by Getty Images, 179. Photos 12/Alamy, 181. Sweetland Films/Jean Doumanian Prods/The Kobal Collection, 182. Howard Earl Simmons/NY Daily News Archive via Getty Images, 183. AF archive/Alamy, 185. Moviestore/Rex, 186. AF archive/Alamy (top & bottom), 188. Photos 12/Alamy, 189. AF archive/Alamy, 191. Everett Collection/Rex, 192. Moviestore Collection/Rex, 193. Everett Collection/Rex, 194-195. Jean-Christian Bourcart/Getty Images, 196. Courtesy Everett Collection/Rex, 197. Sunset Boulevard/Corbis, 199. Moviestore Collection/Rex (top & bottom), 201. Ron Galella/WireImage/Getty Images, 203. Dreamworks LLC/The Kobal Collection/ Clifford, John, 205. Dreamworks/Everett/Rex, 206. Brian Hamill/Getty Images (top), c.FoxSearch/Everett/Rex (bottom), 208. Fox Search/Everett/Rex, 209. FoxSearch/Everett/Rex, 211. Archives du 7e Art/HanWay Films/Photo12, 212. & 213. Dreamworks/Everett/Rex, 215. AF archive/Alamy, 216-217. Focus/Everett/Rex, 219. Canadian Press/Rex, 221. & 222-223. AF archive/Alamy, 224. & 225. Weinstein/Everett/Rex, 227. Sony Pics/Everett/Rex, 228. Moviestore Collection/Rex, 229. Sony Pics/Everett/Rex (top), Moviestore Collection/Rex (bottom), 231. & 233. Moviestore Collection/Rex, 234-235. AGF s.r.l./Rex, 237. Sony Pics/Everett/Rex, 239. Francois Guillot/AFP/Getty Images, 241. AF archive/Alamy, 242-243. Sony Pictures Classics/courtesy Everett Collection/Rex, 245. Joe Klamar/AFP/Getty Images, 246. Moviestore/Rex (top), Archives du 7e Art/Gravier Productions/Photo 12 (bottom), 249. & 250-251. (left & right) AKM-GSI/Splash News/Corbis, 253. Richard Corkery/NY Daily News via Getty Images, 256. Ernst Haas/Getty Images

Every effort has been made to acknowledge correctly and contact the source and/or copyright holder of each picture and Carlton Books Limited apologizes for any unintentional errors or omissions, which will be corrected in future editions of this book.